Electronic Data Interchange: A Total Management Guide

Electronic Data Interchange
A Total Management Guide

Margaret A. Emmelhainz, Ph.D.

VNR VAN NOSTRAND REINHOLD
New York

Van Nostrand Reinhold
115 Fifth Avenue
New York, NY 10003

Van Nostrand Reinhold International Company Limited
11 New Fetter Lane
London EC4P 4EE, England

Van Nostrand Reinhold
480 La Trobe Street
Melbourne, Victoria 300, Australia

Nelson Canada
1120 Birchmount Road
Scarborough, Ontario M1K 584, Canada

16 15 14 13 12 11 10 9 8 7 6 5 4 3 2 1

Contents

ACKNOWLEDGMENTS   xi

PREFACE   xiii

I EDI OVERVIEW AND INTRODUCTION 1

1 EDI OVERVIEW 3
  Background 3
  What is EDI? 4
  Traditional Documentation Flow 6
  Problems with Traditional Flow of Information 9
  How Does EDI Solve These Problems? 10
  Functional Acknowledgment 13
  How Does EDI Differ from FAX and E-MAIL? 13
  What are the Components of EDI? 14
  What Documents Can Be Sent via EDI? 18
  Who Should Use EDI? 19
  How Involved in EDI Do I Have to Get? 19
  What Are the Costs and Benefits
   of using EDI? 20
  How Did EDI Get Started? 21
  Why Should I read the Rest of this Book? 23

2 WHY EDI? 25
  Introduction 25
  Business Survival 25

Cost Savings   28
Improved Operations   33
Improved Customer Responsiveness   36
Improved Channel Relationships   37
Improved Ability to Compete Internationally   38
Summary   40

3   EDI USERS   **41**
Introduction   41
EDI in the Transportation Industry   42
EDI in the Grocery Industry   47
EDI in the Health Care Industry   49
EDI In the Automotive Industry   52
EDI in the Retail Industry   54
Summary of Industry Usage   57
EDI in the Government   57
Summary   60

II   COMPONENTS OF EDI   **61**

4   EDI STANDARDS   **63**
Introduction   63
History of Standards Development   63
Structure of the Standards   64
Formatting Standards   64
Terminology of Standards   65
Transaction Set Standards   67
Electronic Enveloping   74
Communications Standards   74
Standards Development Process   76
Industry Standards   79
Proprietary Standards   80
International EDI Standards   80
Communications Standard X.400   81
Summary   82
ANSI ASC X12 Standards   82
Uniform Communication Standard (UCS) Documents   83
Warehouse Information Network Standards (WINS) Documents   84
Voluntary Interindustry Communications Standards (VICS)   85
TDCC Developed Standards   85

5   EDI SOFTWARE AND HARDWARE   **89**
Introduction   89
Definition of EDI Software   89
The Function of EDI Software   89
Additional Features of Software   93
Make or Buy Factors   94
Selection of Software Vendors   95
Software Costs   96
Software Summary   97
EDI Hardware   97
Communications Modems   100
Summary   100

6   THIRD PARTY NETWORKS   **107**
Introduction   107
Direct Exchanges   107
The Role of Third Party Networks   108
Third Party Mailbox Services   108
Value Added Services   111
Experience of Third Party Networks   114
Issues/Concerns with Third Party Networks   114
Costs of Using Third Party Networks   117
Selecting a Third Party Network   118
Use of Third Party Networks   119
Summary   119

III   IMPLEMENTATION OF EDI   **123**

7   EDI IMPLEMENTATION STEPS   **125**
Introduction   125
Implementation Guide   126
Decide EDI Strategy   126
Obtain Top Management Support   128
Establish EDI Project Team   129
Conduct/Obtain Education Programs   129
Perform an EDI Audit   130
Develop Preliminary Cost/Benefit Analysis   131
Select EDI Participants   131
Mapping with Trading Partners   133
Establish EDI Contracts   134

Conduct Pilot Test   134
Review Pilot Test Results and Modify   135
Expand Usage   135
Publicize Efforts   136
Summary   136

8   EDI STAFFING AND TRAINING REQUIREMENTS   137
Staffing Requirements   137
EDI Leadership Group   138
Operations Group   140
Technical Group   141
Liaison Group   143
Staff Support Group   144
Summary of Staffing Requirements   146
EDI Training   146
Training Requirements   147
Training Matrix   147
EDI Knowledge and Skills   147
EDI Overview Knowledge Requirements   149
EDI Components Knowledge Requirements   150
Implementation Issues Knowledge Requirements 151
Summary of EDI Knowledge Requirements   152
Summary of Training Requirements   153

9   OVERCOMING EDI BARRIERS   155
Introduction   155
We've Never Done It That Way Before!   156
EDI Will Change What I Do!   157
EDI Will Destroy My Relationship With My Buyer (Seller)!   158
EDI Is Someone Else's Problem— It's Not My Department!   159
EDI Is Too Complex to Understand!   160
Perceived Costs and Benefits   161
EDI Will Give Others Access to Our Proprietary Data!   162
EDI Presents All Sorts of Legal Problems!   163
EDI Eliminates the Audit Trail!   165
EDI Communications Are Not Secure!   165
EDI Takes Away My Float!   166
None of Our Trading Partners Are Using EDI!   166
EDI Standards Keep Changing!   167
Summary   168

10   QUANTIFYING EDI COSTS AND BENEFITS   **169**
Introduction 169
Why Document Costs and Benefits 170
Behavior of EDI Costs and Benefits 171
Categories of EDI Costs 172
Categories of EDI Benefits 174
Preparing a Cost/Benefit Analysis 177
Summary 179

11   IMPLEMENTATION CASE STUDIES   **181**
Introduction 181
Mervyn's 181
Mervyn's EDI Applications 182
North American Philips Corporation Introducing EDI in a
    Multidivisional Organization 185
Summary of EDI Implementation 191

IV   THE FUTURE OF EDI   **193**

12   EDI AND ELECTRONIC FUNDS TRANSFER   **195**
Introduction 195
Payment Methods 196
Paper-Based Systems 196
Electronic Payment Methods 196
Examples of EFT 201
EFT Players 204
Benefits of EFT 205
Barriers to EFT 206
The Future of EDI/EFT 207
Relationship of EDI and EFT 208
Summary 208

13   INTERNATIONAL EDI   **209**
Introduction 209
Importance of International EDI 209
International Standards 210
International EDI Activity 212
Specific Examples of International EDI 213
Barriers to International EDI 215
Summary 216

14   THE FUTURE OF EDI   **217**
Introduction   217
Growth in Volume   217
Growth in Applications   218
Growth Through Integration   220
EDI for Competitive Advantage   222
Summary   223

GLOSSARY   **225**

ENDNOTES   **233**

INDEX   **247**

ACKNOWLEDGMENTS

A book of this type rarely reflects the efforts of just one person. This effort could not have been completed without the help and support of a number of people. I owe particular thanks to the EDI Group, Ltd. My experiences as an instructor in the Principles of EDI course provided contacts which were invaluable in completing this book. Special thanks go to Daniel Ferguson and Ned Hill for their support and encouragement, as well as for the permission to use selected materials in this book. Thanks also go to others who provided sources and materials including: Anna Lee Payne of EDI, Spread the Word; Lane Cooper of *EDI News*; Victor Wheatman of INPUT; the Data Interchange Standards Association, the National Association of Purchasing Management, and the Council of Logistics Management.

In addition to those who provided material for the book, I also thank those who reviewed chapters. Those reviews and comments significantly improved the quality of this work. Thanks go to Dan Ferguson and Ned Hill, as well as to two anonymous reviewers. Very special thanks go to Dave Hough of McDonnell Douglas who provided numerous and detailed comments on the entire book.

I also thank Dr. Bill Sekely, my department chairman at the University of Dayton, for his support throughout the entire time it took to complete the book. Finally, this book could never have been completed without the support of my family. To Larry, Lara, and Nathan—thank you for your patience, understanding, support, and love.

PREFACE

Electronic Data Interchange (EDI) is fast becoming the standard way of exchanging business documents, not only in this country but also in the rest of the world. EDI provides a faster, more accurate, less costly method of communication than do traditional methods of business communications such as mail, telephone, and personal delivery. However, EDI is doing more than just changing how businesses communicate; it is changing the way businesses operate.

Electronic data interchange is changing industry. Trading relationships are changing, management philosophies are changing, and production techniques are changing. As one user of EDI has said, "EDI is a whole new ballgame."

The purpose of this book is to help you play the EDI ballgame by providing an introduction to EDI. The book is intended for functional managers in such areas as purchasing, accounting, marketing, sales, and transportation, as well as for systems and MIS managers. The objective of the book is to provide you with a solid foundation of knowledge about EDI. The book brings together explanations of EDI terminology and structure, examples of EDI usage, case studies of implementation efforts, and predictions of EDI's future.

The book is divided into four sections, each addressing a specific aspect of EDI. The sections are written so that they can be read independently of each other, as long as Chapter 1 is read first.

The first section (Chapters 1 through 3) explains the game of EDI. EDI is defined and the key concepts behind EDI are examined. Examples of how and why EDI is currently being used are provided.

The second section (Chapters 4 through 6) explains the equipment you need to play the EDI game. The basic EDI tools of standards, software, and networks are introduced and explained.

The third section (Chapters 7 through 11) provides the rules for playing the game of EDI. EDI strategies are discussed and a step-by-step guideline for implementing EDI is presented. The section also includes a discussion of commonly encountered barriers to EDI, a game plan for estimating costs and benefits of EDI, and case studies of how others have successfully implemented EDI.

The final section of the book (Chapters 12 through 14) predicts what the game of EDI will be like in the future. This section examines the use of EDI for electronic payment as well as for international trade, and examines the future potential of EDI.

Each day more and more businesses begin to play the EDI game. It is estimated that by 1993, over 70 percent of U.S. firms will be using EDI to some extent. The objective of this book is to give you the knowledge that you need to make sure that your company is not left sitting on the bench while your competitors are on the playing field hitting home runs.

I

EDI OVERVIEW AND INTRODUCTION

1

EDI OVERVIEW

"It would be almost unthinkable nowadays for a business not to have a telephone to communicate with customers and suppliers. In the future, it may be almost as unthinkable for a business not to have a computer for the same purpose."

The New York Times, July 10, 1986.

BACKGROUND

Every business organization communicates daily with suppliers, customers, transportation carriers, banks, and other business partners. Communication, in some form, is necessary to place an order, to check status, to send a bill, to pay a bill, to arrange for shipment, and to perform numerous other business functions. Traditionally, these communications have been performed primarily through the use of paper. A 1988 study conducted by EDI Research, Inc., found that 79 percent of document exchange between businesses in the United States is in the form of paper transmitted via mail or personal delivery. Fifteen percent of the communications are exchanged verbally, while 4 percent are exchanged through either facsimile transmission or through electronic mail networks.[1] The remaining 2 percent of business documentation is exchanged through a method often referred to as a "new way of doing business." This new way of doing business is Electronic Data Interchange, or EDI.

Although today only a very small percentage of business documents are exchanged through EDI, the use of EDI is expected to grow significantly and to soon become an accepted way of doing business. Current estimates place the number of U.S. firms significantly using EDI at nearly 5,000 with the expectation that by 1990 over 11,000 organizations will be using EDI.[2] A 1988 study found that 35 percent of Fortune 1000 type organizations were using EDI and that an additional 20 percent were actively planning for its use.[3] EDI is currently being used in over 50 industries including transportation, grocery, automotive, electronics, chemical, retailing, healthcare, warehousing, and others. EDI is also being used by the federal government. In other words, the stage is set for explosive growth in the use of EDI.

It is no longer a question of "if" EDI will become a major factor in business; it is only a question of "when." And "when" is most likely to be within five years. This means that in the very near future your company is going to have to be in a position to participate in EDI. Being in a position "to do" EDI means understanding:

- What is EDI?
- What technology is required?
- What are the benefits of EDI?
- What are the costs of EDI?
- What is involved in implementing EDI?

The purpose of this book is to help you gain that understanding by providing a complete guide to EDI. This book brings together explanations of EDI terminology and structure, examples of EDI usage, case studies of EDI implementation, and predictions of EDI's future. The book will prepare you to meet the challenge of the new way of doing business.

WHAT IS EDI?

> Electronic Data Interchange is the interorganizational exchange of business documentation in structured, machine-processable form.

EDI is often viewed as simply a way of replacing paper documents with electronic documents, and replacing traditional methods of transmission such as mail, phone, or in-person delivery with electronic transmission. However, EDI is actually a way of replacing manual data entry with electronic data entry. The purpose of EDI is not to eliminate paper, but rather to eliminate processing delays and data reentry.

Electronic data interchange can be used to electronically transmit such documents as purchase orders, invoices, shipping notices, receiving advices, and other standard business correspondence between trading partners. EDI can also be used to transmit financial information and payment in electronic form. When used in this application, EDI is usually referred to as EFT, Electronic Funds Transfer.

Application-to-Application EDI

Figure 1-1 shows the use of EDI in place of traditional methods for the transmission of a purchase order between a buyer and seller and demonstrates the key concept

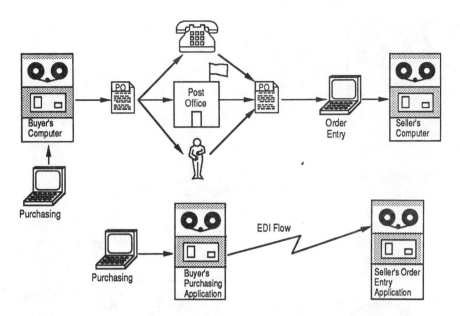

Figure 1-1   EDI vs. traditional methods.

behind EDI. Once data are entered into the buyer's computer system, the same data are electronically entered into the seller's computer, without the need for rekeying or reentry. This is normally referred to as application-to-application EDI. In other words, data are moved electronically, without additional human interpretation or rekeying, between the sender's application program (such as a purchasing system) and the receiver's application program (such as order entry). When EDI is fully integrated with application programs, not only do data flow electronically between trading partners without the need for rekeying, data also flow electronically between internal applications of each of the trading partners. The electronic flow of data between applications within an organization is known as bridging.

The actual movement of the data can take many forms, as shown in Figure 1-2. The transmission can be direct between the two parties; or it can be transmitted indirectly via a third party service provider. Also, the transmission can be made in the form of computer tapes, computer disks, or other forms of physical storage of data as long as the data can be processed by the receiving computer without prior rekeying.

Door-to-Door EDI

EDI in its truest form means that data are not rekeyed between the sender and the receiver; however, much of what is reported as EDI usage involves some rekeying between trading partners. An example of this type of EDI is shown in Figure 1-3.

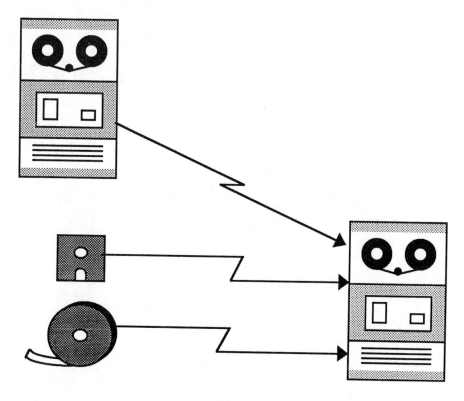

Figure 1-2   Movement of EDI data.

In this case a buyer transmits an electronic purchase order to a supplier. Upon receiving the electronic order, the supplier prints out the order and then manually enters the data into an order entry system. This type of EDI has been labeled "door-to-door" EDI, a term developed by Dan Ferguson of the EDI Group, Ltd. Although this is not "true" EDI, since it does not eliminate redundant data entry, door-to-door EDI does offer significant benefits and is often a good way to get started with EDI.

TRADITIONAL DOCUMENTATION FLOW

The value of electronic data interchange can best be seen by comparing the use of EDI to the traditional flow of documents between organizations. In this example, the flow of documentation between a buying firm and a supplier firm for the purchase of a standard, repetitive item, will be examined. As shown in Figure 1-4, a "typical" transaction between buyer and supplier requires repeated data entry and numerous time delays. Such a transaction may include, based on industry and type of purchase, the following steps:

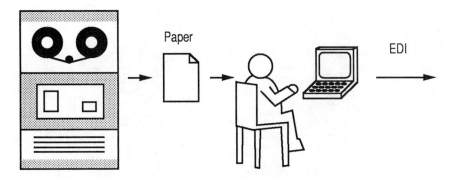

Figure 1-3   Door-to-door EDI.

1. The buyer identifies the item to be purchased. Data are either typed on a purchase order form or entered into a purchasing application and a purchase order is generated. At least one copy of the purchase order is mailed to the supplier. Additional copies are forwarded to other departments within the company such as accounting, finance, and receiving.

2. Upon receipt of the purchase order, the supplier abstracts information from the purchase order and enters the information into an order entry system, creating an order record. A copy of the order record is sent to the invoicing department as well as to the warehouse holding the item (or factory producing the item).

3. Based upon the order record, a purchase order acknowledgment may be created and mailed to the buyer.

4. Upon receipt of the purchase order acknowledgment, the buyer enters the data into the purchasing application system and the item is included in the open order file.

5. At some later time, using the open order file, the buyer may create a status request which is sent/called to the supplier.

6. Upon receipt of the status request, the supplier enters the request into the order entry system.

7. A status reply is created. The status reply is mailed or phoned back to the buyer.

8. The buyer receives the status reply and keys the information into the purchasing application to update status.

9. Upon receipt of a copy of the purchase order (Step 1), the accounts payable department keys the data into the accounts payable application.

10. Also upon receipt of a copy of the original purchase order (Step 1), data are entered into the receiving file.

11. Upon receipt of a copy of the order record (Step 2), data are entered into the invoicing application system by the supplier.

12. Also upon receipt of a copy of the order record (Step 2), data are entered into the warehousing/factory record file.

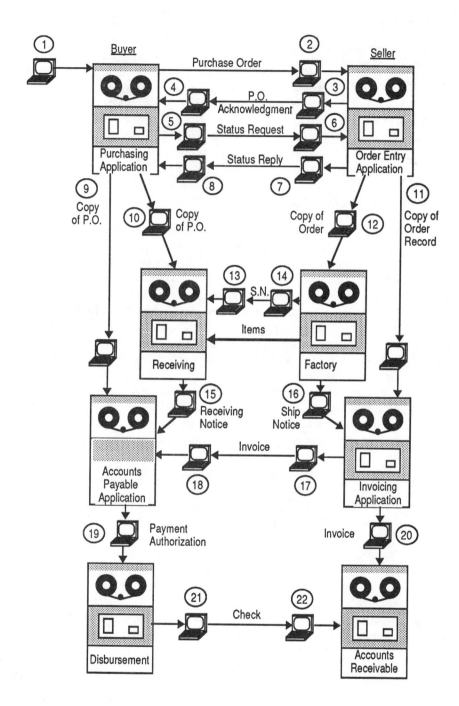

Figure 1-4   Traditional flow (without EDI).

13. The warehouse/factory selects the necessary items and may create a ship notice, which is mailed to the buyer. The product is shipped.
14. Upon receipt of the ship notice, the buyer updates receiving records.
15. Upon receipt of the items, a receiving notice is prepared and sent to accounts payable where the data are entered into the accounts payable record.
16. Upon shipment of the items, a record is created at the warehouse/factory and sent to the supplier's invoicing application, where the data are keyed to update the invoicing file.
17. An invoice is created and mailed to the buyer.
18. Upon receipt of the invoice, data are keyed into the accounts payable application. Usually the invoice, the purchase order, and the receiving document are manually reconciled (compared).
19. A payment authorization is prepared and sent to disbursement.
20. At the time the invoice is created by the supplier (Step 17), a copy is sent to accounts receivable where the data are keyed to update the receivables file.
21. Based upon the payment authorization, accounts payable prepares a check and mails it to the supplier.
22. Upon receipt of the check, the supplier keys the data to update the accounts receivables application and deposits the check.

PROBLEMS WITH TRADITIONAL FLOW OF INFORMATION

Under this traditional flow of information, data are keyed at 22 different steps in the process. And in most cases, the rekeying process involves redundant information. As an example, the original purchase order number is likely to be included in every document produced. In other words, the purchase order number, which does not change from when the order is placed until when the order is received and payment is made, is entered 22 different times. The purchase order number is not the only piece of information used repeatedly; in fact, it is generally accepted that 70 percent of one company's data output eventually becomes another company's data input. The repeated rekeying of identical information in the traditional, paper-based method of business communications creates a number of problems that can be eliminated or significantly reduced through the use of EDI. These problems include:

- Increased time
- Low accuracy
- High labor usage
- Increased uncertainty

Increased Time

Delays are inherent in the paper-based system. One source of delay is the time it takes to physically transmit the information between trading partners. In the example discussed earlier, information was mailed on seven separate occasions, building in a delay each time. Another source of delay in the system is the time it takes to reenter data. At each of the 22 points where data were entered, a processing delay is likely. (Obviously, one additional source of delay which cannot be eliminated, even with EDI, is the time it takes to physically move the product from the supplier to the buyer.)

Low Accuracy

Also inherent in a paper-based system that requires multiple instances of data entry is error. One study has indicated that even "expert-level" data entry operators miss-key 2 percent of the time.[4] Repeatedly entering the same data at various places in the information flow increases significantly the number of key strokes involved in the transaction and thereby increases the opportunities for error.

High Labor Usage

In the traditional paper-based flow of information, manual data entry is performed at each step in the process. In addition, manual reconciliation (comparison of the purchase order, receiving notice, and invoice) is also done. These are labor-intensive operations.

Increased Uncertainty

Also present in a paper-based system is a high level of uncertainty. Due to mailing and processing delays, a sender of information is unsure when, or if, the document is received. It is not unusual that a buyer first finds out that a supplier never received the purchase order when the items are not delivered as expected. This uncertainty often results in constant telephoning to confirm receipt of documentation. On the payment side, it is difficult to predict when a check will clear; thus, there is uncertainty as to which funds are available for use.

HOW DOES EDI SOLVE THESE PROBLEMS?

The use of electronic data interchange can help to eliminate or significantly reduce the problems found in paper-based systems. As can be seen in Figure 1-5, which depicts the use of EDI between a buyer and a seller and the use of bridging EDI within each company, EDI significantly reduces both time and rekeying effort. With EDI the following steps may be performed depending upon industry and type of purchase:

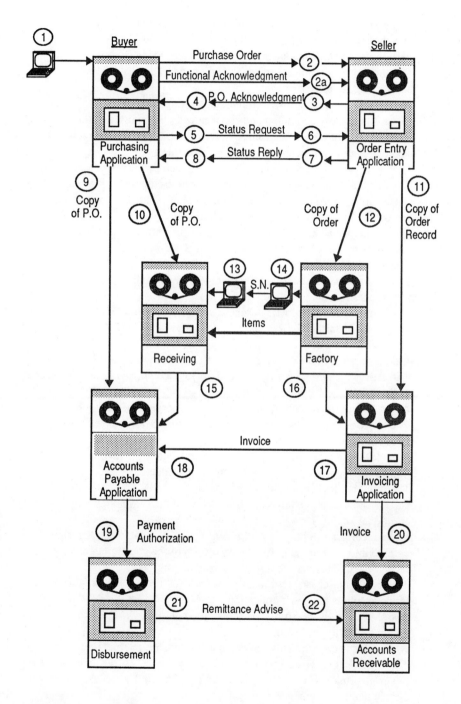

Figure 1-5   EDI flow.

1. As before, the buyer identifies the item to be purchased. Data are entered into the purchasing application program. Translation software creates an EDI purchase order which is sent electronically to the supplier.
2. The supplier's computer receives the order and EDI software translates the order to the supplier's format.
    2a. A functional acknowledgment, indicating receipt of the order, is automatically generated and electronically transmitted to the buyer.
3. The supplier may also electronically create and transmit a purchase order acknowledgment indicating availability of items.
4. The purchase order acknowledgment is received by the buyer's computer, is translated to the buyer's format, and the purchasing records are updated.
5. Based upon the purchase order data, a status request is generated and electronically transmitted to the supplier.
6. Upon receipt by the supplier's computer, the status request is translated into the supplier's format and status is checked.
7. A status reply is electronically created and transmitted back to the buyer.
8. The status reply is electronically received, translated, and used to update the purchasing file.
9. At the time the original EDI purchase order was created (Step 1), bridging software transmitted the data to the accounts payable application where the data were electronically entered.
10. Also at the time of the creation of the original EDI purchase order (Step 1), bridging software transmitted the data to receiving, where files were updated.
11. At the time of the receipt by the supplier of the original EDI purchase order (Step 2), bridging software transmitted data to the warehouse/factory.
12. Also at the time of the receipt by the supplier of the original EDI purchase order (Step 2), bridging software transmitted data to the invoicing application where the invoice file was electronically updated.
13. The order is filled from the warehouse/factory and a ship notice is created and transmitted to the buyer. (The creation of the ship notice may require additional keying.)
14. Upon receipt by the buyer of the ship notice, the data are electronically entered into the receiving file. Upon receipt of the goods, the buyer enters receipt data. (This may require additional keying.)
15. The receipt notice is electronically transmitted, through bridging software, to the accounts payable application.
16. The ship notice is electronically transmitted, through bridging software, to the invoicing application.
17. An invoice is electronically generated and transmitted to the buyer.
18. The invoice is received by the buyer's computer and is translated into the buyer's format. The invoice, receiving notice, and purchase order are electronically reconciled.

19. A payment authorization is electronically created and transmitted to accounts payable.

20. At the time of creation of the invoice, the receivables application is electronically updated to indicate an open receivables.

21. The buyer electronically transmits payment to the supplier's bank through their bank. An electronic remittance advice is transmitted to the supplier.

22. Upon receipt of the remittance advice and notice of good payment, the data are translated into accounts receivable and the buyer is given credit for payment.

The use of EDI, as demonstrated in the example above, eliminates many of the problems with the traditional flow. First, the delays associated with mailing (or other forms of physical transmission) are eliminated. The processing time required for an order entry clerk, buyer, accounts payable clerk, etc., to read and reenter data is also eliminated. Second, since the data are not repeatedly rekeyed (in this case, there are only 3 instances of manual data entry instead of 22 instances), the chance for error is greatly reduced.

Third, because the data are not manually reentered at each step in the process, labor costs can be reduced. Tasks such as data entry, filing, storing, and reconciliation are significantly reduced. Fourth, because time delays are reduced, there is more certainty in information flow.

FUNCTIONAL ACKNOWLEDGMENT

The EDI flow above includes one transfer of information not present in the traditional flow—that of the functional acknowledgment. Whenever an EDI message is received, a functional acknowledgment is generated and electronically transmitted to the sender. This acknowledgment simply states that the message was received. In this way, a buyer knows that the purchase order, for instance, was received by the supplier.

The core concept of EDI, as demonstrated in the above example, is that with EDI data are transferred electronically in machine-processable form. In other words, an EDI message can be immediately processed by the receiving computer, without any additional human interpretation or rekeying. This concept makes EDI very different from other forms of electronic communication.

HOW DOES EDI DIFFER FROM FAX AND E-MAIL?

Facsimile transmission and electronic mail are two forms of electronic communications sometimes thought to be similar to EDI. However, while both of these methods of communication move data electronically, neither are EDI.

Facsimile transmission is the movement of a digitized image of a document over telephone channels. Nearly any document can be "faxed." The data received by the sender are not in a structured format, nor can they be computer processed without rekeying.

Electronic mail (E-mail) is the use of computers to communicate person-to-person (in contrast to EDI, which is a way to communicate computer-to-computer). E-mail is usually used to take the place of phone calls or letters. The data transmitted by E-mail are in a very unstructured or free format, and cannot be processed by a computer without interpretation and rekeying. Because the key concept of "structured, machine-processable format" is missing from both facsimile transmission and E-mail, neither are EDI.

WHAT ARE THE COMPONENTS OF EDI?

What are the essential components of EDI that make it so different from other forms of electronic messaging? While strategically EDI is a new way of doing business, operationally EDI is very similar, in many ways, to paper-based systems. As an example, think about what you would need to send a business letter to a trading partner in Germany. Most likely you would produce or obtain:

- A letter written in "generally accepted business format"
- Translation capability from English to German
- A mail service or other method of transmission

To send or receive an EDI message you need exactly the same three elements:

A "standard" way of writing	EDI standards
Translation capability	EDI software
A mail service	Third party providers (or direct links)

EDI Standards

In normal business communications, most messages follow generally accepted rules of format and syntax. For instance, a business telephone call usually begins with: "Hello, this is John Smith. May I please speak to Sally Jones?" Business letters usually begin with a letterhead showing the sender's name and address, followed by a date, followed by the receiver's name and address, followed by a salutation, and so forth. These rules of format and syntax provide an accepted way of communicating between businesses and ensure that the message sent is understood upon receipt.

Similar rules of format and syntax exist in the world of EDI. The rules that govern electronic data interchange communications are called EDI standards. EDI standards are agreements among EDI users as to what is an acceptable EDI communication. There are two types of EDI standards: formatting standards and communication standards.

Formatting Standards   EDI formatting standards provide guidelines covering:

- What documents can be communicated electronically
- What information is to be included in each electronic document
- What sequence the information should follow
- What form of information (numeric, ID codes, etc.) should be used
- The meaning of individual pieces of information

For instance, one of the most widely used EDI standards for a purchase order states that an electronic purchase must include, at a minimum, the following information (along with additional "enveloping" information):

- Description of purchase order (type, purpose, number, date)
- Organizational information (function, name)
- Item description (quantity, unit of measure, price, product description)
- Hash totals

EDI standards provide much more detail than do the rules of general business correspondence. This is necessary because computers cannot read and interpret different forms of the same information, as can order entry clerks and other personnel who interpret business correspondence. In a paper-based system, an order entry clerk may receive hundreds of orders a day, each in a different format. The clerk can recognize each as an order and can abstract from each the pertinent information such as date, purchase order number, and so on. Further, the clerk can recognize and understand the date of the purchase order whether the date is written in month-day-year format or in year-month-day format. Unfortunately, a computer cannot do the same.

Because EDI is designed to allow processing by the receiver without human interpretation and rekeying, the information must be in a format that is readable and understandable by the computer. This means the information must be in a structured format. EDI standards, therefore, specify how and where information will be written, so that it can be read and processed electronically.

Communication Standards   In the paper world, guidelines also exist for how messages are to be physically moved between trading partners. For instance it is normal business practice that letters are put in envelopes and are sent via regular mail if routine or via express mail if urgent. Similar guidelines on transmission methods exist in some industries in the EDI environment. These guidelines are called communication standards and address such items as:

- What type of electronic envelope is to be used
- At what baud rate and on which protocol a message should be sent
- What times during the day are acceptable to send and receive messages

What Are the Different Types of Standards?

Proprietary Standards   As guidelines for formatting and communication, EDI standards can be either proprietary or common. Proprietary EDI standards are formatting and communications guidelines whose use is limited to one organization and its trading partners. For instance, in an early application of EDI, K mart developed a prescribed method of communication for its suppliers in their communications with K mart.

Common EDI Standards   Common EDI standards, on the other hand, are guidelines adopted by industry-wide or cross-industry users. Two of the most widely known industry-specific standards are those in the transportation industry (known as TDCC—Transportation Data Coordination Committee standards) and those in the grocery industry (known as UCS—Uniform Communication Standards).

A cross-industry standard is also in use. This standard (known as ANSI X12) was developed by an Accredited Standards Committee chartered by the American National Standards Committee whose purpose was to develop standards that could be used by various industries. (The history of standards development and a detailed description of standards is found in Chapter 4.)

EDI Software

The EDI standards provide a common language, in terms of formatting and syntax, for the development of electronic communications. While the standards are flexible enough to accommodate numerous needs and requirements of different companies, it would be highly unusual for a company to have its internal database set up in the same format as the standard. Just as every company has its own paper form on which information is placed, every company has its own unique format and structure for its database. Therefore, some method must be used to take the information from the company-specific database and translate it to EDI standard format for transmission.

A similar operation often takes place in a paper-based system. For a standard purchase, a buyer might provide the following information to a purchasing assistant:

Buy 10 widgets at $5.00 each from Joe at ABC company.

The purchasing assistant would take this information, retrieve additional information (such as ABC's complete address, the catalog number for widgets, and normal terms and conditions) from the company's database, and then "translate" this information into the standard purchase order form used by the company. In the EDI world the translation from company-specific format to EDI standard format is done by EDI software. EDI software, which is discussed in detail in Chapter 5, is commercially available for mainframe, minicomputers, and microcomputers. Usually some in-house software development is also needed in order to do EDI.

EDI Networks

Through the use of EDI software and EDI standards, a company can abstract information from its database, prepare a purchase order or other type of documentation in regular company format, and then translate that document to a standard format for transmission to a trading partner. Just as transmission of paper documents is done through a network made up of transportation and storage facilities, so is electronic transmission done through a network system.

EDI documents are transmitted electronically through phone or data lines from one computer to another. In a direct EDI network the computers of the trading partners are linked directly, usually through dial-up modems. When one of the partners wants to transmit documents to the other, the sender simply dials up the receiving party and transmits the document.

A direct system works well when a company is communicating electronically with only a limited number of trading partners. However, as the number of trading partners increases, the difficulty of maintaining open lines for the trading partners, of coordinating timing of transactions, of assuring communications compatibility, and of maintaining communications security also increases. To overcome these problems, many companies using EDI communicate with trading partners through a third party network.

A third party network, also known as a value added network or VAN, serves as an intermediary between trading partners. The VAN in the EDI world is similar to the post office in the paper world. The post office receives mail from a large number of senders, sorts the mail by receiver, and delivers the mail to a post office box where it is later retrieved by the receiver. A VAN performs the same function for electronic documents. A VAN maintains a mailbox for both the sender and the receiver. In this way, if a company has a large number of electronic purchase orders to send to different sellers, the company would transmit all of the purchase orders to the VAN in a single connect or call. The VAN would then sort the purchase orders by seller and place each seller's purchase orders in the appropriate mailbox. Then at some later time, the seller would dial in and retrieve its mail in the form of electronic purchase orders. This allows each trading partner to create only one electronic transmission to the VAN rather than having to create a separate electronic transmission for each trading partner.

Further, VANs can also perform additional services, similar to the services performed by mailing bureaus. For instance, a VAN will not only receive electronic transmissions in standard format, many VANs will also accept transmissions in company specific format and translate them into EDI standards before placing the transmissions in the mailboxes. The use of the value added services provided by a VAN removes much of the complexity of EDI from the trading partners. EDI third party networks are discussed in detail in Chapter 6.

WHAT DOCUMENTS CAN BE SENT VIA EDI?

In general, any business document for which your company has a standard form can potentially be transmitted electronically. If the information can be organized to fit a form, it can be organized for electronic communication. Currently, there are standards that cover the EDI transmission of nearly 200 electronic documents. The most common documents transmitted electronically include:

- purchase order
- purchase order acknowledgment
- purchase order change request
- purchase order change request acknowledgment
- request for quotation
- response to request for quotation
- planning schedule
- release notice
- invoice
- receiving advice
- functional acknowledgment
- bill of lading
- shipment information
- freight invoices
- status reports
- shipment pickup order
- waybill interchange

In addition to the above documents that can be used by a number of different industries, documents specialized to a particular industry can also be communicated electronically via EDI. For instance, EDI standard documentation formats exist for petroleum industry-unique documents such as nominations, meter tickets, inventories, and gauge tickets.

WHO SHOULD USE EDI?

While the use of EDI is steadily growing in most major industries, certain company or industry characteristics make its use particularly appropriate. If your company or industry exhibits any of the following characteristics you should seriously pursue EDI:

- HANDLES A LARGE VOLUME OF REPETITIVE STANDARD ACTIONS
  An important factor in both the transportation and grocery industry.

- OPERATES ON A VERY "TIGHT" MARGIN
  A strong influence in the grocery industry's decision to pursue EDI.

- FACES STRONG COMPETITION REQUIRING SIGNIFICANT PRODUCTIVITY IMPROVEMENTS
  The major reason the automobile industry has embraced EDI.

- OPERATES IN A TIME-SENSITIVE ENVIRONMENT
  The reason retailing is a strong advocate of EDI.

- HAS RECEIVED REQUESTS FROM TRADING PARTNERS
  The reason for EDI activity in a number of industries.

HOW INVOLVED IN EDI DO I HAVE TO GET?

The example of EDI usage given at the beginning of the chapter could have been taken to mean that EDI is an "all-or-nothing" proposition. In other words, you either do EDI completely (for all transactions and partners) or you don't do EDI at all. However, EDI is not like that.

In fact, doing EDI is, in at least one way, a little bit like entering a swimming pool. Some people dive right in and totally immerse themselves. Others wade in the water and just get half-wet, while some just sit on the side and dangle their toes in the water. You can take any of those approaches to doing EDI.

Dave Hough, Manager of Implementation Programs at McDonnell Douglas, has called these three approaches the "levels of EDI." A level 1 user (a toe dangler) uses EDI to transmit only one or two different documents to a limited number of trading partners. In many cases the EDI effort is handled by just one department within the company and the EDI activity is likely to be performed using a door-to-door approach.

A level 2 user (a wader) is using EDI to communicate with a large number of trading partners across a number of industries. Multiple departments within the firm are involved and numerous documents are transmitted and received electronically.

A level 3 company (a diver) is completely immersed in EDI. EDI is seen as not just a method of transmission but as a new way of doing business. Internal corporate functions are restructured to get the most from EDI, and internal applications are bridged.

WHAT ARE THE COSTS AND BENEFITS OF DOING EDI?

Costs and benefits of EDI vary significantly from one user to another. Both depend upon the level of EDI, as well as on the type of hardware used (mainframe or PC). However, the types of benefits received and the types of costs incurred are similar across all usage of EDI. The discussion below introduces the types of benefits and costs likely to be realized with EDI. A detailed discussion of how benefits are obtained along with specific examples of benefits is found in Chapter 2. Chapter 10 provides a detailed analysis of cost categories and presents a method of doing a cost-benefit justification.

EDI Benefits

- REDUCTION IN TRANSACTION TIME
  EDI reduces the time in the business cycle from order placement to receipt of good funds. This reduction in time can lead to additional benefits of:
  - REDUCED INVENTORY
  - INCREASED CASH FLOW
  - LOWER COSTS

- REDUCTION IN KEYING ACTIVITY
  EDI eliminates much of the keying required under a manual system. This leads to:
  - FEWER ERRORS
  - POTENTIAL PERSONNEL REDUCTIONS
  - LOWER COSTS

- IMPROVED RESPONSIVENESS TO CUSTOMER
  Because EDI reduces delays and provides more accurate information, companies can be more responsive to customers' needs. This may lead to:
  - BETTER CUSTOMER SERVICE
  - INCREASED SALES

EDI Costs

The economic cost of doing EDI can vary from relatively insignificant (under $5000) to the level of a major capital investment. The types of costs that will be incurred include:

- SOFTWARE/HARDWARE COSTS
  Costs for development or purchase of software, internal modifications to in-house systems, and maintenance. Cost to purchase a PC and communications modem and maintenance.

- TRANSMISSION COSTS
  Third party charges or communication costs.

- TRAINING
  Both in-house and purchased training for your company as well as for trading partners.

- TIME VALUE COSTS
  Loss of float from earlier payment.

HOW DID EDI GET STARTED?

Although the use of EDI has just recently "come of age," neither the concept of EDI nor the technology needed to perform EDI are new.[6] The idea of EDI was first introduced in the late 1960s in the transportation industry. In 1968 a number of companies in the transportation industry formed a committee to evaluate the feasibility of developing standards for electronic communication. This committee was known as the Transportation Data Coordinating Committee (TDCC). The actions of the TDCC formed the foundation for EDI as used today. Also in 1968 a number of California banks joined together to assess the feasibility of using some form of paperless exchange of financial information in lieu of checks. The efforts of these banks formed the foundation for the development of EFT as used today.

In the early 1970s efforts to develop EDI standards continued. In 1970 the American Bankers Association formed a committee to study the payment systems used in U.S. banks. The committee recommended that industry-wide standards and a national settlement system be developed for paperless transmission of financial information. In 1972 the first automated clearing house system was established, followed in 1973 by the formation of the National Automated Clearing House Association (NACHA). The purpose of NACHA is to allow the electronic exchange of financial information on a national basis.

In 1975 the first EDI standard was published by the TDCC, leading the way for the electronic exchange of information in the transportation industry. Also in 1975 the government began to use the automated clearing house network to process government payments such as social security checks and military payroll checks.

In 1976 the first major proprietary EDI system was put into operation with American Hospital Supply's (now Baxter Healthcare) introduction of a private order entry network that allowed hospital buyers to link directly to AHS's computer. Other large organizations also developed and implemented proprietary EDI systems. During this period, the development of EDI networks also began. Companies such as General Electric and National Data Corporation developed arrangements to let outside users have access to time-sharing networks for communication. RAILINC, a communications network for the rail industry was also established.

In the late 1970s significant progress was made toward national EDI standards and networks with the creation of a national committee to establish EDI standards. The committee, established in 1978, was referred to as the X12 committee and was officially chartered as an Accredited Standards Committee by the American National Standards Institute in 1979. The committee began work on the development of EDI standards for use across industry groups.

Also during this period, the grocery industry began significant industry-wide efforts toward EDI. In 1978 the grocery industry commissioned A. D. Little, Inc., to study the feasibility of a grocery industry EDI system. The study was completed in 1980; recommendations of the study suggested that the use of EDI in the grocery industry was both technically and economically feasible. It was further recommended that grocery industry EDI standards be patterned after TDCC standards already developed. The grocery industry followed the recommendations and formed the Uniform Communications Standards Committee (UCS) to develop standards along the line of the TDCC standards. Also in 1980 the transportation industry adopted TDCC standards for use by motor, air, and ocean carriers and shippers, as well as by public warehouses.

In the early 1980s the development of EDI standards and the adoption of EDI systems continued to progress. In 1981 the first standard was published by the ANSI X12 committee. The first EDI transmission in the grocery industry was made using the UCS standards, and plans were begun for an industry-wide pilot of the UCS system, which was conducted in 1982. An industry-wide EDI effort was also started in the automobile industry with the formation of the Automotive Industry Action Group (AIAG) to look at ways in which U.S. automakers could become more competitive with foreign automakers. Among items specifically examined by the group was EDI.

During this time, work also continued on the development of standards for the transmission of financial information. In 1982 the National Automated Clearing House Association introduced the first standard format for corporate trade payments.

In the mid-1980s the use of EDI began to expand significantly. Additional standards were published by the X12 committee as well as by TDCC and UCS. A number of large organizations, particularly those in the automobile industry, began to announce that their suppliers were expected to communicate electronically. During this time, efforts were also begun on the development of international EDI standards. The ANSI X12 committee joined with its European counterpart to begin work on international standards.

In addition, a number of industry groups announced the adoption of the ANSI X12 standards. In 1986 the Data Interchange Standards Association (DISA) was created to encourage the use of X12 standards across industry lines, and a common data dictionary was developed for use in the development of EDI standards. In 1987 discussions began between the various standards groups such as TDCC, ANSI X12, and UCS to ensure compatibility among EDI standards. Also in 1987 efforts were begun to increase compatibility between EDI and EFT. NACHA announced efforts to incorporate X12 standards into the automated clearing house payment system. Also in 1987 the Treasury Department announced the initiation of a program to replace vendor check payments with ACH payments. The Department of Defense, in 1988, stated that "EDI is the way to go" and that ANSI X12 standards would be used for electronic communications between the Department of Defense and its suppliers and transportation carriers.[5]

WHY SHOULD I READ THE REST OF THIS BOOK?

Given the benefits of using EDI and the number of industries and companies currently involved in EDI efforts, if your company is not yet using EDI, it is very likely that you will be in the near future. This book is designed to help you enter the EDI market.

It presents an overview of what EDI is and how you can implement an EDI system to best fit your needs. The remaining chapters of Section I provide examples of companies currently using EDI and highlight the benefits. Section II discusses the components of EDI, providing a description of EDI standards, software, hardware, and value added networks and explains their functions within the EDI environment. Section III presents implementation issues of EDI. A detailed guideline on implementation steps is presented, along with a discussion of staffing and training requirements. In addition, common EDI barriers are discussed and recommendations are given for overcoming these barriers. Section III also presents a method of quantifying costs and benefits of EDI. Section IV of the book examines the use of EDI on an international basis as well as for financial transactions (EFT). Also included in this section is a discussion of where EDI is going in the future and its integration with other management technologies such as J-I-T, MRP, and its use with point-of-sale scanning.

2

WHY EDI?

INTRODUCTION

Why should your company invest the time and effort necessary to implement EDI? Will EDI really make any significant difference in your competitiveness and profitability? This chapter addresses those issues.

EDI can provide substantial benefits. At a minimum the benefits include improved efficiency and reduced costs. However, EDI can have a much more significant impact on your company than just a reduction in costs. When EDI is viewed as, and is used as, a new approach to doing business, the benefits from EDI can be substantial. These include:

- Improved internal operations from a reduction in time
- Better responsiveness to customers
- Improved channel management
- Increased ability to compete, both domestically and internationally

A discussion of each of these benefits follows. However, another very important benefit of doing EDI should be discussed first. That benefit is avoiding what might happen if you do not do EDI.

BUSINESS SURVIVAL

One obvious and compelling reason to implement EDI is that EDI is becoming a "requirement of doing business." The ability to receive and send electronic transmissions is becoming a necessity in a number of diverse industries. Many organizations are beginning to believe they have no choice but to implement EDI efforts because EDI is fast becoming the norm in their industry.

EDI Is the Norm

According to a recent Coopers and Lybrand study, EDI is the preferred method of doing business in the automotive, railroad, chemical, and pharmaceutical industries.[1] Another study has reported that EDI's "momentum may be unstoppable in paper products, metals, oil and gas, chemicals, grocery, office products, warehousing, rails, trucking, ocean freight, pharmaceuticals, and medical supplies."[2]

As the use of EDI continues to grow in these industries, the ability of an organization within these industries to conduct business without EDI will decrease. Already, many companies in these leading industries are finding that they must use EDI in order to maintain their business relationships with other firms in the industry. Users of EDI have been putting pressure on their trading partners to join the movement toward EDI since the time EDI was first introduced. And the pressure is continuing as the use of EDI and the benefits received from its use continue to grow.

Pressure from Trading Partners

In a 1986 study of early pioneers of EDI implementation, half of the companies surveyed felt EDI would eventually become a vendor selection criteria. In other words, the companies stated that sometime in the future, their purchasing policy would be "no EDI—no purchase order." A major food manufacturer explained this position by stating that "We will choose suppliers on whether we can do business with them efficiently, and this means EDI." A consumer products manufacturer stated that "EDI will become like the phone. You won't think of doing business with someone you can't reach electronically." An auto manufacturer stated the case for EDI even more strongly. "In the long run our intent is to do business electronically—we will not do business with non-EDI vendors."[3] These early users of EDI predicted that the use of EDI would become a necessity for doing business. This prediction appears to have been accurate.

A number of organizations have publicly informed their trading partners that they must implement EDI. According to one source, the Buick Division of General Motors has sent a letter to its suppliers saying that to continue to do business with Buick, suppliers must implement EDI.[4] The Ford Motor Co. has stated that "it is a requirement for its suppliers to have EDI capabilities."[5] Toys-R-Us has begun the implementation of an EDI system and a corporate spokesman has stated that once EDI is operational within the company, "it'll be very difficult to do business with non-EDI suppliers."[6] In a 1988 study conducted by the Council of Logistics Management and Ohio State University, the percentage of companies that reported they had been required to implement EDI systems by major customers ranged from 45 percent in the chemical industry to 12 percent in the merchandise industry, as shown in Figure 2-1.[7]

"Some of our large customers have required us to develop EDI systems..."

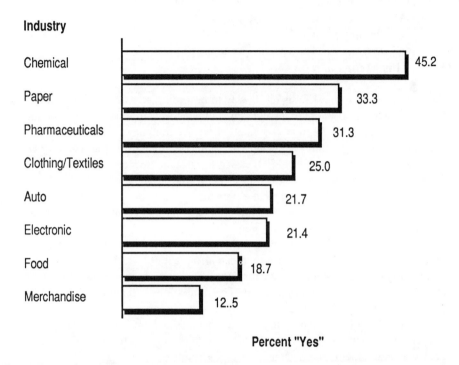

Industry

Chemical   45.2

Paper   33.3

Pharmaceuticals 31.3

Clothing/Textiles 25.0

Auto   21.7

Electronic   21.4

Food   18.7

Merchandise   12..5

Percent "Yes"

Source: *Customer Service: A Management Perspective*
Council of Logistics Management
(Reprinted with permission)

Figure 2-1   EDI implementation required by trading partners.

The pressure from customers to implement EDI is contributing significantly to the growth of EDI. According to a study of Fortune 1000 companies by INPUT, a California consulting firm, the most commonly cited reason for implementing EDI was strong demand by customers.[8] Another study of companies with annual revenues of at least $100 million indicated that 15 percent had implemented EDI in response to customer demand.[9]

Future Growth

This pressure on trading partners from customers is likely to continue. A study by Frost and Sullivan found that of the current users of EDI, 15 percent reported that they will be "urging" over 100 new trading partners to become involved in EDI in the near future.[10] A study conducted by EDI Research, Inc., indicated that of the Fortune 1000 firms currently using EDI, 83 percent plan on adding new trading partners to their EDI systems in 1989, with 16 percent of those planning to add at least 50 new trading partners.[11]

What This Means to You

These figures show that EDI is on its way to becoming an essential requirement for doing business. If your company has not already been approached by a trading partner to implement EDI, it is very likely that your company will be approached in the near future. In some ways a request from a trading partner that you do EDI may make the implementation of EDI easier. For instance, according to Lee Foote, Du Pont's EDI manager, a letter from General Motors indicating that GM was planning to implement EDI helped to eliminate ". . . interior barriers on spending money. We no longer had to spend a lot of time justifying because when your key customer asks you to do something, you obviously respond."[12]

However, being in the situation where you must implement EDI, and you must implement it *now* to satisfy a customer, can also make the implementation effort more difficult. Often companies find that they have a very short time frame in which to respond to their customer's request. This limits how effectively EDI can be integrated with other systems in the company, and may also limit the benefits achieved. EDI requires changes in internal processes and procedures. It takes time to prepare personnel to accept these changes; therefore, it is better to do EDI on your schedule rather than on someone else's schedule.

In other words, it is much better for a company to be proactive rather than reactive in implementing EDI. Establishing an EDI program designed to best meet your needs, and doing so when it best fits your schedule, is likely to make the implementation easier and the benefits to you greater. And benefits from the implementation of EDI can be significant.

COST SAVINGS

One significant benefit of the use of EDI is that it reduces the costs of operations and increases efficiency. Numerous examples of substantial cost savings, which have led to increased competitiveness and profitability, can be found. For instance, one estimate places cost savings due to EDI, across all industries, at between 5 to 6 percent of sales.[13] It has been widely cited that the use of EDI in the automotive industry will save over $200 per car.[14] Estimates for the grocery industry indicate that the current use of EDI is saving the industry approximately $300 million annually, with a potential additional savings of $250 million annually when EDI is used for direct store delivery accounts.[15] IBM estimates that its use of EDI will save the corporation over $60 million in the next five years.[16]

Types of Savings

As indicated, the overall cost savings from EDI can be quite significant. These savings result from improvements in a number of areas, including:

- Reduction in document processing tasks and costs
- Reduction in personnel levels and better use of personnel
- Reduction in inventory and the associated reduction in the cost of carrying and storing the inventory
- Reduction in other costs such as premium freight, special handling, etc., required due to late receipt of information

Document Processing Costs

One of the most obvious savings resulting from the use of EDI is document processing costs. Reported savings in document processing costs vary significantly from company to company. This is due primarily to the fact that cost savings are dependent upon how the document was processed prior to EDI. As an example, purchase order processing and transmittal costs would vary greatly depending upon whether the traditional method of preparing the document was manual or computerized, and whether the traditional method of transmittal was via phone, mail, or personal pickup.

One study by INPUT of 200 U.S. managers reported that EDI offers a 10 to 1 cost benefit in the processing of purchase orders. The study indicated that a paper document that has to be typed, revised, and mailed costs up to $49, while an electronic document costs less than $5.[17] Hewlett-Packard has reported a decrease in purchase order costs from $1.65 per purchase order to $.58 per purchase order, a reduction of 65 percent.[18] The Automotive Industry Action Group (AIAG) estimates that $12 per document is saved through the use of EDI.[19] According to George Klima, former Director of Accounting Systems for Super Valu Stores, that corporation saves approximately $1.30 per purchase order and $10 per invoice through the use of EDI.[20] The Douglas Aircraft Company has reported a reduction of $5 per transaction.[21] RCA, an early pioneer in the use of EDI, was able to reduce the cost of an average purchase order from $62 before EDI to approximately $7.50 after EDI.[22] Digital Equipment Corporation has reported a reduction in purchase order preparation costs from $125 to less than $32.[23] The U.S. Treasury Department has reported a reduction, in just postage alone, of over $60 million annually through the use of EDI for transmitting payment information.[24]

Where do these cost reductions come from? EDI reduces the cost of processing documents by reducing or eliminating the following actitivities:

- Repeated keying of redundant information
- Manual reconciliation of different documents (such as purchase orders, receiving notices, and invoices)

- Correction of errors caused by incorrect data entry
- Sorting, distributing, and filing documents
- Document mailing or telephoning of information

It is obvious that the use of EDI does reduce the cost of document processing and transmittal. While the reported savings vary significantly, even a very small savings in document costs can have a significant impact on an organization's profitability, due to the large number of documents transmitted between trading partners. Across all industries, the average number of documents required to process just one transaction has been estimated at anywhere from 5 to 12 documents, with some estimates ranging as high as 30 documents per transaction. In certain industries the volume of paperwork is staggering. Members of the grocery industry annually exchange over 15 million purchase orders, and another 90 million additional documents.[25] The Department of Defense annually issues 1.4 million bills of lading, each of which normally requires at least another three documents to process.[26] Due to the large volume of paperwork handled, any reduction in document processing costs offers a substantial benefit to EDI users.

Personnel Costs

Another type of cost often reduced due to the use of EDI is the cost of personnel. In a 1986 study of early users of EDI, half of the organizations using EDI anticipated that EDI would allow the company to operate with fewer personnel.[27] In some of these instances, the companies planned to reduce personnel levels; in others, the companies planned to reassign personnel to more productive activities. A reduction in personnal costs results from:

- Elimination of redundant rekeying
- Elimination of manual reconciliation
- Reduced time spent correcting errors
- "Freeing" professional personnel from administrative tasks

Examples of organizations that have experienced a reduction in personnel costs due to EDI include Super Valu Stores, Hasbro, Inc., Digital Equipment Corporation, and LTV Steel Company.

Through the use of EDI in both the purchasing and accounting functions, Super Valu has been able to reduce the number of personnel required in the accounts payable area. George Klima has reported that Super Valu experienced a $600,000 reduction in accounts payable personnel costs due to the reduction of the time and effort needed to reconcile invoices against purchase orders.[28] Hasbro, Inc., a toy manufacturer, is in the process of implementing an EDI system to process invoices, purchase orders, remittance advices, and shipping information. Three divisions are currently processing purchase orders and invoices electronically and have already saved the company the cost of 10 order processing clerks.[29] Digital Equipment Corporation (DEC) anticipates that by 1991, 80 percent of its purchase orders, invoices, and payments will be made electronically. If this level is reached, DEC anticipates being able to either cut or reassign 30 percent of its purchasing personnel.[30] LTV Steel Company is another EDI user that has experienced a reduction in personnel costs due to EDI. LTV uses EDI to exchange freight bills with the railroads. Because of increased accuracy and improved speed in processing bills, LTV has been able to reduce the auditing effort required and saves between $20,000 and $30,000 a month in clerical costs and overcharges.[31]

As mentioned earlier, the reduction in personnel costs due to EDI does not necessarily have to mean a reduction in personnel. According to Janet Madigan of TDCC/EDIA, The Electronic Data Interchange Association, "You may have to rearrange your labor force" due to EDI, but it does not mean "that you have to lose clerical people. You may be able to assign clerical workers to other tasks in places where they might be more productive. It all affects the bottom line."[32]

Inventory Savings

Another type of cost that can be reduced through the use of EDI is inventory. EDI helps to reduce inventory cost by reducing the level of safety stock required by:

- Reducing transaction time, which reduces order cycle time, which may reduce safety stock
- Reducing uncertainty in order cycle time

For many companies, the reduction in inventory costs is the most significant cost savings resulting from the use of EDI. Navistar International Corporation has reported that it was able to cut inventories by one-third, or approximately $167 million, in the first 18 months of its EDI implementation. More recently, Navistar has been able to reduce inventories from a 33-day supply to a 6-day supply, for an 80 percent reduction.[33] According to George Klima of Super Valu, the one-day reduction in lead time that resulted from the use of EDI led to a $10 million reduction in inventory.[34] Bergen Brunswig, the second largest pharmaceutical wholesaler in the United States, reported a reduction in inventory from a 10-day supply to a 4-day supply and states that the reduction is due to the faster lead time provided by EDI.[35] According to the company, under a paper-based system, it took six days for the average order to get to the manufacturer and another four days for the merchandise to be delivered. With EDI the six days of mailing and processing time has been eliminated and only enough inventory to cover the four days of delivery time needs to be carried. These examples show that through the use of EDI, inventory costs can be significantly reduced, without an adverse effect on customer service levels.

Other Cost Reductions

The implementation of EDI can reduce other types of costs as well. EDI has been reported to reduce transportation costs, particularly premium freight charges. Because EDI provides accurate information quickly, better planning and management of transportation can be done. This can lead to a reduction in small shipments (which are more expensive on a per-unit basis than are full truckload shipments), as well as a reduction in premium freight. Navistar was able to reduce freight charges by 5 percent in each of the first two years of EDI implementation and also reduced premium freight charges for expedited shipments by 50 percent.[36]

EDI also reduces error costs by reducing the number of business documents that are either incorrect or lost. An error in a business document can be very costly. Suppose, for instance, that while entering the information from a purchase order into an order entry system, the order entry clerk enters a quantity of 10 units instead of 100 units. In most cases, the error will not be noticed until the order is delivered. At that point, special handling and premium freight may be required to correct the problem created by the incorrect order entry. Along the same lines, a lost order can also be costly; because in many cases the buyer does not know that an order was not received by the seller until after the time when the items were to be delivered. This could lead to a possible shut-down in the production line.

The use of EDI reduces these problems in a number of ways. First, because EDI reduces the number of times the same information is entered into various computer systems, EDI reduces the number of opportunities for errors. In other words, whatever information was transmitted is the exact information received. No new errors can be introduced since no rekeying is done. Second, through edit checks in EDI software, some data entry errors made at the source will be caught early. And third, EDI provides for a functional acknowledgment to be returned to the sender of the electronic message. The functional acknowledgment lets the buyer know that the document was, in fact, received by the seller. Further, an electronic purchase order acknowledgment, confirming the content of the order, can also be sent. While EDI does not eliminate all errors, it does allow for early, and less costly, correction of errors.

The reduction in errors due to EDI can be substantial. For instance, one government agency was able to identify over $125 million in errors in one year through the use of EDI.[37] In another case, PPG reported that through the use of EDI, the company was able to process, in a one-week period, over 800 transactions, worth over $10 million dollars, with General Motors. Of those 800 transactions, only one contained an error.[38]

The use of EDI, then, can result in significant savings to an organization. While the implementation of EDI is not without costs, nearly every organization that has implemented EDI has found that, over the long term, the direct savings derived from the use of EDI far outweigh the costs of implementing EDI.

Importance of Cost Savings

As substantial as the cost savings from EDI are, they do not, in most users' opinions, represent the most significant benefit of EDI. A 1988 survey of several thousand business managers indicated that among companies either currently using EDI or planning to use EDI, their main reason for using EDI was not cost reduction. In fact, a reduction in paperwork was cited as the major reason by only 12.4 percent of the respondents; reduced manpower by less than 4 percent; and inventory savings by only 3.2 percent. The major reasons for using EDI, according to the study, were to provide improved customer service and to have better access to information.[39]

These opinions are also shared by some of the pioneers in EDI usage. Whenever asked to describe the cost savings Super Valu has realized from EDI, George Klima does so reluctantly. While Super Valu has achieved substantial cost savings due to EDI, Klima states that by focusing primarily on the cost savings of EDI, users are missing the real advantages and benefits of EDI. According to Klima, the significant benefits of EDI are improved internal operations and improved responsiveness to customers.

In other words, EDI should be viewed as a whole new way of doing business, not just as a cost saving technique. When integrated with other company operations, EDI provides substantial, strategic advantages. These advantages include:

- Improved operations
- Increased customer responsiveness
- Improved channel management
- Increased ability to compete internationally

IMPROVED OPERATIONS

Although EDI is usually seen primarily as a way of improving communications externally, implementing an EDI effort within your organization provides a chance to improve internal operations. Improvements can result from the review of current operations that should precede the implementation of EDI, from the integration of EDI with other management techniques, from the improved use of personnel, and from the management of more accurate and timely information.

Internal Reassessment

Implementing EDI successfully requires a review of your current operations. Before it is possible to replace paper flows with electronic flows, the paper flows must be understood. Therefore, a first step in the use of EDI is a complete review and evaluation of current operations. This step often forces many companies to "take a hard look at themselves" for the first time. This assessment may include "examining your inventory procedures, your management of multi-division operation, or it might include redefining your relationship with suppliers."[40]

This reassessment will often result in improvements to your internal operations. For instance, when Texas Instruments first implemented EDI, they realized that they had to "examine their [current] methods and see whether incoming and outgoing data can draw on the right sources to be useful." According to Kenneth Shoquist of TI, "what we did first was put the applications in place, then did EDI."[41] Because EDI often leads to the integration of other systems, "once you implement EDI, you may realize other shortcomings" within the organization, according to one EDI consultant.[42] One manufacturer discovered that standard, repetitive purchase orders were regularly being sent through a second and unnecessary review process. Correcting this problem reduced the processing time for the manufacturer, even before any EDI was added.[43]

Integration of EDI with Other Systems

EDI also enhances the performance of other management systems and techniques. The strong growth of EDI in the automotive industry is due, in a large part, to the need for improved communications to support such management techniques as Materials Requirements Planning (MRP) and Just-In-Time (JIT) production and inventory management. Both of these techniques require fast and accurate communication between trading partners, and EDI fills this need. EDI, in this usage, then becomes "not an entity in and of itself, but a link in an integrated manufacturing system," according to one EDI consultant.[44]

As an example, the Ford Motor Company sees EDI as the "key to fine-tuning JIT" because EDI helps to improve production schedule stability. According to a purchasing agent at Ford, EDI represented a major change in dealing with suppliers who provide parts in the JIT environment. With EDI, Ford communicates its parts needs and sends purchase orders electronically, and also reviews suppliers' schedules electronically. The use of EDI, in lieu of mail, as the method of communicating with suppliers has increased schedule stability.[45]

Other auto manufacturers, as well as their suppliers, are linking their JIT and EDI systems together. According to the Woodbridge Group, a car seat manufacturer, "We have a 3.5 hour window in which to perform a complete manufacturing cycle from the time we receive the order through electronic transmission to the time the seat is installed in the car. This includes internal processing, manufacturing, assembly, shipping, and transit time. This would be impossible without electronic transmission of information." On a weekly basis, Woodbridge receives a transmission that forecasts vehicle production for the next 12 weeks and also receives daily electronic transmissions that indicate the production schedule for the next 10 days. Upon receipt, the forecasts and schedules are run through Woodbridge's MRP program, which generates an EDI purchase order, which is forwarded to suppliers.

In this way, "JIT uses EDI as a tool," according to Woodbridge's Director of Information Systems.[46]

Digital Equipment Corporation (DEC) is another company that sees EDI as a way of improving internal operations. DEC's MicroVAXs manufacturing plant has implemented EDI as a part of its MRP system. Because of EDI, the MRP system is fully electronic. The integrated MRP and EDI system electronically determines when and what to order, transmits releases, and acknowledges shipping dates. Since integrating EDI into the MRP system, DEC has been able to reduce inventory by 80 percent and lead times by 50 percent.[47]

EDI cannot only be linked to manufacturing systems such as JIT and MRP; EDI can also be used to improve the performance of purchasing systems. For instance, GTE Valenite Corporation uses a computerized purchasing system for buying MRO (maintenance, repair, and operations) items. The purchasing system, which is linked to the EDI system, is networked into the same central computer as is the maintenance department system. Each morning, the MRO buyer queries the computer system's message center for requisitions placed the day before by the maintenance department. Any requisitions found are then transferred into the purchasing department's system and are automatically transformed from requisitions to purchase requests. The purchase requests are then transmitted by EDI to vendors. Under this system, the vendor receives the purchase order the day after the requisition for the items was generated. The integration of the maintenance and purchasing systems with the EDI system not only speeds placement of the order, but also eliminates the need for the purchasing department to prepare and send a purchase order.[48]

These examples show that EDI is more than just a method of fast communication. It is a tool that can be used to improve current management practices and techniques.

Improved Personnel Productivity

The use of EDI not only improves the management and operation of internal systems, but also improves the efficiency and contribution of personnel. Because EDI eliminates much of the administrative activity usually performed in preparing documentation, its use frees up time for personnel to spend on more productive activity. One estimate shows that the average buyer spends 80 percent of his time on administrative tasks.[49] Because EDI reduces the amount of paperwork required, much of this administrative activity is also reduced. In addition, because EDI eliminates many of the problems with orders, such as incorrect information and lost documents, both buyers and sales representatives spend less time trying to solve administrative problems and more time doing their professional jobs.

According to George Klima, buyers at Super Valu now see their roles as merchandisers, where prior to EDI their roles were primarily administrative.[50] Sales people also see an improvement in productivity with EDI. According to a spokesman for the National Electrical Manufacturers Representatives Association, with EDI, sales reps "are in an ideal position to spend even more time with customers understanding their unique needs because computers will place the order after the sale. Because the computer in an EDX [EDI in the electrical industry] system serves as a support function, the rep will have more time to conduct creative selling, sales forecasting, strategic planning, and customer service."[51]

Access to Better Information

The use of EDI provides one additional, significant improvement to internal operations. Through EDI a company has access to much more accurate information, and has access to that information in a timely manner. When EDI is fully integrated within an organization, once information is received into the company through the EDI system, that information is available for use throughout the company. The 3M company, according to information specialist Hal McDonald, receives as many benefits from the use of EDI internally as it does from the use of EDI with trading partners. McDonald states that because internal systems are linked to the EDI system, "We do not have to rekey any data that we receive via EDI in order to process it in accounting, purchasing, shipping, or whichever departments need access to it."[52] Thus, the use of data received via EDI insures that everyone in the company is working with the same information and that it is both accurate and up-to-date. The availability of timely and accurate information leads to another significant benefit of EDI—that of improved responsiveness to customers.

IMPROVED CUSTOMER RESPONSIVENESS

As previously mentioned, the use of EDI provides management with the ability to use information more effectively. Because information available on a "real time" basis is more accurate, management can more effectively address the concerns of customers. Thus, many companies are finding that they can provide much higher levels of customer service due to EDI. In addition, a large number of EDI users have found that their ability to respond quickly has actually increased sales. EDI's ability to quickly transmit orders, coupled with point-of-purchase sales tracking methods, has allowed manufacturers to adjust quickly to changes in the market-place.

Increased Customer Service

According to a 1988 nationwide study on customer service, "information has moved to center stage in providing efficient and effective customer service."[53] The study, conducted for the Council of Logistics Management by Ohio State University, indicated that the most important ingredient of an effective customer service relationship is "accurate and timely information." The study showed that in almost one out of ten orders, some status information on the order is requested by the customer prior to product delivery and that nearly one-third of the respondents could provide status information to customers in ten minutes. Many of these companies used EDI to provide the information.[54]

Increased Sales

Companies have also experienced increased sales with EDI, particularly when EDI is linked with some form of point-of-sale data collection. One of the leaders in this area is the retail industry. In this industry, the use of EDI, along with Universal Product Code (UPC) bar coding, has led to increased sales in a number of retail sectors. According to Paul Benchener, Director of EDI services at Levi Straus & Co., the combination of UPC and EDI has increased sales by 25 percent over the last three years. As reported by Benchener, "With every retailer that we've hooked up with on EDI, we've seen sales increases."[55]

The sales increases occur because the manufacturer can respond quickly to trends in the market place. As an item is sold, the UPC code is scanned at the register. This provides information on what is selling. Orders are then generated electronically based upon this information and are then transmitted via EDI to manufacturers. The fast transmission of orders translates into a quick replenishment of the "hot sellers," and thus an increase in sales.

Haggar, a manufacturer of clothing, has reported that in a one-year period, retailers were able to increase sales by 27 percent through the use of EDI. In addition, the increase in sales was accomplished with no increase in inventory. In some cases, the retailers were able to increase sales while decreasing inventory levels.[56]

Electronic data interchange can be used, then, to improve responsiveness to customers. Not only will this make your company "easier to do business with" and help you to be perceived as offering quality service; this increased responsiveness can also lead to increased sales and profitability.

Improving responsiveness to your trading partners is likely to also improve your relationships with them and with other organizations in your logistical supply chain. EDI has been found, in many instances, to improve trading partner relationships.

IMPROVED CHANNEL RELATIONSHIPS

In recent years, a number of U.S. companies have begun to focus on improving relationships with trading partners as a way to improve productivity. As global competition has increased, the traditional view of trading partners as adversaries has been questioned; and a movement toward stronger, more cooperative relationships with trading partners has begun. EDI enhances this trend toward improved channel relationships. According to Susan Lesch of Touche Ross & Co., EDI requires changes "in operations, in strategies, and perhaps most importantly, changes in attitudes about suppliers."[57]

Stronger Relationships

When questioned as to whether EDI had an impact on vendor relationships, 87 percent of the respondents to a 1986 study believed that EDI improved relationships. The most important reason cited for the improved relationship was that the cooperation and coordination required to implement EDI tended to build trust between the trading partners. Also cited as important was the fact that EDI enhanced the sharing of information between trading partners, and this was seen as a movement toward longer, more cooperative relationships. One other factor often cited as a reason for improved relationships was that EDI eliminated issues that often caused conflict, such as lost and incorrect orders.[58]

EDI can also be used as a way of "extending" organizational boundaries to include trading partners. The linkage created by EDI tends to strengthen the ties between trading partners by encouraging stronger levels of commitment. Increasingly, however, as the closeness of relationships between trading partners is increasing, the number of trading relationships is decreasing.

Reduced Vendor Base

Many companies have found that one of the side effects of EDI is reduction of number of vendors. According to TI's Shoquist, concentrating volume among a limited number of vendors "is not a requirement of EDI, but EDI helps that to happen."[59] This tends to lead to a fewer, longer-term relationships which, according to the Vice President of Information Resources for Levi Straus, will become the norm in the future because of EDI.[60]

Xerox Corporation is just one of many companies that have improved channel relationships through EDI. According to Xerox spokesman Judith Campbell, Xerox has used EDI to improve the "customer building functions" and in 1987 successfully used EDI as a major bargaining chip with trading partners to win contracts.[61] However, Campbell points out that while EDI will improve already good trading partner relationships, "An EDI implementation effort requires working closely together and the sharing of information, and this will be a struggle with any trading partner with whom you have a very adversarial relationship."

IMPROVED ABILITY TO COMPETE
INTERNATIONALLY

Another significant benefit achieved through EDI is an improved ability to compete on a global basis. According to Anthony Craig, formerly of General Electric Information Services Corporation, EDI can help meet the needs of today's global market. Craig has reported that, "The old methods of communicating simply do not allow [U.S. firms] to compete. They can't give us the productivity gains we need because they can't meet the needs of today's fast-paced global business."[62] EDI can help by more closely linking manufacturers and also by improving the flow of international documentation.

Faster Design/Production

According to Craig, in order to compete internationally, domestic manufacturers have found that they must employ concurrent product/process development where design and production are done simultaneously. Because of increased market segmentation, product proliferation, and shorter product life cycles, manufacturers must be able to respond to changes in the market and to introduce new products quickly. Concurrent product/process development helps manufacturers to respond quickly by cutting down the time it takes to get a new product on the market.

However, for concurrent product/process development to work, the manufacturer and suppliers must be able to exchange information quickly and efficiently. This is where EDI comes in. "The purchasing, engineering, and manufacturing components of a company can respond quickly to requests for quotes, engineering sketches, models, and production drawings. In doing more design work, the auto suppliers are speeding information to [the manufacturers] using EDI."[63] This use of EDI is helping domestic manufacturers to compete with foreign manufacturers who historically have been able to respond to market changes in half the time of domestic manufacturers.

Improved International Documentation

Craig also notes that EDI helps to reduce the number of errors in international documentation and to speed the documentation processing time. According to a study by INPUT, international trade documentation costs $40 billion annually. Further, approximately 40 percent of all paperwork for overseas shipments contains errors.[64] And on the international side, an error can be even more costly than one in a domestic shipment. If any two of the many documents needed for international trade do not match, chances are that the entire shipment may be postponed. EDI, because it reduces errors and eliminates the chance of the introduction of errors after the shipment is initiated, helps significantly in international trade.

One company using EDI extensively for international trade is Union Carbide. The company moves over $1 billion in goods to more than 1200 customers in 100 countries, and generates more than 50,000 export documents a year. All of these documents will, according to the company, be moved electronically in the near future.

Union Carbide's use of EDI has resulted in many of the benefits discussed earlier. Cost savings are conservatively estimated at $1 million a year; the EDI system has helped to streamline internal logistics operations, and the number of freight forwarders and carriers used for international shipments has been decreased. But, perhaps most important, the faster preparation of documents under EDI has resulted in "earlier Customs clearance, boosting the company's reliability as a supplier."[65] Union Carbide's EDI system has significantly increased the company's ability to compete internationally.

SUMMARY

Electronic data interchange is much more than just a faster method of transmitting documentation. When integrated into other systems in the company, EDI enables the company to change how business is done. EDI encourages reassessing current operations, reevaluating relationships with suppliers, and questioning traditional methods. While EDI provides significant cost savings, implementing EDI with only cost savings in mind is short-sighted and limits the benefits that can be achieved. More examples of the benefits of EDI are presented in the next chapter, which discusses how EDI is being used in a selection of industries.

3

EDI USERS

INTRODUCTION

The use of electronic data interchange is becoming pervasive across all industries. As noted, current estimates place the number of United States firms significantly using EDI at nearly 5,000 with the expectation that by 1990 over 11,000 organizations will be using EDI to some degree. Perhaps even more important than the numbers alone are the types of organizations using EDI. According to a 1988 survey, "34 percent of Fortune 1000-class public and private companies, large universities, and government agencies are now using EDI. An additional 20 percent are actively planning and implementing EDI."[1] The use of EDI by the Fortune 1000 firms is distributed across most industries, with over 50 industries having substantial industry-wide action groups working on EDI implementation. The widespread use of EDI by so many major players in so many diverse industries indicates that a foundation for fast, explosive growth of EDI has been set. According to INPUT, a market research company, annual EDI activity should grow at an annual rate of 56 percent through 1993.[2]

The purpose of this chapter is to indicate how EDI is being used in a selection of industries. This discussion of EDI is in no way exhaustive; however, it does show the diversity of EDI usage. It also shows the different ways in which industries and individual companies have become involved in EDI efforts. Discussed are examples of EDI usage in:

- The transportation sector
- The grocery industry
- The health care industry
- The automotive industry
- Retailing
- The federal government

Two additional applications of EDI are its use for electronic payments and its use internationally. Because of the importance and the uniqueness of electronic payments and international EDI, these applications are discussed in later chapters.

EDI IN THE TRANSPORTATION INDUSTRY

> Shippers and carriers alike are no longer just talking about EDI . . . they're actually doing it.

The transportation industry was one of the first to develop electronic data interchange on an industry-wide basis. The industry pioneered the use of common syntax and architecture for the transmission of electronic data, and most current EDI standards are based upon these early efforts.

EDI is being used, to varying degrees, by all elements of the transportation industry. The strongest user of EDI in the transportation industry appears to be the railroads. Major EDI efforts are also underway in the areas of motor transport and ocean transport. In addition, transportation forwarders and brokers are using EDI, as are numerous ports.

According to *Traffic Management* magazine, "EDI appears to have hit its stride [in the transportation industry]. Shippers and carriers alike are no longer just talking about EDI . . . they're actually doing it."[3] Although EDI was started fairly early in the transportation industry, it has taken a number of years for its use to become widespread, due to the complexity of doing EDI in transportation. According to a senior marketing manager at General Electric Information Services, "EDI between a company and its suppliers is fairly straightforward, but when you add the transportation sector with all of its players—the shipper, ocean carriers, railroads, trucking companies, terminal operators, warehouses, brokers, customs—EDI becomes much more complex."[4] However, it now appears that the transportation industry has "reached a critical mass of people who are comfortable with computers and understand and use EDI."[5] The widespread and diverse usage of EDI in the transportation industry can be seen by examining some specific applications of EDI. Examples of how EDI is used by the railroads, motor carriers, ocean carriers, ports, and customs operations are presented.

Rail EDI

The railroads are among the most advanced users of EDI. The rail industry has its own EDI network called Railinc. Railinc is a subsidiary of the Association of American Railroads and acts as a third party network for EDI transmissions. Although originally established to handle only transactions between railroads and their shippers, Railinc has now expanded its services to handle transactions between two nonrail parties, such as a shipper and its suppliers.

Rail Transactions   The primary transactions handled through EDI in the rail industry include rail car location messages and waybills. Rail car location messages are particularly important in the rail industry, because the messages provide a tracing capability that lets shippers and receivers know exactly when a rail shipment will arrive. This information is critically important in production line scheduling; prior to EDI many companies found that they needed two or three full-time people just to call the railroads to check on arrival times. With EDI, this effort is no longer required.[6]

Waybills, which identify the cargo carried in rail cars, also represent critical information to both shippers and the railroads. Currently, approximately 90 percent of all waybills are being transmitted electronically.[7] The fastest growth in rail transactions, however, has been with purchase orders and freight bills.[8]

Users of Rail EDI   Numerous examples can be found of shippers and railroads working together to improve productivity and efficiency for both parties through the use of EDI. One strong supporter and user of rail EDI is Union Pacific. Union Pacific is currently using EDI to transmit car location messages to shippers and is also exchanging electronic bills of lading, freight bills, and freight claims with customers.[9] Conrail, since 1981, has also been a strong user of EDI, using electronic transmissions for the exchange of bills of lading, invoices, rail car tracing, and funds transfer.[10] Burlington Northern also has an EDI program that allows for electronic communications of rail car tracings, bills of lading, and freight bills.[11]

Intermodal EDI   Shippers and the railroads are also using EDI for intermodal movements as well. As an example, Interamerican Transport Systems, Inc., a shippers' agent who moves freight via piggyback (truck trailers moved on rail cars) and truck between the United States and Canada, is a heavy user of EDI. The company handles approximately 10,000 piggyback trailers a year. While the company does not own any of the trailers, it must track the movement of all 10,000 of them. This tracking is done through EDI. With EDI tracking of the trailers, Interamerican has been able to eliminate 16 man-hours of effort per day that were required to manually track the rail cars. In addition, Interamerican also is electronically communicating waybills—a move which is significantly saving time and effort. In the past, communicating waybills to just one railroad, Conrail, took two hours per day through facsimile transmission. Today, through EDI, the transmission takes only about one minute.[12]

Growth in Rail EDI   The use of EDI in the rail industry is expected to continue to grow. According to one Conrail executive, "one day, all shipper-carrier transactions could be conducted electronically. We could reduce all customer/carrier communications to EDI. Starting with sales communications, we could send the customer a bid package, or the customer could put out a general broadcast asking for rates on a certain freight movement. The railroad could respond with rates, electronically. Or the carrier could announce a rate sale on certain corridors and transmit that notice to shippers."[13] This is all in addition to the current use of rail EDI for the transmission of bills of lading, freight bills, invoices, freight claims, and rail car location.

Motor Carrier EDI

The trucking industry has been involved in EDI for nearly as long as the rail industry. However, the level of involvement has been somewhat less, and the reason for the involvement has been different. Current estimates of the percentage of transactions conducted electronically in the trucking industry range from 20 to 30 percent. However, unlike the rail industry, this level of involvement has been "largely customer driven."[14] According to Paul Lemme, a past president of TDCC and an EDI consultant with Lemme Associates, ". . . the motor carriers came on board because their customers demanded it. What we are seeing today is that the ATA [American Trucking Association] has realized that it has to take some control before technology runs it."[15]

Examples of EDI in Trucking

Union Carbide and Yellow Freight   One example of "customers demanding EDI" is Union Carbide. Union Carbide uses specific criteria for selection of motor carriers, and one of those selection factors is EDI. According to one Union Carbide representative, "We would eventually expect carriers to have EDI capability."[16] Union Carbide is currently doing EDI with a number of motor carriers, including Yellow Freight Systems.

One of Union Carbide's major uses of EDI is for electronic freight billing (EFB). According to Yellow Freight, every time a shipment is made, Yellow Freight creates and electronically saves a freight bill. At a designated time the bills are forwarded to Union Carbide's third party network. Once a day, the Union Carbide computer, without human intervention, dials into the third party network and retrieves the stored freight bills. The bills are translated from the TDCC format into Union Carbide format and are then audited against shipments received. Bills that are correctly matched against shipments are automatically routed to the accounts payable system. The bills are then held until the appropriate payment time arrives, and checks are then generated and mailed. In addition, Union Carbide transmits back to the carrier a notification of acceptance or rejection of the freight bill within 24 hours of its receipt.[17]

According to Newton Graves, Vice President of Yellow Freight Systems, use of EDI is an example of "partner shipping" between the shipper and the carrier. Partner shipping means that carriers must work to develop and maintain long-term relationships with shippers. The keys to building these long-term relationships include commitment, cooperation, trust, and communication—and EDI is the key in communications.[18]

Procter & Gamble and Motor Carriers   Another example of the use of EDI between shippers and motor carriers is Procter & Gamble's use of EDI for outbound transportation. Procter & Gamble handles approximately 90,000 freight bills a month, and according to the P & G EDI manager, EDI was seen as a way to improve productivity and also to improve customer service. EDI provided a way for P & G to "reduce the time-consuming aspects of the day-to-day details" and thus allowed customer service representatives to spend more time actually performing customer service tasks.[19]

Procter & Gamble is currently using EDI for the processing of freight bills with 74 percent of its 124 outbound carriers, covering approximately 65 percent of all freight bills received. The use of EDI for freight bills has resulted in benefits to both P & G and to its carriers. Procter & Gamble has experienced a 50- to 75-percent reduction in errors due to the elimination of rekeying efforts. In addition, P & G also experienced a reduction in telephone expenses, improved cash flow, and more productive use of personnel.

Carriers supplying transportation services to P & G have also experienced benefits. One carrier has reported a 17-day reduction in the processing and transmission time for freight bills and a resulting improvement in cash flow. Another carrier has reported a cost savings of about $3.50 per freight bill.[20] The use of EDI by motor carriers is providing significant benefits to shippers and carriers alike. This also appears to be true for ocean carriers and their shippers.

EDI in Ocean Shipping

Another mode of transportation that has found EDI to be beneficial is ocean transport. Ocean carriers, shippers, ports, and customs agencies have all found that the use of EDI saves both time and money while improving customer service. As in the motor carrier industry, the use of EDI in ocean transport is often encouraged by shippers. According to *American Shipper*, "It is becoming increasingly evident that electronics communication capability within the ocean transportation industry is inevitable and that its development is being spurred to a large extent by shippers."[21]

Ocean Forwarders   EDI is also being used by ocean forwarders and by ports in order to improve productivity and service. For instance, the National Customs Brokers and Forwarders Association of America recently formed an EDI committee. According to Paul F. Wegener, President of the Association, in the future "brokers and forwarders will be the managers overseeing the flow of cargo through expanded EDI communications with all of the various transportation modes."[22] The duties of the newly formed committee include educating members about EDI, evaluating the possibility of establishing an EDI network (similar to Railinc) for the forwarders, determining how EDI can best be used, and acting as a liaison on EDI matters to other industries.

Ocean Ports   A number of ports also have substantial EDI efforts underway. The port of Seattle, for one, has established electronic links with a number of carriers. While the port originally set up its system to electronically transmit bills of ladings to railroads, it has now expanded its usage to include brokers, as well as ocean carriers.

The Port Authority of New York and New Jersey also has an EDI effort in place. The EDI system, referred to as ACES (Automated Cargo Expediting System), was developed to speed handling of shipping transactions at the port. The EDI system allows "maritime shipping executives to speedily and efficiently transmit and exchange cargo information at reasonable cost."[23]

The system, which is scheduled to be in place by the summer of 1989, is expected to serve over 400 firms in the maritime industry. Initially, EDI communications will be conducted between steamship lines, terminal operators, and custom house brokers. Later the system is to be expanded to include rail and motor carriers, freight forwarders, and government agencies.

The system is expected to significantly improve document processing. Currently, maritime transactions require the transfer of official documents either by mail or messenger, usually with repeated telephone follow-up. Using EDI to transmit the documents will eliminate the lengthy delays which are common under the current arrangement.[24]

EDI in Great Lakes Shipping

In addition to the EDI activity in the ocean transport segment of the maritime industry, EDI activity has also begun in the Great Lakes segment of the industry. Under consideration is an EDI system for the Great Lakes maritime industry, based upon a 1986 study by the St. Lawrence Seaway Strategic Planning Group. This group recommended that the use of EDI for Great Lakes traffic be investigated since "the rapid advancement of the maritime industry's electronic data interchange programs . . . eventually may automate all maritime transactions."[25] A system similar to the ones currently used by the ports is being planned. The system is expected to provide electronic communications of manifest data, cargo status, vessel scheduling, bills of lading, bookings, purchase orders, and invoices—and would link agents, ports, carriers, brokers, forwarders, inland carriers, warehouse operators, terminal operators, and banks.[26]

Summary of EDI in Transporation

EDI is currently being used in all modes of the transportation industry, and its use is expected to continue to grow. As stated by Stanley R. Rozycki, Operating Vice President of Transportation and Logistics for Federated Department Stores, "Communication, as transportation departments and companies realize, quite clearly is now as essential as the actual movement of the product or goods from point A to point B."[27] EDI is now providing that essential communications ability in the transportation industry.

EDI IN THE GROCERY INDUSTRY

> Savings from EDI from direct store delivery transactions are estimated at over $900 million industry-wide.

The grocery industry was one of the first industries to implement EDI on an industry-wide basis. Characteristics of the grocery industry are such that the use of electronic data interchange is very well suited to the needs of the industry. Margins in the industry are tight, meaning that any method of reducing costs, even to a small degree, could have a significant impact on overall profitability. The grocery industry is also very transaction- and paper-intensive. A 1980 feasibility study on the use of EDI in the grocery industry estimated that over 15 million records flow annually between 5000 manufacturers, 2400 distributors, and 3000 brokers. In addition to the 15 million orders, the industry also processes an additional 90 million documents in the form of order changes, invoices, bills of ladings, invoice changes, payments, price changes, and promotion announcements.[28]

Development of EDI in Grocery

Because of these characteristics, and because of the recognition that the use of EDI could have a significant impact on productivity, in 1978 the grocery industry commissioned a feasibility study on the use of EDI on an industry-wide basis. The study was initiated by a coalition of the six major trade groups in the industry, including the Cooperative Food Distributors of America, the Grocery Manufacturers of America, the National-American Wholesale Grocers Association, the National Association of Retail Grocers, the Food Marketing Institute, and the National Food Brokers Association. The study was conducted by Arthur D. Little, Inc., and focused on "the routine business transaction messages flowing between manufacturer, distributor, and broker associated with the full goods procurement cycle."[29]

The feasibility study indicated that total grocery industry benefits from the use of EDI could be substantial. It was estimated that at a 50 percent usage rate, the direct savings in the form of reduced errors and reduced clerical effort resulting from EDI could reach $84 million annually with operating costs for EDI of approximately $16 million annually. In addition, it was estimated that indirect cost savings, including inventory reduction resulting from more accurate information and more productive use of time, could reach as high as $256 million annually.[30] (While no industry audit of actual costs and benefits has been done, it is generally agreed within the industry that the original estimates were conservative. In other words, net savings are thought to be greater than were projected.)

The major conclusion of the feasibility study was that the use of EDI in the grocery industry was technically feasible and economically justified. In addition, the study indicated that the major impediment to the widespread use of EDI in the grocery industry, or any other industry, was the lack of industry-wide standards. As a result, the study recommended that the standards and format set by the Transportation Data Coordinating Committee be used as a guideline for establishing grocery industry standards. The feasibility study also indicated that because most of the messages to be transmitted were relatively short, the total time to transmit and receive the messages was also relatively short and therefore the use of a large industry-dedicated network to handle the transmissions was not necessary. Rather, the use of public, shared networks for transaction transmissions was recommended.

The grocery industry accepted the recommendations of the feasibility study and in 1980 formed the Uniform Communications Standards Committee (UCS) to develop industry-wide standards. From 1980 until 1982, the grocery industry tested a number of standards, all based upon the TDCC syntax. In 1982 a pilot test involving manufacturers, brokers, and retailers exchanging purchase orders and invoices was conducted. The results of the pilot indicated that EDI was indeed technically feasible and economically justified. In 1982 the use of EDI was expanded to include additional companies and new transactions. Today over 250 members of the industry, including 114 manufacturers, 96 brokers, 22 wholesalers, and 28 retailers participate in UCS and process over 100 million messages electronically annually.[31]

Examples of Use in Grocery

One of the leading users of EDI in the grocery industry is Super Valu Stores. Super Valu is a leading grocery wholesaler with approximately $10 billion in annual sales. Super Valu supports over 3000 stores through 19 distribution centers. Currently UCS is used in 16 of the 19 distribution centers.

Super Valu is one of the true leaders in EDI. The company first began electronic exchange in 1972 with the exchange of punched cards and magnetic tapes with three trading partners: CPC, Kimberly Clark, and General Mills. These three companies and Super Valu agreed on standards to be used for formatting the information on the tapes and the punched cards. However, according to George Klima, former Director of Accounting Systems for Super Valu, no real progress could be made with this electronic exchange until there was some industry-wide standard. Super Valu was instrumental in developing the UCS standard and began to use it as soon as it was available.

Today, Super Valu is an active participant in EDI and is currently using the UCS standard for the transmission of over 6500 purchase orders and over 3000 invoices weekly with 1600 vendors. In addition, the company also transmits promotion announcements and price changes electronically.[32]

The benefits from the application of EDI at Super Valu have been significant. Purchase order transmission costs have been reduced by approximately $1.30 per order; purchase order and invoice reconciliation costs have been reduced by $6000 daily; and significant personnel savings have been achieved in accounts payable and accounts receivable. While these benefits are significant, they are not the most important result of the use of EDI, according to Klima. The most significant benefits have been achieved through better use of more accurate information and through more productive use of buyers' time. Prior to EDI, 40 percent of the buyers' time was spent on clerical activity. Since EDI, buyers have had more time to spend on buying activities and as a result have become "merchandisers" rather than "paper processors."[33] The result of this has been improved personnel productivity. In one Super Valu division, business has increased 50 percent with no increase in the number of buyers.

Future EDI Use in Grocery Industry

Although the results achieved thus far by Super Valu, and others in the grocery industry, have been significant, even greater benefits are expected in the future. The grocery industry is currently in the test phase of using EDI for direct store delivery, which is expected to provide a substantial increase in EDI benefits.

Currently, EDI in the grocery industry is used only on those transactions that take place between warehouse level grocery distributors and their supplying grocery manufacturers or brokers. In other words, EDI is not used for transactions that take place directly between suppliers and the retail level stores (called direct store delivery). Yet, a feasibility study conducted by the Arthur D. Little company estimates that there are "500 million such deliveries annually to food stores in this country, involving close to 10 billion line transactions."[34] The feasibility study indicates that significant benefits can be achieved through the use of EDI for direct store delivery. It is estimated that direct savings to retailers could reach $330 million annually, with annual direct savings for suppliers of $175 million. Indirect savings are estimated at $430 million each for the suppliers and the retailers. The grocery industry is currently in the pilot test stage of EDI for direct store delivery. It is expected that after the brief pilot test, DSD EDI will be expanded and will become common within the grocery industry.[35]

EDI IN THE HEALTH CARE INDUSTRY

EDI has saved one wholesale drug distributor "hundreds of thousands of dollars in uncollectables per year."

While industry action groups took an early lead in establishing EDI standards and in developing industry-wide EDI efforts in the grocery and transportation industry, in other industries the development of EDI was characterized more by the development of private or proprietary EDI systems. In both the health care and the automotive industries, major players in the industry had developed private EDI systems prior to any strong industry-wide activity.

Structure of the Health Care Industry

The health care industry is composed of two major components: wholesale drug distributors and hospital suppliers. Wholesale drug distributors such as Bergen Brunswig and McKesson generally buy low-priced, small items in very large volume from a number of diverse manufacturers. These distributors then sell these items to drugstores and hospitals. Hospital suppliers, on the other hand, buy primarily large, expensive items from a limited number of manufacturers. These items are then sold to hospitals. EDI systems have been developed and are currently used by both types of suppliers.

Wholesale Drug Distributors   Major distributors in the wholesale drug trade developed a number of private ordering systems to help improve the order entry process. As early as the mid-1970s McKesson installed a direct ordering system for its customers. McKesson provided over 15,000 customers with hand-held terminals used as order entry devices. In this way, orders were received quickly and correctly by McKesson. Today, orders received by McKesson through the order entry devices are now transmitted via EDI to McKesson's suppliers.

Use of Wholesale Drug EDI

Bergen Brunswig, which is the second largest drug wholesaler in the United States, also started to use order entry devices in the 1970s to receive orders from its customers. As does McKesson, today Bergen Brunswig also uses EDI to communicate its orders to its suppliers. Currently, Bergen Brunswig is using EDI to submit purchase orders to over 150 suppliers, and has plans to add 450 more suppliers to the system.[37]

The company has recently launched what it calls the "Electronic Partnership Program." The program has been established to allow Bergen Brunswig to transmit all of its purchase orders electronically, whether its suppliers can receive electronic orders or not. The system converts electronic purchase orders to paper purchase orders for those suppliers not yet using EDI. The ability to transmit purchase orders electronically is important because of the time it usually takes for a paper order to reach a supplier. According to one Bergen Brunswig representative, "When we mail a purchase order to a manufacturer, it may take from two to eight days to get there; when we transmit electronically, they go out at midnight and get there at one the next morning."[38] This shortened time means less inventory has to be carried.

Bergen Brunswig has also started to test the use of electronic invoices and has plans to include electronic payments as a part of its EDI transmissions. Currently, the company opens and processes 5000 to 6000 invoices a day, indicating a strong potential for savings if invoicing is done electronically.[39]

EDI to Handle Chargebacks   EDI in the wholesale drug distribution industry has helped to reduce a problem unique to the industry—that of chargebacks. In this industry, a drug manufacturer may often agree to sell a product to one of the wholesaler's customers for a below-normal price. For example, the wholesale price from the manufacturer to Bergen Brunswig may be $15; however, the manufacturer may agree to a price with a hospital or a pharmacy of $7. When the sale is made through Bergen Brunswig, the hospital is charged the $7. Bergen Brunswig then forwards a record of the sale, along with a chargeback reflecting the difference between the price the item was sold at under the special arrangement and the price the item is normally sold at, to the manufacturer. The manufacturer then reimburses Bergen Brunswig for the difference. Not only did this system result in large volumes of paper (70 cases a month for Bergen Brunswig), it also resulted in a large number of uncollectable chargebacks. If the chargeback is not completed within a limited time period, or it has discrepancies, the wholesaler often does not get paid the difference. According to Bergen Brunswig, using EDI for chargebacks has saved the company "hundreds of thousands of dollars in uncollectables per year by eliminating inaccuracies."[40]

Growth of Wholesale Drug EDI

The use of EDI in the wholesale drug trade is expanding. In some cases, manufacturers are receiving the majority of their purchase orders via EDI. For instance, Eli Lilly, one the largest pharmaceutical manufacturers, has begun receiving electronic purchase orders from all of its wholesale trading partners.[41] Not only is EDI used in the wholesale supply side of the health care industry, it is also used by hospital suppliers. And similar to the development of EDI on the wholesale side, EDI on the hospital side initially began with proprietary systems.

Use of EDI by Hospital Suppliers

Three major hospital suppliers all currently have individual order entry systems for hospitals. The first of these systems was introduced in 1976 by Baxter Healthcare (then known as American Hospital Supply). The system was called ASAP (Analytical Systems Automated Purchasing) and connected hospital purchasing agents to the Baxter order entry system. Following the introduction of ASAP, other proprietary systems were also introduced. Johnson and Johnson introduced an order entry system called Coact Plus, while Abbott Laboratories introduced Quik Link.[42]

Initially all of the systems operated differently and required the buyers to learn each system. However, now all of the systems have moved toward the ANSI X12 format and have made the systems more readily available to all users. According to one official in the hospital industry, "the marketplace is forcing these companies to put their systems out in the public domain. It will encourage their use. Proprietary systems aren't used because they threaten the hospitals by tying them to a particular vendor."[43]

Industry EDI Action   Until the move toward the common X12 format, only about 15 to 20 percent of hospitals had the capability of having two-way electronic communications with suppliers. Because of the widespread use of private systems, most hospitals had the ability only to communicate one way with the supplier of the private order entry system. However, in 1988, 23 major multi-hospital buyers, along with representatives of the Health Industry Distributors Association (HIDA) and the Health Industry Manufacturers Association (HIMA), signed a joint agreement saying that EDI would be the way health care providers (hospitals) would do business with their suppliers.[44] The agreement recognized that EDI could provide substantial benefits and stated that hospitals would "work as quickly as possible toward a common goal of communicating business transactions between trading partners." The group agreed that the X12 standard would be the standard used in the industry and that the system would be open to all trading partners from all segments of the industry.[45]

According to industry members the agreement "makes clear the requirement that EDI must be an everyone-to-everyone system just as the telephone technology has developed."[46] The Executive Vice President of HIDA has stated that "the agreement is a milestone and sets the stage for every provider, distributor, and manufacturer to play a supporting role."[47]

Summary of EDI in the Health Care Industry

It appears then that common EDI, based upon the ANSI X12 format, will soon become the accepted way of doing business in the hospital industry. Although this industry started out with strong proprietary systems, it has now moved toward a common, open EDI system. Another industry that has made the same type of move is the automotive industry.

EDI IN THE AUTOMOTIVE INDUSTRY

> The use of EDI reduces the cost of an automobile by $200.

The automotive industry is another example of how the use of EDI has evolved from proprietary systems to common standards EDI. In the mid-1960s all of the big three automakers individually initiated proprietary EDI systems. For the most part, these systems were designed to function primarily as information systems for internal manufacturing systems. Later, the systems were extended to include first-tier suppliers. While the automakers originally operated in a proprietary environment, they all began efforts to move from their proprietary systems to X12 formats when the standards became available. As in the health care industry, this move was encouraged by industry action.

Automotive Industry Action Group

In 1981, the automakers and their suppliers joined together and formed the Automotive Industry Action Group (AIAG). The purpose of the group was to find ways to improve competitiveness of domestic automakers as compared to foreign automakers. The AIAG established a number of subcommittees, each assigned a specific aspect of the manufacturing process. Techniques explored by the AIAG included just-in-time manufacturing, bar coding, computer assisted design/computer assisted manufacturing (CAD/CAM), quality circles, and EDI. AIAG viewed the use of EDI as a critical ingredient in the move toward increased productivity and competitiveness. The EDI subcommittee of the AIAG was charged with "developing and introducing EDI into the automotive industry."[48]

Current Use of EDI

Today all of the domestic automakers are using EDI and expect their trading partners to do the same. It is estimated that nearly 3000 suppliers are currently linked electronically with the automakers. The most common documents exchanged between the automakers and their suppliers include material releases, advanced shipment notices, invoices, and payments.

In the auto industry, EDI has reached the point of being a "must." All of the big three automakers have announced that they expect their suppliers to be able to communicate electronically, and that the capability to do so will become a factor in vendor selection. Two examples show how extensively EDI is used in the auto industry.

General Motors   General Motors is currently using EDI to communicate electronically with suppliers at many of its manufacturing and assembly divisions and is using EDI to pay bills electronically in 17 of its 30 operating divisions. GM's EDI system performs the following actions. First, a GM manager dials up a supplier's computer to get a price quote on an item. The supplier provides the quote electronically back to GM. Then, when GM is ready to order the item, the purchase order is transmitted electronically to the supplier. Upon receipt of the purchase order and shipment of the items, the supplier responds with an electronic shipping notice and an electronic invoice.[49]

In many cases, the supplier is paid electronically as well. GM is currently linked electronically with six large banks. When a supplier is to be paid, GM communicates electronically with one of the banks, which then debits GM's accounts and credits the supplier's account. GM hopes that it will someday be able to use electronic payment for all of the 300,000 monthly checks it currently sends to over 6000 suppliers.[50]

Ford   The Ford Motor Company is also using EDI extensively. Ford is encouraging its suppliers to use EDI and has stated that in the future the use of EDI will be a factor in vendor selection. Ford has integrated the use of EDI with a program called Common Manufacturing Management System (CMMS). CMMS controls all materials management and production operations and integrates data received via EDI with internal operations.[51]

Summary of EDI in the Automotive Industry

EDI has become a requirement in the automotive industry. Its use is being strongly encouraged by all of the major manufacturers. EDI is seen as a tool to combat rising costs and decreasing productivity and to increase competitiveness of the U.S. automakers. While originally the automakers all used proprietary EDI systems, today the auto industry strongly endorses the use of ANSI X12. Another industry which has experienced a similar move from proprietary systems to standard EDI systems in the retail industry.

EDI IN THE RETAIL INDUSTRY

> "EDI is here to stay. It is a fact of life."

"Electronic data interchange may be the hottest trend in retailing communications, but for some big chains, that's the way business has been done for years" says a major retailing publication.[52] For example, Sears orders nearly 90 percent of its goods electronically, while Penney's orders over half of its items electronically. Both of these retailers, along with other large retailers such as K mart and Wal-Mart, originally had proprietary EDI systems but are starting to move toward standard EDI using the VICS format. VICS (Voluntary Interindustry Communications Standards) is the ANSI X12 standard in the retailing industry.

Proprietary EDI in Retailing

While most of the major retailers are moving from proprietary systems to VICS, the move is expected to be gradual. For instance, Sears has used a proprietary system, called Senden, which originally evolved from the teletype, for 20 years. The company is currently in the process of slowly converting its suppliers to VICS. Also currently changing to VICS is Montgomery Ward, which is linked with over 250 suppliers through a proprietary network. Wal-Mart, which has been communicating electronically with its suppliers since 1981, has recently been encouraging its trading partners to move to VICS as well. K mart, which has one of the largest proprietary systems, has also begun to encourage the 7500 suppliers with whom it currently is linked electronically to adopt the VICS standard. Penney's also has stated that it is converting to the VICS system, from its proprietary system, on a vendor-by-vendor basis.[53]

Common EDI in Retailing

It is obvious that the movement in the retail industry is toward common EDI. A number of large retailers have already established ANSI X12 EDI links with a large number of suppliers. Three companies using the VICS standard for communication include Dillards Department Stores, Hills Discount Chain, and Mervyn's Department Store.

Dillards   Dillards Department Stores is a nationwide chain which has had a strong reputation as a leader in retail information systems. According to Ray Heflin, Manager of Retail Electronic Services at Dillards, "The object of the game is to get the goods to the store as soon as possible."[54] EDI appears to play a significant role in meeting that objective.

Currently Dillards is sending purchase orders to over 50 trading partners, with most of them using the VICS format. According to Heflin, "We see the elimination of paper and the speed by which the process of ordering takes place as extremely important. Without EDI purchase orders, you run the risk of wrong addresses, returned orders, printing and stuffing envelopes, on and on."[55] Dillards' goal for 1988 was to have 90 percent of its top 40 vendors on-line, with at least 100 vendors on-line by the end of 1989. Another department store that is making effective use of EDI is Mervyn's.

Mervyn's Department Store   Mervyn's is a western department store chain and a strong supporter of EDI. According to Ron Whiteside, the senior systems analyst at Mervyn's "EDI is here to stay. It is a fact of life. It must be obtainable to stay in business."[56] Mervyn's began EDI with a pilot test program in late 1986, and began to use the VICS standards in 1987. Today, although EDI is used only for outgoing purchase orders, the volume is significant. There are currently 120 trading partners who are either operational or in the test stage of EDI.

Hills Discount Chain   Hills Discount Chain is another retailer who is currently using EDI. Hills, a New England-based discount chain, has been involved in electronic communications with trading partners for a number of years. However, now with the availability of VICS standards, Hills has become very active in EDI.

According to Virginia Rago, Vice President of Merchandising Systems, as soon as the VICS standards were issued, "we made the EDI programming project our number one priority."[57] Hills' EDI goal for 1988 was to have between 50 and 100 vendors on-line and accepting purchase orders. In selecting vendors to put on-line, Hills used a number of criteria. First, Hills looked for vendors who received a large number of frequent orders. In addition, Hills also looked at the products carried by the vendors. Because fast-moving and basic items are ordered frequently, Hills chose vendors supplying these items as the first to bring on-line.

Using EDI for purchase orders is critically important to Hills due to the complexity of its purchase orders. It is not uncommon for one purchase order to specify 200 items, for one or any number of stores. Because of the complexity of the orders, order entry errors were high and it often took vendors as long as two weeks to get the order correctly transmitted into the order entry system. Rago has reported that, "with complex orders, EDI should greatly reduce or eliminate entirely, the risk of errors that translates into overstocks, understocks, or late shipments."[58]

Hills plans to expand EDI usage into the exchange of invoices as well. Hills' invoices are also complex, because not only do vendors ship to different locations from the same purchase order, they also send invoices to different locations. However, the invoices, although sent to the store level, are not paid at the store. Rather, the store verifies the invoice and then forwards it to headquarters for payment. EDI invoices would provide a way for vendors to "send invoices to headquarters electronically, spelling out the distribution of merchandise and costs, and the stores would only have to verify to us what they received."[59]

These examples show how EDI is being used in the retail industry to cut errors and to speed the processing of paperwork. In addition to this use, EDI is also being combined with point-of-sale scanning methods as a way of increasing sales.

Quick Response

The retail industry has combined EDI with point-of-sale scanning in a program called Quick Response. Under this program, products are marked with a Universal Product Code (UPC) bar code. When the item is sold, the bar code is scanned providing a complete and immediate record of what specific item has been sold. This information is then used to update retail level inventory records and to generate a purchase order. The purchase order is then transmitted via EDI to the supplier. In this way, trends can be recognized, and fast-moving goods can be replenished quickly, thus the "quick response" name. The use of quick response has led to increased sales by nearly all retailers and manufacturers using the program, with increases in sales as high as 35 percent attributable to the use of EDI in combination with UPC.[60]

Summary of Retail EDI

The retail industry is another in which the use of EDI is widespread. The industry has found that the use of EDI, particularly when coupled with other technologies, can result in significant productivity gains as well as increased sales.

SUMMARY OF INDUSTRY USAGE

This discussion of EDI usage by various industries is by no means exhaustive. Major industry-wide EDI efforts are underway in a large number of industries, with more industries and companies becoming involved daily. These industries were selected to provide a sampling of how different industries got started in EDI, and the various applications of EDI.

In addition to use by industry, EDI is also being used by the federal government. While EDI efforts by the federal government have been slower to take off than those in a number of industries, the government has recently embraced and endorsed the use of EDI.

EDI IN THE GOVERNMENT

> If there is any process in the government that is made for EDI, and cries out for EDI, it is procurement.

The federal government has made a strong commitment to EDI. In 1985 as a part of its general information management policy functions, the Office of Management and Budget issued a government circular (A-130) entitled "Management of Federal Information Resources." The circular stated that "the application of information technology to government information collection can lead to much greater economy and efficiency."[61] One of the specific information technologies addressed in the circular was electronic data interchange.

Since then numerous government agencies have begun EDI efforts. These agencies, including the Department of Defense, the Federal Supply Service, the General Services Administration, and others are implementing EDI for reasons similar to those found in industry. As James F. Kerrigan, Director of Federal Market Research Programs at INPUT, states, "In an era of fiscal streamlining, agencies are searching for methods to eliminate paperwork, boost productivity, improve public services, and reduce transaction turnaround time."[62] Federal agencies are finding that EDI meets all of these objectives.

Government Support of Standards

In implementing EDI efforts, the various federal government agencies have decided to support and use the ANSI X12 standards. It is the government policy, as stated by David Baker of the Office of Management and Budget, that the government will "work with voluntary standards bodies to develop and refine such documents in lieu of developing government-unique standards, and [will] coordinate agency involvement so that the resulting standards meet the needs of the government as a whole. We are convinced that only through joint standards endeavors, particularly when dealing with the procurement interface between government and industry, can we successfully achieve the promise that EDI makes."[63]

The federal government currently has EDI efforts underway in three major areas. The first is in the area of purchasing or procurement of items for internal use. The second is in the area of purchasing by government agencies of items intended for resale in military commissaries and exchanges. The third major effort underway is the use of EDI for transportation. The following discussion provides examples of each of the three major EDI efforts.

EDI in Government Procurement

"If there is any process in the government that is made for EDI, and cries out for EDI, it is procurement," says Baker of the OMB.[64] Federal procurement is one of the most paper-intensive processes of the government. In 1987, the government issued over 22.3 million different contract actions. The amount of paperwork generated by those actions is "mind-boggling" according to Baker. Numerous federal government agencies have begun EDI efforts aimed at streamlining the procurement process.

The Department of Defense recently announced, in a memo signed by Deputy Secretary of Defense Taft, that it was beginning an EDI program and that vendors supplying goods to the DOD will need to have ANSI X12 EDI capability.[65] This effort has the potential of affecting nearly all of the 300,000 DOD suppliers.

The General Services Administration, which purchases items for a number of federal government agencies, is currently working on EDI implementation policies and regulations. The Federal Supply Service, which also makes purchases for federal agencies, likewise has a number of EDI efforts underway.[66] The Defense General Supply Center provides a specific example of how EDI is being used in government procurement.

The Defense General Supply Center (DGSC) is one of many purchasing agencies for the Department of Defense. The center currently has an EDI effort underway with a number of major suppliers, including Du Pont. DGSC uses an internal computerized purchasing system known as Paperless Ordering Purchasing System (POPS) to generate purchase orders. The purchase orders are transmitted electronically in the POPS format to the McDonnell Douglas network (DGSC's VAN). The VAN translates the POPS orders into ANSI format and places them into Du Pont's electronic mailbox. Daily, Du Pont retrieves the orders entered into its order entry system. The DGSC is expanding EDI usage to include other vendors and other transactions.[67]

Other federal agencies have similar EDI efforts underway. The use of EDI by federal procurement agencies should provide significant benefits in streamlining internal operations. Most federal procurement agencies not only have purchase order formats that are different from every other agency, many agencies have multiple in-house formats.[68] The use of EDI should help make the procurement process less complex for both the government and the vendors.

EDI in Government Resale Activities

In addition to using EDI for procurement of goods for internal use, the government is also using EDI for the procurement of items intended for resale. The Department of Defense operates a number of commissaries (similar to grocery stores) and exchanges (similar to department stores) for military personnel. Commissaries and exchanges in all branches of the military have begun EDI efforts.

The DOD has obtained a UCS identification number for all of its military stores. "Each service has found that EDI is the way to go."[69] Major General John E. Long, USA, Commander of the Army and Air Force Exchange Service (AAFES), which oversees both commissary and exchange operations, has stated that "EDI appears to be the wave of the future."[70] The AAFES is currently transmitting purchase orders to 14 vendors, averaging 100 to 120 orders a day with such companies as Procter & Gamble, Nabisco, General Foods, Kodak, and R. J. Reynolds. The Marine Corps is actively testing EDI at its East Coast Commissary Complex and is currently processing 40 percent of its orders electronically.[71]

The military exchanges and commissaries are using EDI for the same reason that other retailers do. William Wallace of AAFES has stated that the major benefit of EDI "is a reduction in administrative lead time that leads to a reduction in order processing time. The order processing time reduction has allowed a 5- to 6-day reduction in safety stock."[72] The military stores have found that inventory has dropped, while sales have increased.

EDI in Government Transportation

In addition to the EDI efforts initiated on the purchasing side, the federal government has also initiated efforts to use EDI in transportation activities. The primary efforts to use EDI for transportation have been in the Department of Defense. The DOD is the largest shipper in the world, with total annual transportation costs exceeding $9 billion (FY86) and over 1.35 million shipments moving annually under government bills of lading.[73] With this level of transportation activity, the DOD is constantly looking for ways to "streamline and enhance operations, reduce administrative costs, provide timely information for managers," as well as meeting "mobilization and wartime needs."[74] EDI is seen as a way of meeting these objectives.

In 1987, the DOD conducted a pilot test of electronic transmission of the government bill of lading involving twelve DOD activities, three motor carriers, and three finance offices. According to Ken Stombaugh of the Office of the Secretary of Defense for Transportation Policy, the pilot test showed that EDI reduced both costs and paperwork.[75] In the near term the DOD hopes to expand the use of EDI to include other DOD activities. Long-term plans call for the expansion of EDI to include other transportation documentation.

Summary of Government Use of EDI

These examples show that the federal government is committed not only to EDI, but to ANSI X12 EDI. Use of EDI is expected to grow within the federal government. Numerous agencies have personnel who are voting members of standards-setting groups and who are active in the EDI process. Both the Department of Defense and civilian agencies have tested EDI and have found the results to be positive. In the words of Jack Bartley, of the Office of the Secretary of Defense, EDI "supports a commitment to improved interoperability, increased productivity, and a move toward a paperless environment."[76] EDI is here to stay in the federal government.

SUMMARY

This chapter highlighted a few of the industries that are using EDI. The examples were not intended to be exhaustive, but only to present a sampling of the many diverse ways in which EDI is being used. The following chapters discuss, in detail, the various components which "make up" EDI: standards, software, and third party networks.

II

COMPONENTS OF EDI

4

EDI STANDARDS

INTRODUCTION

As defined earlier, EDI is the intercorporate exchange of business documentation in structured, machine-processable form. EDI is designed so that the receiving computer can "read" and process data without additional human intervention. This means that the data must be in coded rather than textual format.

Although an order entry clerk can review two completely different purchase orders and abstract the pertinent information from those purchase orders with relative ease, a computer cannot. A computer is incredibly efficient and accurate; however, a computer cannot recognize as the same, similar information in different formats or in different positions. Therefore, the computer must be told, in advance, what information to expect and in what format; and then the information must be transmitted in that specific manner for it to be read and understood by the receiving computer. EDI standards provide the structure required for computers to be able to read, understand, and process business documentation.

HISTORY OF STANDARDS DEVELOPMENT

EDI standards are, in essence, agreements between users of EDI on how data are to be formatted and communicated. The first attempt to develop standards occurred in the late sixties in the transportation industry.

In 1968 a group of companies in the transportation industry joined together and formed the Transportation Data Coordinating Committee (TDCC). The purpose of this committee was to develop a common language, or standards, for use in the transmission of transportation documentation. The committee published its first standard in 1975 and has since developed and published standards used primarily in the air, motor, rail, and water industries. Other industries followed TDCC's lead and developed EDI standards for their own industries, most notably the grocery and the warehousing industries. The standards for the grocery industry are termed "Uniform Communication Standards" while the standards for the warehouse industry are termed Warehouse Information Network Standard (WINS). Both are administered by the Uniform Code Council. Industry-specific standards, while slightly different from transportation standards, followed the same general rules, format, and syntax requirements established by TDCC.

In 1978, the American National Standards Institute (ANSI) recognized the need for national EDI standards that could be used across industries. ANSI is a coordinator and clearing house for national and international standards whose membership represents nearly all technical disciplines and all areas of trade and commerce. ANSI coordinates standards for all facets of business.

In 1979 ANSI chartered a new committee, labeled the Accredited Standards Committee (ASC) X12, to develop uniform standards for cross-industry electronic communications. According to the X12 committee, its function is to "develop standards to facilitate electronic interchange relating to order placement and processing, shipping and receiving information, invoicing, payment, and cash application data."[1]

The ANSI ASC X12 committee, using the basic structure and syntax established by TDCC, developed and continues to develop EDI standards. While TDCC-based standards and the ANSI X12 standards are not identical, they use the same basic architecture and employ similar syntax rules. In addition, both sets of standards use a common data dictionary and efforts are now underway to further narrow the differences between the standards.

STRUCTURE OF THE STANDARDS

Because every organization has its own way of formatting information, and because information needs vary from company to company, at first glance it would seem impossible to establish one format that all companies could use and that would adequately meet the needs of companies of varying size and in diverse industries. However, the standards have been designed for flexibility and to accommodate differing levels of information needs. This flexibility can best be seen by examining how information is translated from a manual format to an electronic format through the use of an ANSI ASC X12 standard.

FORMATTING STANDARDS

The X12 standards provide guidelines on formatting electronic communications. The guidelines establish rules for structuring the data to be transmitted between trading partners. Specifically, the formatting standards address:

- What documents can be transmitted electronically
- What information can be included in each document
- What sequence the information should follow
- What form of information (numeric, I.D. codes, etc.) should be used
- The meaning of individual pieces of information

TERMINOLOGY OF STANDARDS

In EDI terminology a specific document, such as a purchase order, is referred to as a *transaction* set. Each transaction set is given a numeric code similar to the way in which most paper forms are assigned a form number. For instance, an ANSI X12 purchase order is called the 850 transaction set. In addition, each transaction set has its own specific standard, which is also numbered. As an example, the portion of the standards addressing purchase orders is known as X12.1. Figure 4-1 shows some common documents, their transaction set number, and their corresponding standard identification.

A typical paper document contains numerous lines of information. In a purchase order, the name of the buying organization generally constitutes one line of information, while the address of the buying organization constitutes another line

X12 Document Number	Transaction Set I.D.	Document Title
X12.1	850	Purchase Order
X12.2	810	Invoice
X12.7	840	Request for Quotation
X12.8	843	Response for RFQ
X12.9	855	P.O. Acknowledgment
X12.10	856	Ship Notice
X12.12	861	Receiving Advice
X12.12	832	Price/Sales Catalog
X12.14	830	Planning Schedule
X12.15	860	P.O. Change
X12.16	865	P.O. Change

Figure 4-1   Common documents.

of information. Further, within each line of information, there are a number of individual pieces of information. The address line, for example, is usually made up of three separate pieces of information: one for the city, one for the state, and one for the ZIP code.

In EDI terminology, each line of information, such as buyer's address, is called a data segment. Each individual piece of information, such as "city," is called a *data element*. Figure 4-2 illustrates the correspondence between a paper document and the components of an EDI standard.

The EDI standards precisely define how information is to be taken from the paper format and structured in electronic format in terms of transaction sets, data segments, and data elements. The definition of how information is written in EDI standard format is provided in three different sections of the standard guidelines:

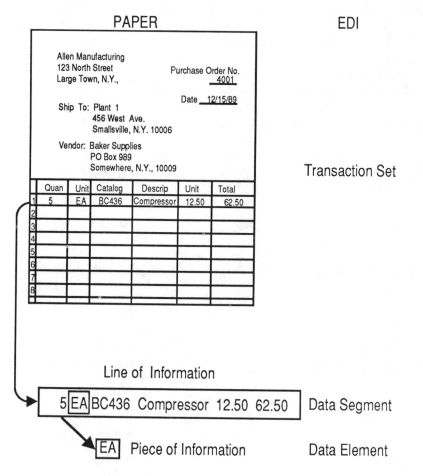

Figure 4-2   EDI terminology.

- Transaction Set Standards
- Segment Directory
- Data Dictionary

TRANSACTION SET STANDARDS

Individual transaction set standards can best be defined as a specification list for an electronic document, since they define the content requirements for each transaction set. In other words, the individual transaction set standards show what lines of information (data segments in EDI terms) belong in each electronic document and also show in what order the lines of information should appear.

Standards committees recognize that some data segments will be found on all purchase orders regardless of the industry, the item being purchased, the size of the company, or other variables. As an example, every organization includes some form of identification of the item being purchased on the purchase order document. Therefore, this data segment has been made mandatory in the transaction set standard.

However, the inclusion of other information on a purchase order may vary from organization to organization. Some organizations always include a buyer's name and phone number on all orders, while others do not. Therefore, in addition to mandatory data segments, transaction set standards also identify optional segments that may be used at the discretion of the sender.

In addition to identifying mandatory and optional data segments, the transaction set standard also indicates whether a data segment can be repeated, and if so, how many times. Most purchase orders include at least two address blocks, one for the buyer and one for the seller, and often also include additional organizational information for the ship to and bill to addresses. The X12 transaction set standard for purchase orders, therefore, allows for the repetition of address information. Shown in Figure 4-3 is an excerpt from the transaction set standard for a purchase order, indicating some of the data segments that are a part of a purchase order transaction set.

Although the purchase order transaction set standard identifies a large number of data segments that can be included in an electronic purchase order, most EDI transactions will, in fact, be fairly short. For example, although the purchase order transaction set standard allows for the inclusion of over 70 data segments, many of which can be repeated, the EDI transmission of the sample purchase order shown in Figure 4-4 would include only 14 data segments.

Segment Directory

The transaction set standard identifies the data segments or lines of information that constitute the transaction set; however, the transaction set standard does not

Data Segment	Requirement	Max Use	Loop
ST Transaction Set Header	M	1	0
BEG Beginning Segment for P.O.	M	1	0
.			
.			
.			
N1 Name	O	1	100
N2 Additional Name Information	O	1	100
N3 Address Information	O	2	100
N4 Geographic Information	O	1	100
PER Administrative Contact	O	3	100
FOB F.O.B. Related Instruction	O	1	100
PO1 Purchase Order Baseline Info	M	1	200
CTT Transaction Totals	M	1	0
SE Transaction Set Trailer	M	1	0

REQUIREMENT: M=Mandatory
                       O=Optional

MAX USE: Number of times the data segment may be repeated within a loop.

LOOP: Number of times that a series of segments can be repeated.
              (For example an electronic purchase order could have 100 name
              and address combinations– for ship to or build to, etc. Each of
              those address combinations could have only 1 name line, 1
              additional name line 1 geographic location line, but 2 address
              lines.)

Figure 4-3   850 purchase order transaction set standard (excerpt).

specify what is to be included in each data segment. This is done in the segment
directory. The segment directory identifies, for each data segment, the specific data
elements (pieces of information) to be included in each data segment. The identification of the data elements is done through the use of a data segment diagram.

The data segment diagram is a critical feature of the standards. It shows all of
the data elements that can be included in a specific data segment, and the sequencing of the elements. Further, the diagram indicates whether the use of each element
is mandatory, optional, or conditional. The diagram also describes the specific form
of each piece of information (i.e., number of characters, numeric or alphabetic,
etc.). Figure 4-5 shows a data segment diagram for the PO1 segment, a mandatory
segment of the purchase order transaction set.

Allen Manufacturing
123 North Street
Large Town, N.Y. 10001

Purchase Order No.
4001
Date 12/15/89

Ship To: Plant 1
456 West Ave.
Smallsville, N.Y. 10006

Vendor: Baker Supplies
PO Box 989
Somewhere, N.Y. 10009

	Quantity	Unit	Catalog No.	Description	Unit Price	Total Price
1	5	EA	BC436	Compressor	12.50	62.50
2						
3						
4						
5						
6						
7						
8						

Figure 4-4   Sample purchase order.

Although at first glance the diagram looks confusing, it is actually very straight-forward and provides all of the information needed to translate information from paper format to structured standard EDI format. The basic structure of every segment diagram is the same, and each contains four basic components:

1. Data Segment Identifier indicates which data segment is being described.
2. Data Element Separator is a character selected by the sender that precedes each element and acts as a position marker. NOTE: The separator is needed since the data elements are of variable length (i.e., the unit price can range from 1 to 14 characters). In other words, the separator indicates when one

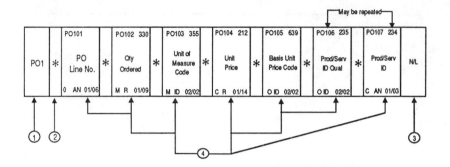

Figure 4-5   Data segment diagram PO1 segment.

element has ended and another element has begun. If an optional element is left out, the separator is entered to mark the position of the data element. The * is the most commonly used data element separator.

3.   Data Segment Terminator is a character selected by the sender to indicate the end of a segment. Usually the new line character (either return or enter key) is used.

4.   Element Diagrams are boxes which describe each data element.

Data Elements

In addition to establishing the sequencing of the data elements the diagram (Figure 4-5) also defines the content of each data element. Examining one of the data elements in detail, as highlighted in Figure 4-6, shows how this is done.

As indicated in the figure, the diagram identifies in words what the data element is. In this case, the data element is the unit of measure. The diagram also provides a data element sequence number, indicates the length and format of the data element, indicates whether the element is mandatory or not, and provides a reference to the data dictionary for more detail. The meaning of the components of the data element diagram are as follows:

5   Data Element Reference Designator
A two-digit sequence number preceded by the data segment identifier. In this case, we have element 03 of segment PO1.

6   Data Element Title
The name of the data element.

7   Data Dictionary Reference Number
A reference number to the data dictionary where additional information on the content of the data element can be found.

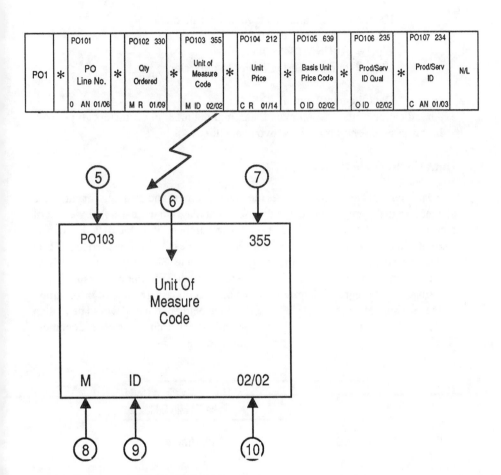

		PO101		PO102 330		PO103 355		PO104 212		PO105 639		PO106 235		PO107 234	
PO1	*	PO Line No.	*	Qty Ordered	*	Unit of Measure Code	*	Unit Price	*	Basis Unit Price Code	*	Prod/Serv ID Qual	*	Prod/Serv ID	N/L
		O AN 01/06		M R 01/09		M ID 02/02		C R 01/14		O ID 02/02		O ID 02/02		C AN 01/03	

⑤ ⑥ ⑦

PO103   355

Unit Of
Measure
Code

M   ID   02/02

⑧   ⑨   ⑩

Figure 4-6   Data element definition.

8   Data Element Requirement Designator
An indication of whether the element *must* be included:
        M = mandatory—must be used
        O = optional—used at discretion of sender
If an optional element is not used, the data element separator is entered to mark the position.
        C = conditional

9   Data Element Type
An indication of the form of the data:
        N = numeric
        R = decimal

ID   = identification code found in data dictionary
AN   = alphanumeric string
DT   = date in YYMMDD form
TM   = time in HHMM form (24-hour clock)

10   Data Element Length
An indication of the minimum and maximum number of characters allowed.
In this case the entry must have two characters.

Data Element Dictionary

The data element dictionary provides the precise content and meaning for each data element. In the example above, the data segment diagram indicates that the unit of measure is an I.D. code described at reference number 355 in the data dictionary. The data dictionary lists acceptable identification codes that may be used to indicate unit of measure and shows the meaning for each code. Shown in Figure 4-7 is an excerpt from the data dictionary for reference number 355, unit of measure.

Using the data segment diagram and the data dictionary, the line of information on the purchase order that describes the first item being purchased would be written in electronic format as shown in Figure 4-8 and the entire purchase order document would be written in electronic form as shown in Figure 4-9.

355	Unit of Meadure Code Type ID Min 2 Max 2
Code	**Definition**
01	Actual Pounds
05	Lifts
.	
.	
.	
BA	Bale
BC	Bucket
BD	Bundle
CA	Case
CN	Can
CT	Carton
EA	**Each**
FT	Foot
.	
.	
ZZ	Mutually Defined

Figure 4-7   Data element dictionary (reference 355 excerpt).

1. 5   EA   BC436   Compressor $12.50 $62.50

PO1∗1∗5∗EA∗12.50∗∗VP∗BC436∗ PD∗ Compressor N/L

(double asterick indicates optional
information left out)

Figure 4-8   First item purchased written in standard format.

Paper Purchase Order	X12 EDI Document
Start of Transaction	ST*850*0001 N/L
P.O. No. 4001 Date 12/15/89	BEG*00*NE*4001***891215 N/L
Buyer: Allen Manufacturing 123 North Street Large Town, N.Y., 10001	N1*BT*Allen Manufacturing N/L N3 *123 North Street N/L N4 *Largetown*NY*10001 N/L
Vendor: Baker Supplies PO Box 989 Somewhere N.Y., 10009	N1*VN* Baker Supplies N/L N3*PO Box 989 N/L N4 *Somewhere *N.Y * 10009 N/L
Ship To: Plant 1 456 West Ave. Smallsville N.Y., 10006	N1* ST *Plant 1 N/L N3 *456 West Ave. N/L N4 *Smallsville *N.Y * 10006 N/L
5 EA BC436 Compressors @ 12.50 each	PO1*1*5*EA*12.50**BC436*PD* Compressor N/L
Number of Line Items	CTT*1 N/L
End of Transaction	SE*14*0001 N/L

Note: N/L indicates new line character

Figure 4-9   EDI purchase order.

ELECTRONIC ENVELOPING

In the sample electronic document shown above, it can be seen that the first and the last data segments (ST and SE segments) in the electronic purchase order do not correspond to any of the lines of information in the paper document. These segments are necessary to separate electronic documents sent together in one transmission.

In the paper world, an organization often sends a number of purchase orders or invoices together in the same package. Because each purchase order or invoice is a separate document, it is easy to see where one purchase order stops and the next one starts. However, in the EDI world, the documents are simply a series of characters. Therefore, something is needed to separate the series of characters that represent the first purchase order from the series of characters that represent the second purchase order. The ST segment (transaction set header) and the SE segment (transaction set trailer) perform the function of separating each document from other documents included in the same transmission. These segments form the innermost envelope of an electronic transmission.

In addition to having data segments that separate one document from another, EDI standards also use similar segments to separate groupings of documents. Often an organization will send one envelope, containing both purchase orders and invoices, to a trading partner. In most cases the purchase orders are paper-clipped together, as are the invoices. EDI also provides a way to "paper clip" together like documents. The electronic form of a paper clip is the functional group. In EDI terminology, a functional group is a group of like documents. In place of a paper clip to designate the functional group, EDI standards use two data segments: a functional group header (GS segment) and a functional group trailer (GE segment). The functional group data segments form the next level of enveloping provided by EDI.

A third level of enveloping, in both paper and electronic transmissions, is an outer envelope that designates the addresses of both the sender and the receiver and encloses all of the documents being sent. In EDI transmissions, this outer envelope is known as the interchange envelope and consists of two data segments: the interchange control header (ISA segment) and the interchange control trailer (IEA segment). Figure 4-10 shows the enveloping structure of a typical EDI transmission as compared to "enveloping" in a paper transfer.

COMMUNICATIONS STANDARDS

In paper-based transactions there is usually a general agreement between trading partners on how documents are to be delivered (by mail, by express mail, by courier, etc.). The same holds true in EDI. Certain EDI standards (such as the UCS standards), in addition to providing formatting guidelines, also provide guidelines

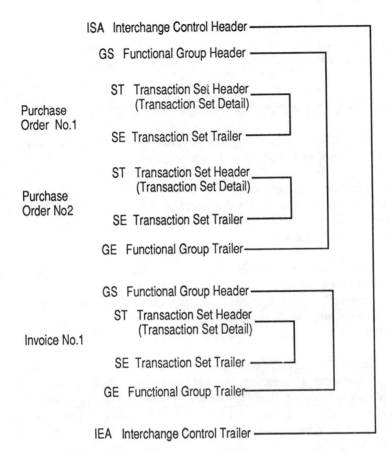

Figure 4-10   EDI envelope structure.

on how electronic messages are to be communicated. These guidelines are referred to as Communication Transport Protocols and address such issues as:

- Communication passwords and identification codes
- Baud rate and transmission modes
- Line protocols (asynchronous or bisynchronous)
- Network availability and service level
- Communication links (such as public phone lines)

For instance, in the grocery industry EDI standards designate that the baud rate must be at least 2400 baud, the line protocol must be bisynchronous, and network communication through public dial-up lines must be used. (A discussion and explanation of communications issues such as baud rate and line protocols is included in Chapter 5.)

EDI standards, in essence, are agreements between users on what information is to be communicated and how that information is to be transmitted. These agreements are reached through the standards development process.

STANDARDS DEVELOPMENT PROCESS

The ANSI ASC X12 standards development process is done on a consensus basis by a committee of volunteers from a wide range of organizations. This process encourages participation from a wide range of industries and functions and ensures standards that meet the needs of users. The X12 organization is structured into committees and subcommittees as shown in Figure 4-11. The two major committees are the Steering Committee and the Procedures Review Board who are responsible for the following:

- Steering Committee: Performs administrative functions for X12 and provides coordination among subcommittees and task groups.
- Procedure Review Board (PRB): Reviews all project proposals submitted to the committee. Also manages draft standards, standards maintenance, and compliance guidelines.

In addition to the two major committees, there are nine standing subcommittees. Six of the committees represent functional area interests (product data, materials management, purchasing, finance, transportation, and government), three of the subcommittees deal with issues of a broader nature. The Communications Committee oversees communications protocols and related issues. The Technical Assessment Committee reviews draft proposals to determine if they are within the scope of X12's activities and also ensures consistency within X12 standards. The Education and Implementation Subcommittee acts as the public relations arm of the committee.

In addition to the two major committees and nine subcommittees, two other groups play a part in the X12 organization. The Data Interchange Standards Association (DISA) acts as the secretariat for the X12 organization. In this role, DISA performs administrative functions such as printing, distribution, and storage of the standards. The X12 organization also participates in development of standards on an international basis by having X12 members serve as representatives to the North American EDIFACT Board.

New Standards Development

Any individual or organization, whether a member of the X12 committee or not, can request that a new standard be developed, or that a change be made to an existing standard. A work request is usually submitted to the secretariat, who

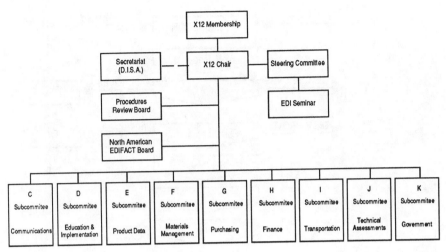

Source: ASC X12

Figure 4-11 ANSI X12 organization.

forwards the request to the technical assessment subcommittee, as shown in Figure 4-12. If the request is within the scope of X12, the technical assessment subcommittee forwards the request to the pertinent subcommittee for review. The subcommittee prepares a formal project proposal based upon the work request, which is submitted back to the technical assessment committee for a consistency check with other standards. If the proposal passes this check, it is sent to the Procedure Review Board for one more vote on whether the proposal is within the scope of X12 and is consistent with other standards. If this vote is positive, then the proposal is referred back to the original subcommittee for actual standards development.

The subcommittee is then responsible for preparing a draft proposed standard, which is sent through a Technical Assessment review as well as a Procedures Review Board check. The draft proposal is then sent to all X12 committee members for review, comment, and vote. The subcommittee reviews the vote and comments, responses to the comments, and allows time for additional open discussion on the draft proposed standard. If, after this process there are no unresolved issues, the draft proposed standard is sent to the Procedures Review Board, which ensures that proper procedures were followed and votes on releasing the draft proposed standard. Upon a positive vote of the procedures board, the draft proposed standard is released for "trial" use by the EDI community and is referred to as a dpANS. However, at this point it is not yet a fully approved standard.

Final approval authority for all business related standards, not only EDI standards, rests with ANSI. Whenever ANSI receives a proposed standard from any Accredited Standards Committee, such as X12, ANSI sends the proposed standard out for public review and comment, a process that can take two to three years. Only after the review process is completed is the standard approved and released as an

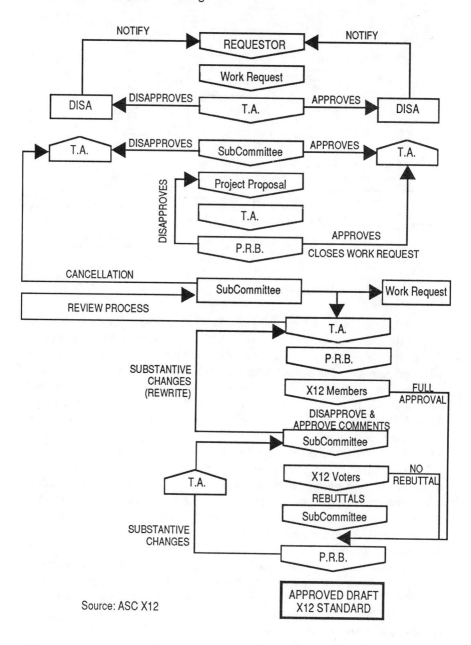

Source: ASC X12

Figure 4-12   ANSI X12 maintenance/development flow.

ANSĩ approved standard. In the EDI community, standards are considered approved once they have been accepted by the X12 committee. So, although most ANSI EDI standards carry the official title of "draft standards," they are the standards in use and accepted by the EDI community.

Changes to Standards

Just as paper forms are changed over time, so are electronic forms. As a result, standards do not remain stable. Approximately every two or three years, following its normal review cycle, ANSI releases an updated set of standards. The updates released by ANSI are called "versions" and are numbered with a 6-digit number ending in 000. For instance, the set of standards released in 1984 was called version 001000 and the set released in 1986 was called 002000.

In addition to the changes released by ANSI, the X12 committee also issues changes to the standards. Up through 1989, X12 released a revised set of standards reflecting new or updated transaction sets every six months. These are known as "releases" and are numbered as a part of the ANSI versions, such as release 002001 (indicating ANSI version 002000, X12 release 1). Starting in 1990, the X12 committee will be releasing changes to the standards on a yearly rather than a semi-yearly basis.

Versions of Standards

The distribution of a new version or release of the standards does not render previous versions and releases of the standards obsolete. EDI software is usually designed to support numerous versions and releases, since not all EDI users update their software and their operations upon receipt of a new version or release.

INDUSTRY STANDARDS

As mentioned previously, the first EDI standards were developed for the transportation industry based upon the syntax and architecture established by the Transportation Data Coordinating Committee. These standards covered transactions for the air, motor, rail, and ocean industries, as well as for freight claims transactions, and are generally referred to as TDCC standards. In addition, a number of other industry groups used the TDCC syntax and architecture to develop industry standards. These groups included the grocery and the warehousing industries.

The ANSI ASC X12 Committee was established to develop a generic standard that could be used across all industries. Currently, over 50 industries, including automotive, banking, aircraft, paper products, petroleum and pharmaceuticals, as well as the federal government, support and use the ANSI ASC X12 standards. Although the X12 standards were developed to be cross-industry standards, they often are not used until groups of users agree upon "conventions."

Conventions are agreements among members of industry groups that specify how the X12 standards will be used in that particular industry (i.e., what optional segments will or will not be used). One example of this is the development of industry conventions based upon the X12 standards by the retail industry. This industry has established a set of standards for use by nonfood retailers. Called VICS (Voluntary Interindustry Communications Standards), these standards are simply a modification of existing X12 standards.

This seems to say that there are many different "standards." However, TDCC, X12, UCS, and VICS (and other industry standards) all follow the same general rules of format and syntax. Further, they all use the same data dictionary and follow the same segment structure. In addition, the various industry-specific standards developing committees coordinate their activities to ensure compatibility among the standards. In May of 1988, the ANSI X12 committee and TDCC/EDIA, the Electronic Data Interchange Association (the new name for TDCC), issued a public statement of the relationship between the two groups. The groups stated that they will work together to develop a common maintenance system for EDI standards and will also work to develop a clear delineation of organizational relationships and responsibilities between the two organizations.

There are differences in "standards" depending upon industry. However the differences are minor and are narrowing. Further, most commercially available software supports multiple standards and multiple versions and releases. For practical purposes, the EDI community has developed one common architecture for electronic communication.

PROPRIETARY STANDARDS

It should be noted that some organizations have proprietary EDI systems. These are systems in which the organization has developed a "standard" format used in communicating only with that organization's trading partners on a closed system. While these types of systems are often referred to as EDI, they do not use common EDI standards as the format or method of communication.

INTERNATIONAL EDI STANDARDS

EDI efforts are also underway on an international basis. And similar to what has happened in the United States, different industries have developed different standards. Some of the most well-known and widely used standards overseas include:

- TDI (Trade Data Interchange): Used primarily in the U.K. and in Europe for warehousing and distribution
- ODETTE (Organization for Data Exchange and Teletransmission in Europe): Used in the European automobile industry
- DISH (Data Interchange for Shipping): Used in European transportation industries

In 1987, efforts to create an international standard, EDI for Administration, Commerce, and Transport (EDIFACT), were undertaken. EDIFACT activity is the responsibility of two international organizations. The International Standards Organization (ISO) is responsible for developing syntax rules and the data dictionary. The United Nations Economic Commission for Europe is responsible for the development of the document standards.

Currently Western Europe, Eastern Europe, and North America have representatives participating in the development of EDIFACT. The international standard groups are using the ANSI X12 standards and the TDI standards as a basis for the EDIFACT standard.

COMMUNICATIONS STANDARD X.400

In addition to the EDI standards, another standard has begun to play an important role in the transmission of electronic messages. This standard, referred to as X.400, addresses the issue of how messages are to be sent, rather than the content of the message, as addressed by X12. In other words, X12 is a language standard, while X.400 is a "postal service" standard.

X.400 provides guidelines for the movement of information and is most often used for the transmission of free-formatted electronic transmission, as opposed to the structured transaction sets used in EDI. Originally developed as a standard for electronic mail, X.400 has developed into a message handling system that includes a method of enveloping electronic content and passing the information on to a second party.

The components of X.400 are similar to those of EDI. In X.400 terms, a User Agent (UA) is a computer process that provides a link between the user's computer and the X.400 standard. A Message Transfer Agent is a network through which X.400 messages pass. The system of all Message Transfer Agents and all users is called the Message Transfer System. The envelope used to surround electronic messages is called the P1 Message Transfer Protocol, and includes an addressing scheme referred to as the Originator/Recipient Name (O/R Name). Under the X.400 standard, users are connected to User Agents which pass messages to Message Transfer Agents. In most cases the receiving Message Transfer Agent passes the electronic message on to a second Message Transfer Agent who passes it on to the recipient as identified by the O/R Name in the P1 envelope.

Although the widespread use of X.400 is still a long way off, its development is important in EDI because it is seen as a way to communicate messages between third party networks. As the use of EDI has grown and expanded across industries, a number of organizations have found that they must deal with trading partners who are not using the same third party network. This problem with communication between third party networks has been dealt with in a number of ways. In some cases, organizations have established accounts with more than one third party network. However, this tends to be an expensive and inefficient method of using EDI. In other cases, the third party network has used an open mailbox or gateway approach. Under the gateway approach, one network will have an account with another network and will transfer electronic messages to the second network for its customers.

The use of X.400 is seen as an effective and cost-efficient alternative to either of the two approaches. Under the X.400 approach, EDI messages will be enveloped in the X.400 P1 envelope. The P1 envelope will be constructed using current EDI interchange control information. Once the EDI message is enveloped as an X.400 message, the X.400 message will be sent through the Message Transfer System. Upon receipt, the X.400 envelope will be removed, and a standard EDI message, including interchange control data, will remain.

SUMMARY

For a telephone conversation to be effective, both parties must speak the same language. The same holds true for the use of EDI. In order for computer-to-computer communication to be successful, both of the computers involved must be able to read and understand data in the same way. EDI standards provide the common language needed for EDI to work.

Following are listings of the standards discussed in this chapter.

ANSI ASC X12 STANDARDS

Released Standards as of April 1989

810 Invoice
819 Operating Expense Statement
820 Payment Order/Remittance Advice
822 Customer Account Analysis
823 Lockbox
830 Planning Schedule with Release Capability
832 Price Sales Catalog
840 Request for Quotation

843 Response to Request for Quotation
844 Product Transfer Account Adjustment
845 Price Authorization Acknowledgment/Status
846 Inventory Advice
849 Response to Product Transfer Account Adjustment
850 Purchase Order
855 Purchase Order Acknowledgment
856 Ship Notice/Manifest
860 P.O. Change
861 Receiving Advice
862 Shipping Schedule
863 Report of Test Results
865 P.O. Change
867 Product Transfer and Resale
869 Order Status Inquiry
870 Order Status Report
997 Functional Acknowledgment
X12.22 Segment Directory
X12.3 Data Element Dictionary
X12.5 Interchange Control Structure

For information on the X12 standards, contact:

Data Interchange Standards Association
Suite 355
1800 Diagonal Road
Alexandria, Virginia 22314
(703) 548-7005

UNIFORM COMMUNICATION STANDARD (UCS) DOCUMENTS

UCS is the electronic data interchange standard used by the grocery industry and other retail-oriented industries. The UCS standard is administered by the Uniform Code Council, which provides identification numbers for members and also provides support services such as education, a technical hotline, and publications.

Uniform Communications Standards are developed by two user committees. The UCS Advisory Council is made up of management representatives from member companies who make recommendations to the Council regarding UCS goals and progress. The Standards Maintenance Group is a committee made up of technical representatives from member organizations. This group is responsible for the actual development of the standards.

UCS Transaction Sets

874 Purchase order—Multipoint
875 Purchase order
876 Purchase order change
877 Purchase order adjustment
878 Product authorization/deauthorization
879 Price changes
880 Invoice
883 Invoice-multipoint
881 Credit memo/Debit memo
884 Shipment Advice
885 Receiving Notice
888 Item Maintenance
889 Promotion Announcement
890 Prepayment Adjustment Advice
891 Promotion Announcement Change
892 Promotion Announcement Confirmation Change
895 Delivery/Return Acknowledgment and/or Adjustment
905 Remittance Advice
999 Acceptance/Rejection

Uniform Code Council, Inc.
8163 Old Yankee Road, Suite J
Dayton, OH 45459
(513) 435-3870

WAREHOUSE INFORMATION NETWORK STANDARDS (WINS) DOCUMENTS

WINS is the electronic data interchange standard used by the warehouse industry and those industries which do business with the warehouse industry. WINS is administered by the Uniform Code Council, which serves as the Secretariat for WINS. Standard development is done by the WINS committee, made up of technical representatives from member companies.

Wins Documents

940 Warehouse Shipping Order
941 Warehouse Inventory Status Report
942 Warehouse Activity Report
943 Stock Transfer Shipment Advice

944 Stock Transfer Receipt Advice
945 Warehouse Shipping Advice
946 Delivery Information Message
999 Acceptance/Rejection

VOLUNTARY INTERINDUSTRY COMMUNICATIONS STANDARDS (VICS)

The apparel and general merchandise industry has formed the VICS steering committee for the development of EDI standards for the industry. The standards are based upon ANSI X12 syntax and are administered by the Uniform Code Council.

810 Invoice
856 Advance Ship Notice
846 Inventory Advice
850 Purchase Order
867 Product Transfer and Resale
832 Price/Sales Catalog

TDCC DEVELOPED STANDARDS

Air Industry Standards

101 Flight Confirmation
104 Shipment Information
105 Container/Equipment Transfer
107 Shipment Information for Export Declaration
108 Shipment Information for Import
109 Shipment Information for Pick-up/Delivery Order
110 Freight Details and Invoice
111 Freight Details and Invoice Summary
113 Inquiry
114 Shipment Identities and Status Reply
115 Status Details Reply
116 Repetitive Pattern Maintenance

Motor Industry Standards

204 Shipment Information
205 Container/Equipment Transfer

206 Shipment Pick-up
207 Shipment Information for Export Declaration
208 Shipment Information for Import
210 Freight Details and Invoice
211 Freight Details and Invoice Summary
213 Inquiry
214 Shipment Identities and Status Replies
216 Repetitive Pattern Maintenance

Ocean Industry Standards

300 Reservation
301 Confirmation
302 Containers/Specialized Equipment Pickup Orders/Cancellations
303 Cancellation
304 Shipment Information
305 Container/Equipment Transfer
306 Dock Receipt
307 Shipment Information for Export Declaration
308 Shipment Information for Import
310 Freight Details and Invoice
312 Arrival Notice
313 Inquiry
314 Shipment Identities and Status Reply
315 Status Details Reply
316 Repetitive Pattern Maintenance

Rail Industry Standards

404 Shipment Information
407 Shipment Information for Export Declaration
408 Shipment Information for Import
410 Freight Details and Invoice
411 Freight Details and Invoice Summary
413 Status Inquiry
414 Status Information
415 Fleet References Update
416 Repetitive Pattern Maintenance
417 Waybill Interchange
418 Advance Interchange Consists
419 Empty Car Advance Disposition
420 Car Handling Information
440 Shipment Weights

Freight Claims Transaction Sets

920 Lost or Damaged Claim—General Commodities
921 Acknowledgment of Receipt of Claim Transaction Set
922 Resolution of Claim
924 Lost or Damage Claim—Automotive
925 Claim Tracer
926 Claim Tracer Reply
927 Claim Status Report

TDCC Business Applications (BUSAP)

810 Invoice
850 Purchase Order
980 Functional Group Totals
994 Administrative Message

Cross Industry Standards

800 Commercial Invoicing
900 Functional Group Totals
901 Completed Payments
980 Generalized Feedbacks
999 Acceptance/Rejection Advice

For more information on TDCC standards, contact:

TDCC/EDIA: The Electronic Data Interchange Association
1101 17th Street, N.W., Suite 712
Washington, DC 20036-4775
(202) 293-5514

5

EDI SOFTWARE
AND HARDWARE

INTRODUCTION

As explained in Chapter 4, EDI standards provide the structure and the common format for electronic messages. However, since no organization has its data file structured in EDI format, and since manual input of data in EDI format would be tedious and time consuming, some method of transforming data from a company-specific format to the EDI standard format is needed. EDI software performs this function.

DEFINITION OF EDI SOFTWARE

EDI software consists of computer instructions that translate information from unstructured, company-specific format to the structured EDI format and then communicates the EDI messsage. EDI software also performs this activity in reverse (receives the message and translates from standard format to company-specific format). EDI software can be developed in-house or it can be purchased from a number of commercial software vendors. EDI can be performed on various types of computers and software is currently available for EDI applications using mainframe computers, minicomputers, or microcomputers (personal computers).

THE FUNCTION OF EDI SOFTWARE

As shown in Figure 5-1, three basic functions of data conversion, data formatting, and message communication must generally be performed for an EDI message to

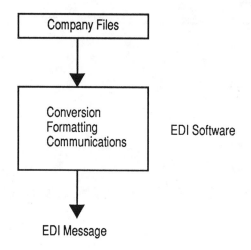

Figure 5-1   Software tasks.

be created and transmitted (or to be received and interpreted). These functions are also often referred to as extraction, generation, and communication.

Formatting

The major function that EDI software performs is formatting or translation. Formatting software translates data from a company-specific format to an EDI standard format. As an example, formatting software can accept as input a purchase order number, date, product description, quantity, unit of measure, price, etc., and would arrange that data into an electronic transaction set with the appropriate data segments.

Formatting software generally uses a table structure to perform the translation. The software includes tables consisting of the standard data dictionary and syntax rules for the data segments and elements of a given EDI transaction set. Whenever a transaction set is to be generated, the software selects the appropriate table to perform the translation.

After the formatting software has arranged the data into the appropriate transaction set format, an edit check is normally performed to make sure that there are no errors in the data and that they are indeed in the appropriate standard format. The transaction sets are then arranged into functional groups and the segments that form the functional group and interchange envelopes are generated.

Formatting software can accept input from two sources. One source is manual data entry. In this case the software takes the data that are entered, reformats if necessary (for instance changing a date from a month-day-year format to the EDI year-month-day format), arranges the data in the correct element and segment order, and adds data element separators and terminators as needed.

The second source of data input for the formatting software is a data file. Any organization that uses computerized systems for internal operations is likely to have most of the data necessary to create an EDI document already on file in a database. Computerized purchasing programs, accounting systems, and order entry systems (all referred to as application programs) are normally supported by a database.

An EDI document can be generated using the data in the application program databases. However, since the structure and syntax of application program databases vary from company to company, formatting software cannot take the data necessary to generate EDI directly from the databases. The information in the database must first be "converted" or restructured so that it can be read by the formatting software. This conversion is also known as "mapping" the application program to the EDI translator.

Conversion

Conversion software performs this function. The data are abstracted from the database and restructured into a flat data file. A flat data file usually consists of records 80 characters in length that have data in fixed positions. Once the data are in a flat file, the formatting software can read the data and then perform the translation function.

Conversion software must be customized to each application and usually requires in-house programming. Many commercially available EDI software packages provide a program shell, usually written in COBOL, or a code generator that will produce a program shell, for performing the conversion.

Communication

The result of the formatting function, coupled with either manual input or data conversion from a database, is an EDI message ready to be sent. The actual transmission of the EDI message is controlled by communications software. This software manages and maintains phone numbers of trading partners, performs automatic dialing, and also produces an activity log. The software interfaces with the communications modem to establish the speed and type of transmission and can perform limited error detection during data transfer. Communications line protocols and speeds are discussed later in this chapter.

For incoming EDI, the same process occurs but in reverse. The communications software receives the transmission. Formatting software interprets the transmission and also generates a functional acknowledgment, notifying the sender that the message has been received. The software then sorts the data from the received transaction sets back into a flat data file that can be used to update application programs. Figure 5-2 shows the normal sequence of activities performed by EDI software for both incoming and outgoing EDI (assuming that the data source is a data file).

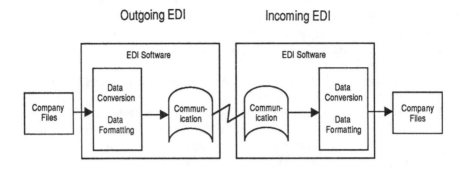

Figure 5-2 Function of EDI software.

Bridging Software

The EDI software described thus far is generally referred to as translation software. Its function is to translate data back and forth between company-specific format and EDI standard format. However, to achieve the full benefits of EDI, one additional form of software is needed: that of bridging software.

As shown in Figure 5-3, bridging software links the various applications programs within an organization and allows for the incoming EDI messages to be used to generate outbound EDI messages. In other words, just as EDI eliminates the need for rekeying operations between firms, bridging software eliminates the need for rekeying between various departments within a firm.

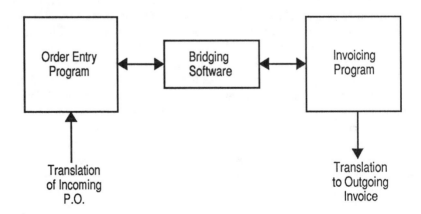

Figure 5-3 Bridging software.

As an example, in an organization with bridging software, data from an incoming purchase order would be used to update purchasing files. The same data, without rekeying, would also be used to update the accounting files so that an invoice could be automatically generated.

Because bridging software is specific to each company's application programs, this software must also be customized. This makes the software expensive in terms of both time and dollars. However, the benefits from bridging software can be significant. For instance, bridging between outgoing purchase orders and incoming invoices eliminates the need for manual reconciliation of the two documents prior to payment. When the EDI invoice is received, the software would compare the invoice information to the purchase order information that was forwarded to the accounting application from purchasing when the purchase order was generated. This is all done electronically rather than manually.

ADDITIONAL FEATURES OF SOFTWARE

In addition to the basic functions of data conversion, formatting, and communication that all EDI software must do, a number of other functions are helpful. Most of these features are available in commercially developed software, and should be included in any in-house developed software. These include:

- Table-driven structure
- Editing capability
- Customizing ease
- Audit options

Table-driven Structure

One very important feature in EDI software is that the software is table-driven. In table-driven software, all of the transaction sets, data segments, and data elements are described in tables rather than in the program code. In this way whenever changes are made to the standards, only the tables, and not the program code, must be changed. While table-driven software is usually more difficult to develop initially, it is much easier to maintain.

Editing Capability

EDI software should include editing and error-checking capability. The software must have the capability of checking messages for compliance with standards. This should include the validation of identification numbers and codes; the verification of interchange, functional group, and transaction set control numbers; the check of segment sequencing; and the verification of the presence of all mandatory segments and elements. The software should be designed to not only indicate when an error has occurred, but also to indicate exactly what the error is and how it should be corrected.

Customizing Ease

The software should allow for users to customize EDI options. As discussed in Chapter 4, EDI standards allow for great flexibility and provide a number of options in terms of segments, elements, interchange control, separators, and terminators. In addition, the standards allow for the use of any of a number of versions and releases. Any EDI software should allow the user to enter defaults for the optional items, and then the software should reflect the default values until changed by the user.

Audit Options

EDI software should include some auditing and control features. The software should be able to report, by time and day, what interchanges, functional groups, and transaction sets were sent and received. The software should also have the ability to match functional acknowledgments with previously sent or received messages. In addition, the auditing function of the software should include the capability of generating printed report summaries of activity.

MAKE OR BUY FACTORS

EDI software can either be developed in-house or purchased from software vendors. As late as 1985, only a very few software packages were available for EDI, particularly for mainframe computers. However, today software is readily available for all types and sizes of computers. Three major factors should be considered in determining whether your organization should buy a commercially available software package or whether it should develop the software in-house. These include:

- In-house resources
- Maintenance required
- Company policy

In-house Resources

The first major factor to consider is the availability of in-house resources, measured in both time and talent. Obviously, purchasing a package requires less time and less expertise than does developing software in-house. By using a package, the user does not need to become an expert on the EDI standards. However, even with a purchased software package, some in-house programming will be required (except if all data entry is by manual input and the EDI program is not linked to any internal applications).

Maintenance Required

A second major factor to consider is maintenance activity. EDI standards change fairly frequently, which means that the software must be frequently updated. If the software is developed in-house, in-house maintenance will also need to be performed. However, if a commercial package is used, the maintenance will be performed by the software vendor.

Company Policy

Some companies expect, or require, that all systems software be developed internally by MIS staff. In these companies, getting approval for the purchase of EDI software may be difficult. While some users see EDI software as being similar to word-processing or spreadsheet software, many MIS departments see EDI software as being within the normal realm of systems development.

SELECTION OF SOFTWARE VENDORS

If your organization decides to buy rather than develop software in-house, you will be faced with selecting among a number of software vendors. In evaluating commercially available software packages and vendors, four major factors should be considered:

1.   Does the software meet your needs, both current and future?
2.   Is the company experienced in your industry?
3.   Is the software user friendly?
4.   Is the software vendor user friendly?

Meeting Needs

Obviously a major factor that must be considered in the purchase of any item is whether the product will meet the organization's needs. This is true with EDI software as well. The software should be reviewed from a number of perspectives. First, does it support the transaction sets your organization will use? Does it support all of the versions and releases your trading partners use? Second, does it have the capability to be run on your system, with minimal additional effort on your part? For instance, if the software is designed for a microcomputer, does it have an easy uploading and downloading procedure? Third, does the software include options for adding security in the form of encryption and authentication in messages?

(Encryption is the coding of data to ensure secrecy; authentication is sending both a coded and an uncoded message to ensure that the data were not changed during transmission.) Fourth, can the software be used with all of the third party networks with which you will deal? While most software is compatible with all networks, some are not.

Company Experience

One very important factor in selecting a software vendor is the level of experience of that vendor. Does the company have experience in *your* industry, with *your* application? EDI is still a growing field, and new software vendors are entering the market. Your company should not be the training ground for a new vendor, or for a vendor expanding into a new application area.

User Friendly Software

The third major question to address is whether the software is user friendly. This is particularly true for microcomputer software that will use screen entry as the data input method. User friendly software provides easy-to-follow screen input directions. For instance, the use of a menu-driven program that takes a new user through the process step-by-step is much easier to use than one without a step-by-step approach. Does the software have built-in safeguards against data entry errors? A number of software packages are designed to not allow a mandatory data element to be skipped. If the user tries to bypass the mandatory element, the computer "beeps" and the cursor refuses to move beyond the required element.

Vendor User Friendly

In addition to the software being user friendly, the software vendor should also be "user friendly." Does the vendor have a hotline staffed with knowledgeable technical people, who can be used to get quick answers to problems? Does the company have an account representative who is willing to come to your location to assist in the installation and to help with any problems after the software is installed? Does the vendor sponsor a users' group of customers currently using the software? Considering all of these factors in the selection of a software vendor should help to assure that the software you purchase will effectively meet your EDI needs.

SOFTWARE COSTS

In general, there are two kinds of EDI software costs: the initial program development or purchase cost and on-going maintenance. The prime factor that determines initial cost is the type of software developed or purchased. In general, mainframe software is much more expensive than microcomputer software. As a general rule of thumb, mainframe software is likely to cost at least $25,000 for the initial development or purchase, while initial costs for microcomputer software can be as low as $500. On-going maintenance costs to keep the software current with standard changes will also vary depending upon the type of computer. Annual maintenance charges can vary between $200 for some microcomputer software to over $2000 for some mainframe software.

SOFTWARE SUMMARY

EDI software is the set of instructions that translates company formatted data into standard EDI and generates and communicates electronic exchanges. However, those exchanges actually take place between two computer systems. Obviously the computer hardware is also an essential part of EDI.

EDI HARDWARE

There is actually no such thing as unique "EDI hardware"! As mentioned earlier, EDI software is available for mainframes, minicomputers, and microcomputers. All it takes to do EDI is a computer of some type, a communications modem, and software. The most common hardware and software combinations used to perform EDI are shown in Figure 5-4. As shown in the chart, three basic options exist:

- Mainframe only
- Microcomputer only
- Microcomputer as a front-end processor to a mainframe

Mainframe Application

One method of configuring an EDI system is to have all of the EDI software reside on a mainframe (or minicomputer) and to have that computer perform all EDI functions. This type of arrangement has a number of advantages. First, it allows fast processing of high volumes of transactions. Second, because all activity is done on the mainframe, there is no uploading or downloading and no rekeying of data. Finally, using a mainframe configuration allows bridging between internal operations such as purchasing and accounting.

While this arrangement has a number of advantages, it also has some limitations. The most significant limitation of this arrangement is the cost. Mainframe software is considerably more expensive than microcomputer software. Further, setting up a mainframe EDI system usually takes a considerable amount of time. A mainframe

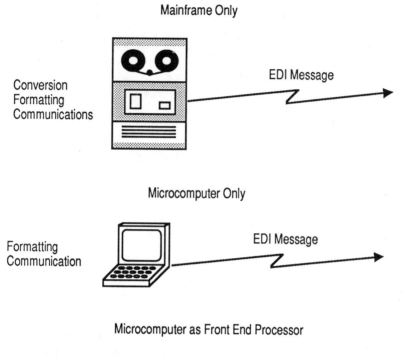

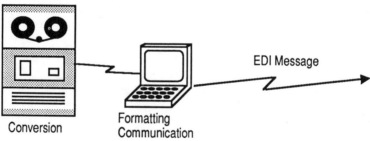

Figure 5-4   Software/hardware options.

system is most appropriate for organizations planning to use a high volume of EDI over a long period, and which have integrated or are planning to integrate EDI with internal operations.

Microcomputer Application

A second arrangement is to have all of the EDI software reside on a microcomputer (PC) and to have the PC perform all EDI functions. This arrangement is referred to as stand-alone EDI, since the EDI activity "stands alone" from any other computer activity within the company. For instance, if the company uses a computerized purchasing program that resides on the mainframe, data are printed out from the mainframe and manually entered into the PC for the EDI application. In a stand-alone configuration, all data entry for outgoing EDI is manual. Further, all incoming EDI is printed out by the PC and then reentered manually into any application systems. (This is sometimes referred to as door-to-door EDI, and is not EDI in the truest sense since that data received on the PC must be rekeyed before being processed.)

There are a number of advantages, however, to this arrangement. First, a microcomputer-based system is relatively inexpensive and can be set up quickly. Stand-alone systems can be purchased (software and hardware) for under $3000. Further, a stand-alone system can often be installed and working within a matter of days. In addition, due to the wide availability of microcomputer software, microcomputer applications tend to be fairly easy to use.

The stand-alone system does have some disadvantages. First, because data input is through screen entry, there is a chance for keying errors. Second, this arrangement tends to be slow and to have limited volume capability. Finally, and perhaps most important, with a stand-alone system, the user does not receive many of the benefits of EDI. The results of the EDI system cannot be bridged to internal operations, nor is clerical activity significantly reduced since all messages must still be rekeyed between the EDI system and internal operations.

A microcomputer stand-alone system is appropriate under a number of conditions. When faced with a demand from an important trading partner that EDI be done *now*, a stand-alone system is appropriate. If top management is reluctant to do EDI, a stand-alone system is an easy and inexpensive way to demonstrate that EDI does work and does produce benefits.

Microcomputer as a Front-End Processor

A third way to configure an EDI system is to use a microcomputer as a front-end processor to a mainframe. In this setup the PC is linked to the mainframe computer. Data stored in the mainframe are put in a data file, which is transferred to the PC (downloading). Likewise, a data file that resides on the PC can be transferred to the mainframe (uploading).

In this arrangement, the file conversion software that sorts data out of applications databases and converts the data to a flat file is normally used on the mainframe. The translation of the data to EDI standards and the generation of transaction sets is usually done on the PC.

This arrangement has some of the same advantages of both the mainframe and the stand-alone configurations. Using a PC as a front-end processor is not as expensive as a mainframe application and does provide more volume and speed than the stand-alone. Because this is a PC application, software is readily available. Because the data are downloaded and uploaded, rather than being manually entered, rekeying is eliminated. On the negative side, this arrangement is not as inexpensive as the stand-alone system, nor is it as fast as a mainframe alone. This is a logical arrangement for a company that wants to begin to perform EDI quickly but anticipates extending the use of EDI in the future.

COMMUNICATIONS MODEMS

In addition to deciding on the type of hardware to be used to generate EDI messages, EDI users must also decide on the communications method that will be used. Communications between computers is actually performed by a modem. A modem is a device that converts computer signals to audio tones, which can be sent over telephone lines.

There are a number of different speeds at which data can be transmitted through modems. Speed of transmission, measured in bits per second (baud rate), generally ranges from 1200 baud to 9600 baud.

There are also different ways in which the characters of data that comprise the message can be grouped during transmission. These methods are called line protocols; the two most common are asynchronous and bisynchronous. In asynchronous transmission, characters are sent out one character at a time. This is normally used at baud rates of no more than 2400 baud. Bisynchronous transmission on the other hand moves characters a block at a time and therefore can move data at higher baud rates. It also has more error-checking and error-correcting features.

In general, bisynchronous protocols and higher baud rates are used when a mainframe application is used, while asynchronous transmission is used for PC applications. In selecting the communication options to be used, it is important to realize that with any direct link between trading partners, both partners must use the same communications method (protocol and speed). If a third party network is used, the communications methods between the trading partners do not have to be compatible since the network will make any necessary conversion.

SUMMARY

Basically, any type of computer equipment can be used to perform EDI. EDI software accepts data from either a data file or from manual input and formats those data into EDI transaction sets. Then communications software takes over and transmits the EDI message to the receiver. The receiver can be either a trading partner or a third party network. The next chapter discusses the functions and use of third party networks.

The following pages provide comparisons, prepared by *EDI News*, of some of the commercially available software packages.

EDI Software: Mainframe

	TranSettlements, Inc. TranSlate	Metromark Translator* MVS	Control Data REDINET REDI-EXCHANGE	EDI Solutions/ ORDERNET EDI TranGentran	American Custom Software Business Partner Network
Composition of Basic Software Package	– Send and Receive – Written in Cobol – Source code given for increased flexability customer's application – Control validation – Table driven on line maintenance interface with user application system	– EDI management software – Data base approach to incoming and outgoing documents – Selective antenna for transmitting and processing documents – Multiple versions of industry standards documents – Comprehensive documentation	– 3 versions of the packages – 1st version prints transaction set into human readable format – 2nd version creates, receives and processes transactions set into and from flat file – 3rd version customized package translates into and out of private format to ANSI	– Link up aid to users internal application – Adhoc reporting facility – Full compliance checking – Mapping feature into users fit and – Error suspense, fix, and acknowledgement – Supports all versions and all transaction sets	– Local area Network – Receives, translates and generates functional acknowledgement simultaneously – Doesn't tie up mainframe time with translations/communication process – Acts as in-house 3rd party network
Basic Package Cost	$25,000 for entire package $15,000 for limited package w/ZTS*	$25,000 1st year increase	1st and 2nd version $7,500 each 3rd version quoted after examination of internal application system	$11,000-$25,000 depending on user's hardware	$25,000 including software, hardware and services
Translation Available for Which Standard	ANSI X12, TDCC, UCS, WINS	ANSI X12, TDCC at public standards	ANSI X12 and subsets plus proprietary	ANSI X12 and subsets, TDCC, UCS, WINS, support select draft standards. EDI lact	ANSI X12 and subsets, any standard available plus proprietary demands
Additional Charge per Standard	none	none - can handle 16 versions of the standards simultaneously	none	none	Yes - per hour programming fee
Additional Charge per Transaction Set	$2,000 per TS for limited package	none	none	none	Base figure includes two sets $500 per additional transaction sets
Annual Maintenance Charge	$2,700 for complete package $2000 + $200 for each additional TS	$3,750 annual license fee includes maintenance	none	$3,000 - annual license fee includes maintenance	10% off software price
Maintenance Charge Include	– 2 standards maintenance updates – Enhancements and new features – Hotline support	– Standards updates – Program enhancements – Hotline	– Hotline support – Standards updates Note: included in basic cost	– Software enhancement – Standards maintenance – Hotline support	– Standards update – Hotline support – Upgrades/ enhancements to software
Start-Up Time/Costs	1 - 4 weeks 2 people to 1 day training session	2 weeks for first time user 2 days of onsite installation assistance for expense costs only	version 1 - 1 hour version 2 - 3 days version 3 - depends on system	2 days on site installation longer depending on internal system application	1 - 2 month time total of 6 - 8 hours/ week at $40/hour
Compatible with Which Systems	IBM MVS or use Tandem, Honeywell, Sperry, Burroughs DEC/VAX, HP3000	Any mainframe that runs on MVS SP or MVS XA operating system	IBM MVS and MVS XA	– All IBM mainframes – HP 3000 – DEC Vac systems	All IBM mainframes
Interfaces with Which Networks	Independent of network No communication feature	– Package does not include communications software – Software is not limited to any network's access	Primarily REDINET and any network utilizing proprietary communications module	No communications module, but compatible with all networks	Any network - experience with GEIS, CO, REDINET, Kleinschmidt, Translink-IBM's Information Network
Value-Added Services	– Scheduled biweekly training – EDI consulting – Installation/implementation – EDI workshop – Powerful user group meets twice a year	– EDI training – EDI consulting – EDI education/vendor seminars	– EDI consulting – EDI training – Extended support program – Effective EDI implementation program for bringing trading partners on board	– Phone consultation support – Customer application link up – Technical EDI consulting – Compression of banks	– Seminars on VAN development – EDI support for trading partners – EDI consulting

* Transaction Set

Source: EDI NEWS, April 6, 1988
Reprinted with permission

EDI Software: Mainframe

	GEIS	American Business Computer	EDI, Inc.
Composition of Basic Software Package	– Translation, Compliance checking, acknowledgement generation, control number generation	– Translates from flat file to ANSI X12 and vice-versa; – Table driven based on three types of tables • Defines content and format of flat file • Defines ANSI X12 syntax and mapping instruction • Trading Partner parameter tables – Online maintenance utility using CICS or IMS	– Accepts files from applications in fixed record layouts; – Offers translation/communication; – Generates functional acknowledgements; – Receive any information in third-party network mailbox
Basic Package Cost	$9,500 for one copy	$24,000	$30,000
Translation Available for Which Standard	ANSI X12, TDCC, UCS, and X12 subsets also protocols not yet approved by X12, if there is a need	ANSI X12, TDCC, and X12 subsets	TDCC, ANSI X12, UCS, WINS
Additional Charge per Standard	none - unless variants are added	none	none
Additional Charge per Transaction Set	none	none	Pricing and number of TS* included with basic package available 5/88
Annual Maintenance Charge	One free year of maintenance, option of annual maintenance after first year $1,200	$2,400	$4,000 for base system
Maintenance Charge Include	– 24 hour hotline support; – Document updates; – Any new feature chooses to distribute	– Hotline support; – Standards update; – New features update	– Standards updates; – Software updates; – Hotline support
Start-Up Time/Costs	Purchase of software	16 - 24 hours of on-site assistance over a on week period per transaction set	2 - 3 days for 1 TS if all hardware is in place
Compatible with Which Systems	Developed for the IBM OS MVS environment, but also complies with Burroughs, VAX, Honeywell DPS6, and IBM DOS	IBM 43XX and 30 XX and DOS or MVS systems	Tandem, DEC VAX in future
Interfaces with Which Networks	Nothing to inhibit communications with any network	No communications package, but does not limit transmission to any network	McDonnell-Douglas, GEIS, Western Union, Kleinschmidt, TranSettlements, Telecom Canada, Ordernet, Railinc. CDC on request
Value-Added Services	– Installation assistance $1,800, includes two days of on-site assistance to help you load the tape, compile the program, test the package, but does not include program; – Professional services for consulting, programming, Turnkey implementation at our professional services	– Provides consultative and/or contracting assignments for such projects as migration of software to other systems such as HP or VAX; – Full range of EDI consulting	– Identical to Telink PC

* Transaction Set

Source: EDI News May 4, 1988
Reprinted with permission

EDI Software: Microcomputer

	EDI, Inc.	Advanced Communications Systems	Birmingham Computer Group	Control Data Corp. REDINET	GEIS+
Composition of Basic Software Package	- Combination stand-alone and front-end to mainframe options - Table and parameter driven - Supports all transaction sets, supporting system utilities, turnkey	- Multiple version support of ANSI X12 - Partner activated acknowledgement - User customized transaction sets, auto compliance tracking	- Document Transmission Software - Receives and Transmits EDI documents - Unattended communications capabilities - Menus based on available data - Report generator database	Create, receive, and process transaction sets using ANSI X12 and all related transaction sets	- Document processor creates standard messaging - Stand-alone - Front-end to mainframe capabilities
Basic Package Cost	$2900	$1995	$1990	$500 + $200 communication package	$950
Translation Available into Which Protocol	X12 + all subsets, UCS, WINS, TDCC Air, Ocean, Motor, Rail	ANSI X12 and TDCC transaction sets and all available subsets	Any protocol requested by customer, also handles fixed and variable length standards	ANSI X12 and all related transaction sets	ANSI X12 (in June will offer translation to TDCC and EDIfact)
Additional Charge per Standard	none	none	none	none	Pricing not available till June
Additional Charge per Transaction Set	typically $300	none	minimum of $500 per transaction set, but package never exceeds $4000	none	none
Annual Maintenance Charge	$750	$150	$600	none	$180
Maintenance Charge Includes	1) training maintenance 2) hotline support 3) software update every 6 mos.	1) new version every 6 months 2) unlimited training	1) hotline support 2) quarterly software update	Basic software cost includes: 1) hotline support 2) standards updates	1) software updates 2) hotline support
Start-Up Time/ Costs	1/2 day	1 day – no start up cost	1 day onsite training, customer incurs expenses only	1/2 hour	1-2 days, training additional cost (in June will include computer based tutorial)
Compatible with Which Systems	IBM Micros and Compatibles	640 k systems with available board slots for modem & printer	IBM MS PC DOS Compatibles	IBM MS PC DOS Compatibles	512k IBM PC, w/10 megabyte harddisk dependent on traffic volume
Interfaces with Which Networks	All major networks	All major networks	GEIS, IBM, CDC REDINET, others as requested	REDINET, and any network that requires communication modules	GEIS network
Value-Added Services	- Password protection - Reconciliation - Duplicate checks - System configuration functions - Timed execution on annual schedule - Technical support	- EDI consulting services - ACS Lazar BAR & SCANLOG software for using scanner and bar codes	- Interface to operational systems - Integration/Consulting services - Offer trade-in to multisystem upgrade - Network registration	Professional services training, consulting, Extended Support Program – one day onsite support	- Interface w/PC - Mail box and user's word processor - System crash protection

+ Formerly GEISCO

Figure 5-13

Source: EDI NEWS March 1988
Reprinted with permission

EDI Software: Microcomputer

	Metromark	American Business Computer EDE	Railinc EDI Synapse	RMS VLT	Can/Am Tech EZ-Order
Composition of Basic Software Package	Create, receive and process documents in all available transaction sets, Translation	Create, receive, and process documents, translate into all available transaction sets	Create, receive, and process documents, translate into all available transaction sets	Dictionaries and Segment directories for all X12, Translator, Create, receive and process documents	Create, receive, and process documents – translation into all ANSI X12 transaction sets
Basic Package Cost	$1995.00	Link to one trading partner $2000.00	$1985.00	$1950.00 Single User Package	$3,000
Translation Available into Which Protocol	ANSI AIAG, UCS, TDCC, ANSI X12	ANSI X12 and all subsets, AIAG, UCS and WINS available 2nd quarter '88. All Proprietary Automotive	US, WINS, TDCC, ANSI X12, EDIFACT	ANSI X12, TDCC coming up now	ANSI X12, Steel and Aluminum sets
Additional Charge per Standard	none	none	none	none	none
Additional Charge per Transaction Set	none	none	none	none	none
Annual Maintenance Charge	$399.00	12% of software price for package #1, 12% for #2 and 20% for #3 (see below)	$200.00	$550.00	15% of software price
Maintenance Charge Includes	1) updates of standards 2) enhancements 3) hotline support	1) software enhancements standards updates 2) hotline support 3) both of the above	1) online help capability 2) 1 day training 3) updates to standards 4) product enhancements	1) software enhancements 2) standards updates 3) hotline support	1) software enhancements 2) standards updates 3) hotline support
Start-Up Time/ Costs	2 days	5 hours – 1 day	1 day	4 hours	1 day
Compatible with Which Systems	IBM PC's and Compatibles	IBM PC's and compatibles	IBM PC's and Compatibles AT or above	IBM PC's and Compatibles UNIX scheduled for 2nd Q '88	Any MS/DOS Compatible PC
Interfaces with Which Networks	McDonnell Douglas, ORDERNET, GEISCO, CDC, Redinet, Western Union, IBM	McDonnell Douglas, IBM, CDC, McDonnell Douglas, Kleinschmidt, Martin Marietta later in '99	Railinc, GEISCO, McDonnell Douglas, Testing on IBM	GEISCO, Redinet, IBM, McDonnell Douglas, CompuServe, GM Net, Chrysler, Ford	GEISCO, CompuServe
Value-Added Services	Purchase price applies to future upgrades	Training and consulting services	Flat-file conversion	Integrated bar coding, Product customizer	

Figure 5-14

Source: EDI NEWS February 1988
Reprinted with permission

EDI Software: Minicomputer

	Metromark Integrated Systems	American Business Computer	Future Three Software	ACS Network Systems	INTEC
Composition of Basic Software Package Offering	– Full function table and menu driver EDI microcomputer software- includes feature for designing proprietary standard communications capabilities provide direct or via network transmission	– EDI minicomputer management software - table and menu driven - communications sub - systems - external systems application for programmer manipulation - UNIX environment	– EDI minicomputer software to handle automotive releases - on-line inquiry - feeds into other applications. - puts proprietary automotive formats into common format	– EDI management software for minicomputer platform – Written in RPG+ – Menu and table driven – Mail box capabilities	– LAN architecture based mid-range to larger scale solution- support national and proprietary standards on line composition and editing functions, compliance checking and data validation capabilities
Basic Package Cost	System 34 - $5000 System 36 - $5500 System 38 - $6000	$15000	System 36-38 - $5000 - $15000 AS 400 - $22000	System 36 - $5000 / System 38 - $8000 -/AS 400 -Model 10- $7000 / Model 20 - $8000	Mid range networks start at $9000
Translation Available into Which Protocol	ANSI X12, UCS, WINS, TDCC	ANSI X12, other standards upon request	Specialize in ALAG X12, ANSI x12, and proprietary	ANSI X12, UCS< TDCC (all versions) proprietaly on request	ANSI X12, UCS, TDCC as well as proprietay
Charge per Standard	No	No	No	No	Yes - based on user requirements
Charge per Transaction Set	No	Yes - additional charge per group of transaction set	No	No	Basic offering supports 3 transaction sets : Incoming, outgoing and functional acknowledgement
Annual Maintenance Charge	Included in 12% annual license	20% of package price per year	18% of package price per year	12% of package cost per year	Generally 1% of installed cost per month
Maintenance Charge Includes	Upgrade of tables and software - hotline support	Updates to tables and software and hotline support	Updates to tables and software and hotline supports	Updates to tables and software and hotline supports	Updates to tables hotline support
Start-Up Time/ Costs	No additional Costs - start up time range between 3 days and a month	Start up cost and time depends on customer premise	No extra cost, full integration within 1 month	No extra cost - installation in as little as 1 - 2 days	Typically a 90 day installation cycle
Compatible with Which Systems	IBM 34 - 36 - 38 - AS 400	UNIX - ZENIX operating systems, but also runs on DOS PC's	Systems 36 - 38 and AS 400	IBM Mid-range systems	Novell operating system, LAN operating environment
Interfaces with Which Networks	All major Third Party Networks	Anybody that has 3780 standard Bisync access	IBM, GEIS, REDINET	All Networks	Currently interface with IBM Information Network, but nothing to prevent other networks
Value-Added Services	– Provide user group forum – Training services under development	– Consulting and training services – Installation programs and implementation planning	– Consulting and educational support – Software modification services.	– Training class being developed – Consulting – Installation	– Full range business consulting support – Technical support – Customer requested training

* HW/ SW - Hardware/ Software   + RPG - Computer programming language

Figure 5–15

Source: EDI NEWS Sept. 7, 1988 Reprinted with permission

6

THIRD PARTY NETWORKS

INTRODUCTION

For electronic data interchange to take place between two trading partners, the trading partners must in some way be linked. The linkage can be done in one of two ways: direct or indirect.

DIRECT EXCHANGES

In point-to-point, or direct, EDI, two trading partners exchange electronic communications directly. In other words, there is a direct access from the computer of the sender to the computer of the receiver, as shown in Figure 6-1. This direct access is most commonly done through the use of telephone lines and a computer modem. One trading partner, using the computer modem, simply dials into another trading partner's computer.

For this direct linkage to work, the organizations must be compatible from a communications standpoint. In other words, the trading partners must use the same communications protocols in terms of line speeds, baud rates, and the like. The two parties must also either use the same standards or have the capability of translating from one standard (such as X12) to another (such as UCS). Further, because the sender calls each trading partner directly, the parties must agree upon the hours of availability of each system. In other words, the receiving computer must be open and available when the sending party transmits a message.

A direct system is workable when an organization is communicating electronically with only a few trading partners. However, as the number of trading partners increases, the complexity of linking with all of them directly also increases. While a number of organizations are currently exchanging electronic documents with a large number of trading partners through point-to-point or direct systems, many

Seller   Buyer

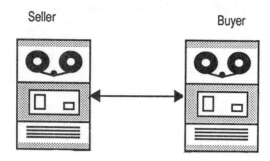

Figure 6-1   Direct links between trading partners.

organizations find that direct linkages are too hard to maintain with a large number of trading partners. As Figure 6-2 indicates, to link directly with a large number of trading partners generally requires the ability to support a number of different communications protocols, time zones, and variations in transaction sets.

THE ROLE OF THIRD PARTY NETWORKS

Third party networks have evolved in the EDI community as a source of resolving the issues involved in communicating with a number of different trading partners. Most third party networks developed out of time-sharing networks. For instance, the first UCS message was transmitted in December of 1983 via TYMNET, a public network owned by Tymshare, Inc. (since acquired by McDonnell Douglas Corporation).

Recent EDI experience shows that most companies consider the use of a third party network when they reach an EDI volume of between four and six trading partners. In essence, what a third party network provides are the EDI communications skills, expertise, and equipment necessary to communicate electronically. In addition, a third party network can also provide value added services such as translation to standard, international connections, connections to other third party networks, and training. A third party network can be used in one of two major ways: simply as an electronic mailbox, or for additional services in the role of a value added network.

THIRD PARTY MAILBOX SERVICES

The most basic service a third party network can provide is that of an electronic mailbox. In providing this service the third party network performs a function very much like that performed by the U.S. Postal Service. The Postal Service receives

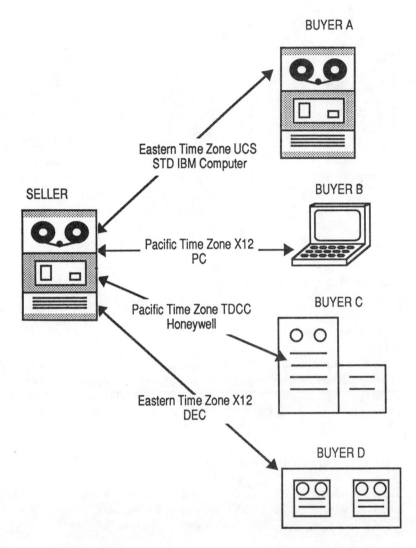

Figure 6-2   Direct linkages.

mail from senders, sorts the mail by receiver, and delivers the mail to the receiver's mailbox. Third party networks function exactly the same in providing an electronic mailbox for EDI messages.

As shown in Figure 6-3, a third party network establishes an electronic mailbox for each trading partner. The sending trading partner transmits electronic messages, usually by dialing-in over phone lines, to the third party network. The network receives the electronic messages and sorts them by receiver. The electronic mes-

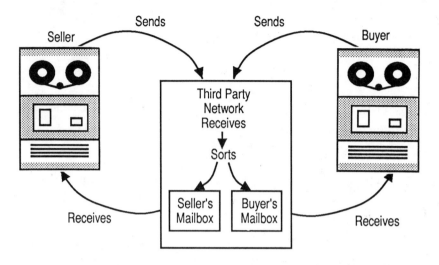

Figure 6-3   Third party network as an electronic mailbox.

sages are then stored in the receivers' mailboxes until they are called for by the receiver.

An electronic mailbox can be used whether you only send EDI messages, only receive EDI messages, or whether you do both. Most third party networks allow you to "pick up" your incoming messages at the same time that you drop off your outgoing messages. In addition, most third party networks allow for 24 hours a day, 7 days a week access to the electronic mailbox.

Advantages of an Electronic Mailbox

Using a third party network in this manner eliminates a number of the problems associated with direct links with trading partners. Advantages received from the use of a third party network as an electronic mailbox include:

- Elimination of communications compatibility problems
- The ability to reach all trading partners with just one call
- The ability to receive audit information
- The existence of a buffer between your computer and that of your trading partner

Communications Compatibility   One advantage of the use of a third party network electronic mailbox is that your organization is dialing out to only one other organization, the third party network. Therefore, the organization needs to be compatible with only one set of hardware and communications specifications. Further, most third party networks have the capability to receive and send via numerous communications protocols and at several line speeds. In addition, because of the 24 hours a day time period, time zones are not a problem. As an example, one large consumer goods company regularly sends to and receives messages from its electronic mailbox at 3 A.M. daily. This allows the company to keep both its phone lines as well as its computer system open during the day for other activity; it means that the company receives discounted communication charges since the calls are made during off-peak times.

One Call or Connect   Another major advantage of using third party networks as an electronic mailbox is that only one call needs to be made to reach all trading partners. The sender calls the third party network who then calls all the trading partners. Further, the call to the third party is usually made through either a toll free number or through a local access number. So regardless of where the trading partner is, the dial-up call is considered a local call.

Audit Trail   In addition to receiving, storing, and sending electronic messages, third party networks in their role as electronic mailboxes will also provide audit information. Most third party networks generate an activity log showing what was received from you and where it went, as well as a log showing what was placed in your mailbox. In many cases, the activity log can be set up on an exception basis reporting only those messages that were put in a mailbox but not picked up in a set time period, such as 24 hours.

Security Buffer   Another advantage provided by the third party network is that the network acts as a buffer between your computer and your trading partners. By using a third party network, you can do EDI but still not have any other computer linked directly with yours.

VALUE ADDED SERVICES

In addition to providing simple electronic mailbox services, third party networks will also perform additional value added services for EDI customers. When additional services are performed, the third party network is usually referred to as a "value added network" or VAN.

In its role as a VAN, a third party network is similar to a mailing bureau. Some common functions performed by mailing bureaus include preparation of mailings, labeling of mailings, and transmission of mailings. Electronic versions of these functions are performed by third party networks in their role as value added networks. These added services include:

- Translation
- Paper conversion
- Dial-out services
- Encryption and authentication
- Installation and training

Translation Services

An important value added service that a VAN provides is translation. A third party network can receive data in your company-specific format and translate that information to EDI standard. This allows you to "do" EDI without changing any of your internal software. All that is required is that the data to be sent are extracted from your application files and formatted to a basic data flat file. Then the software that is resident on the VAN's computer will do the translation to EDI standard prior to sending the data to a trading partner. Having a VAN do the translation activity is likely to reduce software development and implementation time and may also reduce the effort required to maintain the software to reflect standard changes. However, it should be noted that over the long run, using the VAN to do translation is most likely a more expensive option than either developing software in-house or purchasing commercially available software and may make it more difficult and costly for the organization to either change VANs or to change to in-house translation at a later time.

Paper Conversion Services

Some value added networks offer the capability of converting electronic messages to paper messages before sending them on to your trading partners. Even after an organization reaches the point where a majority of its transactions are being transmitted electronically, there will still be some trading partners who cannot receive electronic messages. Conversion services provide a way for you to communicate electronically with trading partners who cannot receive electronic communications. Under this arrangement, your EDI system would generate EDI messages and would send all of the messages to the value added network. Upon receiving the electronic messages, the VAN would sort the messages by trading partners. For those trading partners with no EDI capability, the VAN would convert the electronic message to a printed format. The printed copy would then be sent to the trading partner via either facsimile machine or the mail system. In this way you can "do" EDI even with trading partners who cannot receive EDI.

This paper conversion method can also be used if a large and important trading partner requires that you do EDI before you are ready to implement a full EDI effort. By using the VAN to receive your incoming electronic messages and by then having the VAN convert the electronic messages to paper format for your organization, you can quickly meet the requirements of an important trading partner without having to "do" EDI internally. Although this method allows for a quick response to a major customer, your company receives no additional benefit from EDI under this approach.

Dial-Out Services

Another service provided by VANs is dial-out. A number of large organizations often make data available on their in-house systems to trading partners. However, the trading partners are required to dial-in to the large organizations' computers in order to retrieve the information. A VAN, through a dial-out pickup service, will initiate the necessary calls to retrieve information and will place the messages in your electronic mailbox. The dial-outs can be scheduled as often as required by either you or your trading partner. Through the use of dial-out services, your organization needs to make only one call, to the third party, to both send and receive electronic messages, even if those messages reside on the computer of a trading partner who does not transmit to a third party network.

Encryption and Authentication Services

Encryption and authentication is another important feature offered by some of the third party networks. Encryption is the process of changing an EDI message into a coded message that cannot be read unless the receiver has the key to the code. The use of encryption ensures secrecy of the data. Authentication, on the other hand, does not ensure secrecy but does ensure that the data are not altered. Authentication can be used as a form of electronic signature since its use verifies the identity of the sender. With authentication, the EDI message is changed into a coded message and both the EDI message and the coded message are sent to the receiver. The receiver then uses the key to code the EDI message and compares the result with the coded message that was received. If the two are the same, the receiver knows the message was not altered in transit. While not used for all EDI messages, encryption and authentication are used in the banking industry and in other industries for the transmission of financial and other sensitive information.

Installation and Training Services

Value added networks also offer installation assistance and training. This assistance usually takes the form of working with your trading partners to get them on-line, as well as providing internal assistance to your company. VANs will normally provide documentation, an implementation guideline, and a hotline for questions or problems. In addition, a sales representative is usually available to help with the installation and implementation of your EDI effort.

EXPERIENCE OF THIRD PARTY NETWORKS

There is one additional advantage to using a VAN that is not actually a "service" but is often critical in EDI implementation. That advantage is the experience in EDI that a VAN brings to your implementation effort. Because VANs have experience in working with other users of EDI, they are likely to have faced any implementation problem that may arise. By using a VAN, you gain the benefit of other companies' experiences with EDI. The use of a VAN can mean that you do not make the same mistakes that have been made by others who have implemented EDI before you.

ISSUES/CONCERNS WITH THIRD PARTY NETWORKS

The use of third party networks as both electronic mailboxes and value added networks is growing. The availability of third party networks is crucial to the future growth of EDI. However, as the use of EDI third party networks increases and as more third party networks enter the marketplace a number of issues need to be addressed by the industry. These issues include interconnectability between third party networks, security of third party networks, and legal liability of the networks.

Interconnectibility

Third party networks provide a link between trading partners. But what happens when two trading partners have selected and use different third party networks? As shown in Figure 6-4, organizations have often found that they must deal with trading partners using a number of different third party networks. This is particularly true for organizations that do business in a number of different industries.

For the use of EDI to work smoothly and efficiently across industries, there must be some method of transferring messages between various third party networks. In other words, the third party networks must interconnect in some way. If the networks do not interconnect, organizations using third party networks are left with one of two options, with neither option being very desirable. The first option is to ensure that all of their trading partners use the same third party network (very unlikely); or the second option is for every organization to have an account and an electronic mailbox on every third party network (very inefficient and costly).

The third party networks have addressed this problem by interconnecting through what are called "gateways." A third party gateway allows your organization to deal with trading partners who are using a different third party network without the need of establishing an account with each third party network. Rather, your third party network establishes an account with any other third party network your trading partner may be using. When your third party receives a message for a trading partner on the second network, your network sends the message to its

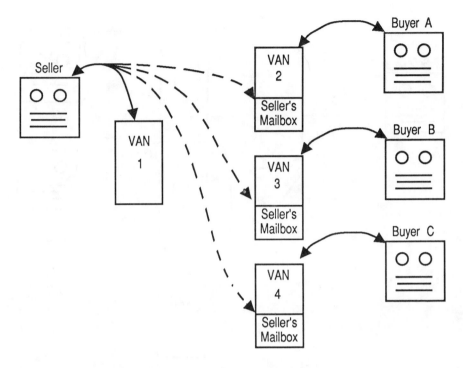

Figure 6-4   Trading partners with different third party networks.

mailbox at the second network. The second network views this incoming message just as it views any incoming message and sorts out the messages to the appropriate electronic mailbox. In this way, you can communicate with trading partners who are not using the same electronic network, as shown in Figure 6-5. Currently, most of the third party networks interconnect through gateways. However, not all of the networks interconnect to every other network. In addition, some networks charge additional fees if the gateway connection is used in the transmittal of a message, while others do not charge anything additional for this service.

In addition to gateway service, another important value added service provided by some third party networks is the ability to connect internationally. A number of the VANs have private networks overseas that can be used for EDI with foreign trading partners. Other VANs interconnect through international common carriers, or use private international gateways.

Security of Third Party Networks

A major concern of many EDI users is that an unauthorized user might gain access to company data. However, third party networks, in general, have numerous security measures in place to assure that data is not lost or sent to unauthorized

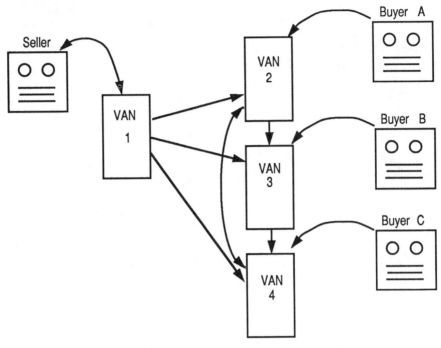

Figure 6-5   Gateway between VANs.

receivers. All data passing through a third party network is routed via the receiver identification codes in the standard envelopes. Access to a mailbox normally requires both a specific mailbox identification code and a password. Document flow between mailboxes within the third party is controlled through the use of an identification and authorization data file maintained by the third party.

In addition to basic security measures, some third party networks offer encryption and authentication of messages, as discussed earlier. (And the X12 standards provide specific formats for encrypted and authenticated data.) This provides another layer of security that protects against data tampering. Further, the way in which networks physically move data also works to prevent data alternation. VANs use packet switching to move data. This means that messages are broken into packets of characters that are moved separately and then rejoined. In this way, it would be very difficult for an outside party to intercept and either read or alter a complete message.

Because of the data security measures maintained by third party networks, many organizations see the use of a third network as a way to *increase* data security. Linking with trading partners indirectly through a third party means that no other organization is dialing into your computer. Many companies view this indirect linkage as an extra buffer of security.

Third Party Network Liability

Another issue of concern to users of third party networks is that of liability. For instance, what happens if a third party network does, somehow, lose an important purchase order and thus cause a company to lose a sale? The liability of third party networks appears to be similar to that of the U.S. Post Office. When the post office loses a piece of mail, liability, if any, is normally limited to only the cost of the mail service. This is often true when using express delivery services as well. If the item is not delivered on time or is lost, in most cases the only compensation is the cost of the transmittal. The same type of limited liability applies to EDI transmissions sent through a third party network.

If an electronic data interchange message is "lost" in a third party network, in general the only liability of the third party is actual costs of transmission. The third party is not liable for any form of consequential damages. This limited liability is usually very clearly stated in the third party network contract. However, in most cases, the third party network will work to recreate the lost data, if possible, and will do so at no charge.

This limited liability of VANs is based upon a number of factors. First, the chance of data getting "lost" is remote. Second, the cost of guaranteeing against such a loss would be prohibitive. Third, with EDI the sender of an electronic message has the ability to know if the message was received or not. The functional acknowledgment provides this information, thus giving the sender the opportunity to retransmit the message.

COSTS OF USING THIRD PARTY NETWORKS

Although not every third party network charges for services in the same way, a number of types of costs are common across all third party networks. In many ways, these costs are similar, in type, to the costs of using a telephone system.

To begin with, most third party networks charge an initial start-up fee to add you to the network. In addition to this "installation" fee is a fixed monthly charge for mailbox use. These charges are fixed and occur whether any messages are sent through the system or not. In addition to the fixed charges are variable charges for message transmission (similar to long distance calling). The variable charges are usually based upon the number of either characters or documents transmitted. Normally an organization establishes an agreement with trading partners, in advance, identifying who will pay transmission charges. For instance, in the grocery industry the sender pays the transmission charge.

The fixed start-up costs, the monthly fees, and the variable usage costs are fairly common across all networks. In addition, other charges may be included depending upon the network used and the services selected. For instance, in some cases a per-session fee may be charged for each transmission session. There may be a minimum monthly charge regardless of usage. There may also be a separate charge for verifying trading partner information or for interconnecting to another third party. Regardless of how a third party charges, it is common to provide both volume and time (off-peak) discounts.

SELECTING A THIRD PARTY NETWORK

As the use of EDI has grown, so has the number of third party networks. In selecting a third party network, a number of factors should be considered. These include:

- Services offered
- Experience level
- Customer orientation
- Cost

First, the services the third party network provides should be examined. Are translation services offered, and, if so, for what standards and what transaction sets? Are additional services such as dialing-out and conversion to paper format available? What kind of training and support is offered? In examining the services provided, both current and future needs of the organization should be considered.

In addition to looking at services offered by the third party network, the experience level of the network should also be examined. How long has the network been in the EDI business? Who else is currently using the network? Are others in the industry trading through this network? Ideally, you would want to find a network that has experience in your industry, with your type of application.

Another question that should be addressed is "how customer-oriented is the network?" By talking to current customers of the network, you should be able to find out how easy or how difficult it is to get started with a particular network. For instance, current users should be able to tell you if network personnel were willing to "walk the organization through" all of the steps necessary to get started. Further, current users can also provide information on how service-oriented the network was after the contract for services was signed.

A final factor to be examined in selecting a network is cost. While cost may not be the only or even the most important factor, it is still a consideration. One of the goals of EDI is cost reduction, and therefore it would not be logical to select a third party network, or any other component of EDI, without consideration of the costs involved. Because the networks charge differently, the best way to compare costs is to estimate a usage volume over some time period and price out what it would cost on the networks under consideration. Most of the cost data are readily available, and therefore using an estimated volume would provide a way to compare the networks.

USE OF THIRD PARTY NETWORKS

Third party networks are not used by all organizations that have implemented EDI. However, recent estimates place the percentage of organizations that have implemented EDI and are currently using third party networks at approximately 60 percent of all EDI users.[1] While it might seem logical that large organizations would be the least likely to use third party network services, approximately 75 percent of the Fortune 500 companies who perform EDI use third party networks to some extent.[2]

Further, as the use of EDI continues to expand, the use of third party networks is also expected to expand. Most of the growth in EDI is likely to come from the implementation of EDI by small and middle-sized companies as their larger trading partners begin to demand EDI transactions. Many of these companies do not believe that they have the in-house resources and skills necessary to establish direct EDI linkages with trading partners. Further, even in organizations where resources are available, many organizations have found that the use of a third party network relieves much of the systems development burden. For instance, one study of EDI users found that organizations that use third party networks do so for a variety of reasons, including lower costs than direct linkages, the shifting of the technical risk of changes in standards and technology to the third party network, and the use of the third party as an added security buffer for data security.[3]

SUMMARY

A number of third party networks are currently available. Although most of the networks offer the same basic services, there are differences in costs, in specific services provided, and in experience in specific industries. The charts on the following pages compare the major third party networks that currently offer EDI services.

	AT&T	COMPUSERVE	EDS of Canada Bulk Data Switch (BDS)	GEIS	Harbinger	IBM Information Network	McDonnell Douglas EDI*NET
Basic Message Cost	$1.00 for 7500 characters. $.40 for up to 400 characters.	$3.75 hourly connect charge and $.15 per 1000 characters.	GM Suppliers retrieve and send messages to and from EDS at no cost. Private EDI mailbox for General Motors, not a commercial offering.	$.12 per document plus $.02 per 100 characters.	$.10 per message plus $.02 per 100 characters; volume discounts available.	$.30 header (ie ISA) + $.07 per 100 characters peak. 50% less off peak.	$1.00 monthly minimum. $.60 per 1000 characters, send $.30 per 1000 characters receive. 33% off peak discount. Volume discounts up to 45%.
Network Translation	No.	Yes, on customized basis. Encourage use of EDI translation software 'certified' by Compuserve.	No.	Yes.	No.	Yes.	No.
Standards Supported	ANSI X12 document formats (and derivatives such as VICS, AIAG, etc.).	ANSI X12 and subsets, all TDCC standards, UCS WINS and more. EDIFACT will be supported in 1989.	AIAG sub convention of ANSI X12 & CISCO (GM format).	ANSI S12, TDCC, WINS, UCS EDIFACT, EDIFICE, ODETTE, GALIA and VDA $ more.	X12 and subsets.	ANSI X12, UCS, EDIFACT, UNTDI, TDCC, AIAG.	ANSI X12 and subsets, TDCC, UCS WINS, some proprietary.
Translation Charges	NA	Charges for custom developed translation software include one time development fee and ongoing surcharge per 1000 characters.	NA	On network—$.60 per 1000 characters.	NA	Prices are per job—volume sensitive.	NA
Asynchronous Access	Yes, included in Basic Message Cost (BMC).	Yes, charges are same as BMC.	No Async access.	Yes, included in BMC.	Yes.	Yes, same as BMC for messages, for Dial up. $.027 per 1000 characters (50% less off peak).	$25 per month mailbox fee.
Bisynchronous Access	Yes, $2,000 per month for private port. $50-$250 per month for shared ports, depending on volume.	Yes, $19 per hour surcharge.	Yes, no cost to the GM supplier.	Yes, included in BMC.	Yes.	Yes, same as above.	$200 per month for initial mailbox, $100 per month for each additional mailbox.
SNA Services	Available 2nd quarter 1989. Pricing to be provided at a later time.	No.	Not for EDI.	Yes, BMC $.04 per 1000 characters.	Yes.	Yes, leased line attach—monthly rate based on line speed and service provided.	Scheduled to be supported by EDI*NET 2.0 system.
Startup Time/Cost	PC-1/2 day, UNIX-1/2 day, other 1-9 days, bisyc host 2-5 days.	If client is EDI ready 1/2 day, one time setup fee $250.	Start time on average is 5 days. No startup cost.	1 week and there is a $250 initiation fee.	$100 setup fee, no setup charge for users of INTOUCH*EDIPC software.	$168 one time charge per account + $44 per month + usage.	1-3 days with EDI certified software. No startup fees.
International Services	Yes.	Yes, can be accessed from 200 countries.	No.	Yes, have a joint venture in UK with ICL called International Network Services (INS) Limited.	Yes, through internetwork connections.	Yes.	Yes.
Interconnect Policy	Negotiating for interconnects now. Pricing to follow upon completion of negotiations.	Interconnect with any and all EDI VANs that share policy of interconnecting at no cost to participating EDI networks.	Does not presently interconnect.	Will connect to any EDI VAN at request of client. Price is $25 per month per connection.	Connect with any and all third parties at cost of $25 per month to the user.	Interconnect with several EDI VANS. Now, will connect others as business needs—$25 per month. Admin. charge $.10 per 1000.	Public network gateway—No charge selective private network access.
Security	Network supports embedded binary data in an X.400 envelope, which allows end-to-end management of encrypted data.	Four levels of access security, 2 ID's & 2 passwords. All passwords are encrypted, continuous monitoring of access attempts.	BDS is password protected. Point to point EDI banking system uses Authentication and Encryption.	High level of security for system access.	Multiple levels of security including private changeable passwords.	Dual user id/acct + passwords at network & mailbox extended security option for those requiring it.	Do not provide but can support.
Other Value Added Services	Consultation, integrated electronic mail, support services.	E-mail, electronic publishing & conferencing, database access, database management and application software, value added network services for business clients.	EDI translation software EDI*ASSET.	Implementation services, electronic mailbox services, etc.	Complete implementation programs for any company that wants to significantly expand their EDI trading partner base of customers and/or suppliers. Free EDI software for trial period.	Same mailbox for E-mail. Network services from SNA hosts. Interactive EDI type service.	24 hour customer service, envelope translation, detailed billing report, message status report, partner setup, immediate outdial, scheduled outdial.

ORDERNET	CONTROL DATA-REDINET	SEARS Communication Network	TELENET	Telecommunication Interface Corp.	TranSettlement	WESTERN UNION
$.05 per transaction set. $.0075 per segment. Charges are for both send and receive.	Annual subscriptions of $900. Includes up to 420,00 characters per month. Beyond that $.025 per block (blocks = 1000 - 1400 characters). Above monthly level of 15000 block, this rate is reduced to $.15 retroactively.	Basic: $30 per month or $330 per year plus $3.35 per 1000 characters. Send only. Basic Plus: $65 per month or $725 per year includes first 125 kilocharacter per month 126-1000 $.25 per kilocharacter, 1001-5000 $.20 per kilocharacter. Above 5000 discount available.	$.005 per ANSI 12 segment. $100 monthly minimum.	$.31 transaction set. $133 monthly minimum.	$.24 per 100 characters.	Rapid send/receive (delivery within 1 min. standard). $.017 per 100 characters (off peak) all documents sent to one address in one session $.10.
Yes.	Yes.	Yes.	Yes.	Yes.	Yes.	No. EDI to free-form text message conversion available 2nd quarter, 1989.
ANSI X12 and all subsets, all TDCC transactions, WINS, EDIFACT, ORDERNET, COMNET and EAGLE.	Any standard or private format including ANSI X12, WINS, TDCC, AIAG, VICS, EDIFACT, etc., as long as data is wrapped in valid header and trailer.	ANSI X12, VICS, TDCC, UCS, AIAG software available to support all standards.	ANSI X12, UCS, Eagle, COMNET ORDERNET.	ANSI X12, UCS VICS.	ANSI X12, TDCC, UCS, WINS, and EDIFACT. X12 drafts as requested.	All ANSI X12, TDCC, WINS, UCS formats.
For translation between standard to fixed format—$.015 per standard segment. Translation between standards—fixed $25 per month.	Network translation costs $.30 per 1000 characters.	Pricing based on resources required.	$.003 per X12 segment.	Included in BMC.	$.20 per 1000.	NA
Yes, MNP protocol. Connect charge is $.45 per connect minute.	Yes. All costs are built into the character clock rate (CBR)	No. Available first quarter 1990.	Yes. $.45 per minute up to 4.8 Kbps.	Yes, same as BMC.	Yes, $.24 per 1000 characters.	Yes, no additional charge.
Yes, connect charge is $.45 per connect minute.	Yes, through WATS dial-up and dedicated facilities. Built into CBR.	Yes, provide 2780/3780 bisynch messages.	Yes, $.55 per minute up to 9.6 Kbps.	Yes, same as BMC.	Yes, same as above.	Yes, no additional charge.
Yes, dial-up SNA now available, connect charge is $.45 per connect. Will support dedicated line soon.	Yes, through WATS dial-up and dedicated facilities. All costs built into CBR except dedicated lines and hardware.	Yes, 3770 SNA and also SNI gateway connections.	Yes.	Yes.	Yes, same as above.	Yes, no additional charge.
Most companies are up within 30 days. There is a $300 utilization fee.	Less than a week. In an emergency less than a day. No startup costs other than annual subscription charge.	1-2 weeks includes testing. One time installation charge of $150.	$250 initiation fee and 1-2 weeks for full integration.	No starting fees, 24-48 hrs.	Startup in one day or less. No startup fee.	48 hour turnaround. $50 installation and setup. $25 per additional site billed to master account.
Yes, ORDERNET services provide international access to 70 countries through the Telenet network.	Yes, access available from 80 countries.	No.	Under development.	Yes.	Yes.	Yes, internationally deployed packet network. Connectivity to 100 countries.
ORDERNET charges its customers a flat $25 per month fee for each interconnect modem telephone no matter how much traffic flows over the line.	No extra charges, a user's bill for an interconnected transmission will look identical to that of a transmission between REDINET customers.	Will connect with any and all networks. $15 per month to connect with as many networks and $.10 per kilocharacter after over 100 kilocharacters per month.	Support interconnections, no charge for receive side. $.01 per segment to send.	Yes, will interconnect with any VAN.	No interconnect charges.	Open interconnection, no setup cost. $.01 per 100 countries.
Can handle both encrypted and authenticated data. We are not privy to the keys and do no validation of the data.	Encryption and extensive password mechinisms.	Authorized user ID required to logon system.	Security available.	Yes, password.	Security codes, passwords, unique account IDs.	Logon, password, username ID algorithm.
Vendor Info Program—structured program to facilitate mass implementation. EDI Fax—generation of print format document from EDI transaction set, EDI laser mail, EDI linked database services consulting, EDI software for micro/mini/mainframe platforms.	Dial-out, consulting, custom & packaged software, education, complete and extensive trading partner installation, coordination, management, feedback support.	Automatic delivery of data—$20 per month plus: scheduled $.01 per kilocharacter received, data ready $.02 per kilocharacter received. Archive retrieval. Dedicated line option.	Hub & Spoke training day, executive training dedicated access facility, dial services, PC/mini/mainframe translation support capabilities.	Comprehensive business systems for small vendors. Provide translation services into proprietary systems. Full software services. Complete EDI turnkey package. Mapping support.	Customer support hotline, initialization and startup, EDI education, on line document archiving.	Access to BCD databases & other info services. Broadcast and polling capabilities. Trading partner survey service seminars. EDI educations. Flexible billing options.

III

IMPLEMENTATION OF EDI

7

EDI IMPLEMENTATION STEPS

INTRODUCTION

Implementing EDI is not an easy task. One leading expert in the EDI field has described the EDI process as "not something where you turn on the switch. It's a long hard slog."[1] An early user and strong supporter of EDI has described the implementation process as difficult, time-consuming, and frustrating.[2]

Implementing EDI requires a two-prong approach: one for the technical issues and one for the organizational and cultural issues. Although understanding the details of exactly how EDI operates may take some time, technologically EDI is not complex. Further, the EDI structure of standards, software, and networks is in place and is working. The technological implementation issues need to be understood and addressed by firms using EDI; however, these issues do not usually present significant difficulties to most firms.

On the other hand, the organizational and cultural issues involved in EDI implementation are significantly more difficult for most firms to deal with. EDI does change the way in which a business operates and relates to other organizations. According to Dennis McGinnis, it is the "depth of the changes [that] efficient use of the technology demands" that makes EDI implementation so difficult.[3] Because EDI changes relationships and interactions both within and outside of the organization, managing the change process is very difficult. By its very nature, the complete integration of EDI within a company requires the coordination of purchasing, accounting, transportation, systems, legal, and auditing personnel. Further, because EDI is intercorporate, the departmental coordination needs to be mirrored in the trading partner's organization. All of this makes the EDI change process one that requires careful planning and close management.

125

IMPLEMENTATION GUIDE

The purpose of this chapter is to present a guideline for EDI implementation. The guideline offers a pattern to follow in deciding to use EDI, in determining the type of EDI, and in establishing the EDI program. Figure 7-1 shows the basic steps that must be completed in order to successfully implement an EDI program. While the steps are shown and are discussed in sequential order, often multiple activities are performed concurrently.

DECIDE EDI STRATEGY

The first decision that must be made in implementing EDI is to determine the overall approach or strategy for EDI. This involves two components:

1.   How comprehensive the EDI effort will be
2.   How integrated EDI will be with internal applications

The level of comprehensiveness deals with how widely used EDI is to be within a corporation. At one extreme EDI can be implemented for just one transaction, within one department, to be used with just one trading partner. At the other extreme EDI could be implemented to include multiple transactions, at all divisions, with all trading partners.

The level of integration deals with how EDI is linked with internal application programs. At one extreme a door-to-door approach can be taken where data transfer between partners is electronic but the link to application programs is manual. At the other extreme is complete integration where all data transfer between partners is application-to-application and where all application programs are bridged.

EDI implementation in most organizations is an evolutionary process progressing through a number of different levels of comprehensiveness and integration. As introduced in Chapter 1, Dave Hough, Manager of Implementation Programs at McDonnell Douglas, has identified three levels of implementation.

In a level 1 implementation EDI is done by a single department for a single transaction set. Only a few trading partners use EDI and its use is optional on the part of the trading partners. In many cases a PC door-to-door approach is used.

In a level 2 implementation EDI is used by multiple departments in the organization. Multiple transaction sets are exchanged with a large number of trading partners. The use of EDI is highly encouraged and may be "required" of trading partners. EDI is linked to internal application programs.

In a level 3 implementation EDI is integrated completely within the organization. All EDI is linked to internal applications that have been restructured and bridged. EDI is considered by the company to be a "way of life" and is expected of all trading partners.

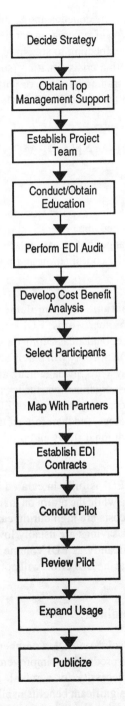

Figure 7-1   EDI implementation steps.

The selection of an EDI strategy depends upon a number of factors. If faced with limited resources, lack of interest from trading partners, or indifferent top management, starting at level 1 (and expecting to stay in level 1) is the most appropriate choice. However, if faced with a crisis situation (such as the auto manufacturers have been), with demanding trading partners, or with "excited" top management, it is more appropriate to plan for a level 2 or 3 implementation from the start.

OBTAIN TOP MANAGEMENT SUPPORT

Why Is Support Needed?

Regardless of the strategy selected, support from top management is needed. And the sooner the support is obtained, the better. Support from the top is important for any major organizational change, but is particularly so for EDI. This is because EDI requires interdepartmental coordination and also may have a long payback period.

Interdepartmental Coordination   The implementation of EDI requires a boundary spanning effort. In other words, EDI implementation usually significantly affects a number of functional areas within the organization. In fully bridged application-to-application EDI, not only will purchasing, accounting, and transportation be affected, so will systems management and, in many cases, sales or marketing. In addition, in most organizations the legal and audit staff are also very much interested in changes occurring as a result of EDI. Further, not only can EDI impact all of these functional areas, and therefore require the support of these areas, EDI also tends to change traditional flows and processes. These changes require strong support from the top.

Long Pay-back Period   If EDI is fully integrated into the organization, initial investment is likely to be high, while the return on that investment, at least initially, may be low. In general EDI costs are high during early implementation and then decrease significantly. Dollar savings are usually low during initial implementation, and then increase significantly as EDI volume increases. Top management support is needed to ensure that the EDI effort will not be canceled because of early "losses."

How Can Support Be Obtained?

If top management must be "sold" on EDI, a number of approaches can be used. EDI can be presented as (1) a productivity improvement program, (2) a strategic competitive move, or (3) a necessity for survival. As discussed in Chapter 2, companies have experienced significant benefits in all of these areas through EDI.

ESTABLISH EDI PROJECT TEAM

While top management support is critical for the success of EDI, so is a wide base of support within the organization. Because the implementation of EDI affects so many functional and staff organizations within the firm, an EDI team with members from across the organization is necessary for successful EDI. The EDI team, which must have total responsibility for the EDI implementation plan, should include representatives from four major areas:

1. Functional areas such as purchasing, accounting, transportation
2. Staff areas such as legal and auditing
3. Technical areas such as information systems and data processing
4. Liaison areas such as sales, customer service, or marketing

It is important that the team includes representatives from all departments that will use, or will be affected by, EDI. Their participation on the team is likely to result in a feeling of "ownership" of the EDI idea. In other words, the users will feel that they were a part of making EDI happen and are more likely to work to see that its use succeeds.

Team Leader

A competent and enthusiastic EDI team leader is essential to a successful implementation effort. A study of early EDI users indicated that the one most significant factor leading to successful implementation was a vocal and talented EDI advocate within the organization.[5]

While EDI is often seen as the application of a new computer technology, most EDI users have found that the team leader should not come from the systems area. Because EDI is such a boundary-spanning activity, the team leader needs to have a broad business perspective. According to McGinnis, "You need someone with a business orientation who understands the needs of the company." The team leader must "understand the disciplines of marketing. The person really should be in a customer-related or a distribution-related function."[6] Further, because EDI requires a selling job, both internally to the functional areas and top management and externally to trading partners, it is important that the team lead be a persuasive advocate of the EDI effort.

CONDUCT/OBTAIN EDUCATION PROGRAMS

Education of potential users and vendors of the EDI system is absolutely essential to the success of an EDI implementation effort. The organization needs a thorough understanding of what EDI is and how it works. EDI information and training is readily available through industry action groups, standards committees, and EDI vendors. All of these sources should be used to educate members of your organization as well as trading partners about EDI. Chapter 8 provides additional detail on the training required for various EDI team members.

PERFORM AN EDI AUDIT

For EDI to be successful, the operation of the system EDI is to replace must be fully understood. Both the flow of information (in paper, verbal, or electronic form) and the data structure of application programs must be known. The following items should be reviewed prior to implementing EDI:

- What information is traded with business partners? Should include formal documents such as purchase orders, invoices, etc., as well as informal documents such as messages, memos, phone calls to check status.
- How and where is the information initiated? Manual input, screen entry, computer generated?
- What is the internal flow of information? How many copies are produced, and in what form? Who receives copies? For what purposes? For how long are copies stored and in what form?
- What control and reporting measures are used? Status reporting? Audit trails?
- What specific information is needed for current application programs? Form of data? Flow between applications? Entry of data?
- What information is available from application programs? What results are produced? What is the form of the output?

Once the current flow of information is outlined and understood, the changes necessary for EDI should be identified. These may include:

- The use of electronic data entry rather than manual
- The development of a data link between the application program and the translation package
- The need to bridge between applications if multiple departments use the same information

Once the current "paper" flows as well as the EDI flows are outlined, then software development should be started. To use an EDI translation package, data must first be abstracted from application programs and placed in a fixed-field flat file. Understanding in advance what data is needed for EDI, and determining where the data resides and in what format, is essential for this programming effort to take place.

DEVELOP PRELIMINARY COST/BENEFIT ANALYSIS

Although many companies are now implementing EDI systems for strategic rather than cost reduction reasons, a cost/benefit analysis is still useful and often necessary to obtain corporate support for the EDI program. Items addressed in a cost/benefit analysis should include the following:

Costs:
        Start-up costs
            Hardware
            Translation software
            Training
        Ongoing Costs
            Transmission costs
            Software maintenance costs
            Training

Benefits:
        Direct
            Reduction in keying
            Personnel savings
            Reduced inventory due to faster information
        Indirect
            Improved use of personnel
            Improved access and use of information
            Strategic advantage gained through the use of EDI

Chapter 10 provides a more detailed discussion of quantifying EDI costs and benefits and includes a cost justification worksheet.

SELECT EDI PARTICIPANTS

Once support for the EDI concept has been developed and an EDI team has been formed, operational decisions concerning the implementation must be made. These include:

- Will a third party network be used? If so, which one(s)?
- Will software be developed or purchased? If purchased, which vendor?
- Which transaction sets will be implemented?
- Which corporate divisions will be involved?
- Which trading partners will be involved?

Transaction Sets

Although many organizations plan on using EDI for all appropriate transaction sets, usually just one or two documents are selected for the initial testing and operation of EDI. Selection of the specific transaction sets to be implemented should include consideration of the following factors:

- Request from major trading partner
- Expected payoff in terms of paperwork reduction
- Standards availability
- Use by others in the industry

Corporate Divisions or Departments

In selecting the initial divisions or departments to use EDI a number of factors should be examined. First, the division should have personnel who are interested in EDI. Second, the division should have a high volume of the type of transactions being considered for the EDI effort. Third, the division should have the resources and capability necessary to implement the EDI effort. And finally, if a number of geographically dispersed divisions are being considered for EDI, selecting the division closest to corporate headquarters tends to encourage closer coordination and a higher level of support.

Trading Partners

In selecting trading partners to begin an EDI system with, it is usual to look for trading partners who:

- Represent high transaction volume, low dollar value per transaction
- Are currently "doing" EDI
- With whom you have a good relationship

In identifying potential EDI trading partners, your organization should first identify its key trading partners in terms of volume and importance. A careful analysis of trading partners should identify those 20 percent of your partners who account for 80 percent of your transactions. These are the trading partners who are likely to provide the biggest payoff in terms of reduced paperwork and increased accuracy.

It is also helpful to find a trading partner who is already doing EDI with someone else. Implementation of EDI becomes significantly easier each time a new trading partner is added to the system. Therefore, if you can identify a key trading partner who is already communicating electronically with someone else, your organization's implementation will be much smoother. In this way you can take advantage of your trading partner's knowledge and prior learning about EDI. If none of your trading partners are currently "doing" EDI, it is important to identify a trading partner who has a strong interest in EDI. Although EDI can be forced on trading partners by major customers or suppliers, the implementation is much easier when both parties are truly enthusiastic about the effort.

EDI requires cooperation and coordination between trading partners. The effort requires sharing of information, agreeing on a large number of very small details, and working closely together. The chance of succeeding in EDI is enhanced when there is a high level of trust in the trading-partner relationship prior to EDI implementation.

One final note on the selection of trading partners should be added. Although it is completely logical to do EDI with your largest-volume, most-trusted trading partner, you may want to consider starting EDI with someone other than your "best" customer. The first time through with EDI, as with any new system, there will be a number of "bugs" that will have to be worked out. According to Dave Hough, if possible it is better to start EDI with a good trading partner who already has done EDI with someone else, rather than with your very best customer. In this way you are not risking alienating your best customer while you learn EDI.

MAPPING WITH TRADING PARTNERS

While EDI standards establish the basic structure of EDI messages, the standards alone are not sufficient to establish exactly what is to be communicated between trading partners. For instance, the standards allow for a product to be identified through the use of a product identification code. However, the standards do not specify which code (seller's catalog number, buyer's part number, etc.) should be used. These decisions are left to the trading partners to decide.

Once an electronic trading partner relationship is established, the trading partners must determine such things as:

- Which transaction sets are to be sent?
- What optional data segments and elements are to be used?
- What types of identification will be used for
  - products
  - companies
  - shipping points
- What communications protocols will be used (if direct)?

This is a time-consuming but essential part of doing EDI. The mapping establishes the ground rules for your EDI effort with each trading partner.

ESTABLISH EDI CONTRACTS

In some cases, the issues raised above are addressed in EDI contracts. Because the use of EDI changes both the format of information and the flow of that information, many companies prepare EDI contracts to be used with trading partners:

- Transactions to be sent electronically
- Use of a third party network
- Allocation of transmission costs between the trading partners
- Terms and conditions that apply to electronic transmissions
- Identification of a project manager or contact point at each location

While not all EDI users establish trading partner contracts, use of contracts appears to be growing. Trading partner contracts are particularly useful when purchase orders and invoices are transmitted electronically. A traditional paper purchase order contains written terms and conditions on the back of the purchase order form. This is obviously not the case with an electronic purchase order. Therefore, the terms and conditions that apply to electronic purchase orders are often stated and agreed to in a trading partner contract. In fact, some of the terms may be different for electronic purchase orders than for paper purchase orders. This is particularly true in the area of payment terms. The use of EDI, particularly when coupled with electronic payment, often changes the timing of payments. If the timing of payments is changed, the cash discount terms (for instance, 2/10, net 30) may also need to be renegotiated.

Other Contracts

Some EDI users also have contracts with third party networks and software vendors. The third party contract usually spells out the responsibilities and the liabilities of the third party, as well as specifying pricing methods. Software contracts spell out responsibilities, liabilities, and costs and include any restrictions on the software use (such as restrictions on the number of sites at which the software can be used). In general, contracts with third party networks and software vendors tend to be standard contracts provided by the vendors. However, trading partner contracts are unique to each situation and are negotiated between the trading partners.

CONDUCT PILOT TEST

Once the EDI system has been designed, vendors selected, trading partners and transactions established, a pilot test of the system should be conducted. Normally the pilot test is conducted in three stages: transmission of dummy data, parallel test of electronic and paper transmission, and electronic transmission with no paper backup. If possible, an organization should run its pilot test with a limited number of trading numbers who have EDI experience with other trading partners.

Dummy Transactions

The first stage of the pilot test should be the transmission of "dummy" data. The purpose of this stage is to make sure that all of the linkages have been made correctly, that software is working, and that messages can be sent and received.

Parallel Test

The next stage of the pilot is a test of the transmission of actual purchasing documents. However, this portion of the test should be run in parallel with the transmission of paper documentation. In other words, the same action (purchase order, for instance) is sent both electronically through the EDI system and manually. This parallel test allows for a comparison of the EDI and manual system and also allows users to become used to the system prior to "giving up" the paper system. It is also a useful way to identify any of the paper flows which were overlooked during EDI audit.

Electronic Test

The next stage of the pilot test is to use the EDI system for a limited number of transactions, without the parallel paper system. This is the final step in testing of the EDI system prior to more widespread implementation.

REVIEW PILOT TEST RESULTS AND MODIFY

The pilot test is usually run until all of the trading partners involved feel "comfortable" with the EDI system. This time will vary from organization to organization. Further, in many instances some pilot partners may be ready to move to the implementation stage before others. In general, the pilot stage may last anywhere from a few weeks to several months. After the pilot test is completed, a review of the entire EDI effort should be made to determine if any changes need to be made prior to expanding the system.

EXPAND USAGE

When the company is ready to expand the EDI system beyond the pilot stage, an implementation schedule should be established. Most companies have found that an incremental expansion schedule works best. Under the incremental approach either new trading partners are added to the system or new transactions are added, but both are not added at the same time. In other words, the expansion is done in one of the two following ways:

- Exchange of the pilot transactions with additional trading partners, or
- Exchange of new transactions with the trading partners used in the pilot

PUBLICIZE EFFORTS

A final step that is very important to a successful EDI effort is to publicize your activities. As mentioned before, it takes two to do EDI. Additionally, the greater the number of EDI partners, the greater the benefits. Therefore, once your EDI effort is operational, announce it to the world.

Publicity should start in-house. Establishing an EDI newsletter sent to functional managers and systems staff at all locations will encourage the use of EDI throughout the company. Emphasizing the benefits achieved through the use of EDI will also encourage its growth within the company.

Publicity to external parties is also important. Attendance at EDI conferences and trade shows provides a chance to exchange ideas and problems with other EDI users. Participation at these EDI meetings can also be used as a way to find new trading partners who are interested in exchanging documents with you. Participation in software or third party network users' groups is also useful. In these meetings you have a chance to discuss EDI with companies that are likely to be using similar applications and methods. These forums provide an excellent opportunity to find out how others may have solved problems similar to ones you may be experiencing.

Activity in standards committees and industry EDI action groups is also important. Participation in these activities provides you with a way to keep current on changes in the EDI environment. And, perhaps even more important, participation in such groups allows you to let your concerns be known and provides a way for you to influence the future direction of EDI.

EDI cannot be accomplished without intercompany cooperation. Most EDI users realize that an entire industry benefits when industry members cooperate and participate together in developing EDI standards, holding EDI conferences, and sharing EDI experiences. Your participation in such activities should increase EDI benefits for you as well as for your entire industry.

SUMMARY

This chapter provided a guideline for EDI implementation. Obviously, no list of steps can fit every situation; however, the steps outlined here should provide a good foundation for your EDI implementation planning and execution. The next chapter discusses the specific staffing and training requirements necessary for successful EDI implementation.

8

EDI STAFFING AND
TRAINING
REQUIREMENTS

STAFFING REQUIREMENTS

Introduction

Implementing Electronic Data Interchange (EDI) requires the coordination and cooperation of personnel from numerous areas both within and outside of your organization. Therefore, the staffing for the implementation effort requires expertise from a number of different areas. This chapter discusses the tasks that must be performed for EDI to be implemented. For the purposes of this chapter, it is assumed that EDI is to be integrated across functional lines, into current operations. However, even in an EDI stand-alone environment, most of the tasks discussed below still must be performed.

This chapter presents the staffing requirements as roles or functions that must be accomplished. While all of the functions discussed below must be done in order to have a successful EDI implementation, each of the roles or functions does not have to be performed by a separate person. A number of current EDI users have only one or two people responsible for the entire EDI effort, while in other organizations, there are as many as 20 people directly involved in the EDI effort. The number of people involved in EDI will depend upon the size of the company, the type of EDI system being used, the volume of transactions being transmitted, and the organizational priority placed on EDI.

Regardless of the size and make-up of the EDI team, the team must have distinct organizational visibility. In other words, the EDI team should have designated members, a designated team or group leader, and should report to upper management. Shown in Figure 8-1 are roles, classified into staff groups, which must be

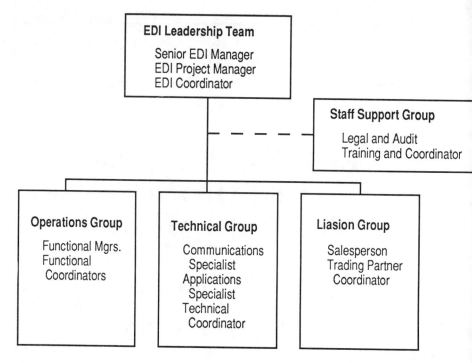

Figure 8-1   EDI staffing requirements.

enacted for a successful implementation of EDI. Those roles are based upon the
tasks described in McDonnell Douglas's EDI∗Net Implementation Guide.[1]

EDI LEADERSHIP GROUP

The EDI leadership group is responsible for overall EDI planning and project
management. The leadership activities consist of three duties: Senior EDI Manager,
EDI Project Manager, and EDI Coordinator. Specific tasks performed by the
leadership group are shown in Figure 8-2.

ACTIVITIES OF THE LEADERSHIP GROUP

— Provide overall direction and supervision
— Determine scope and design
— Communicate with top management
— Obtain resources

Figure 8-2   Activities of the leadership group.

Senior Manager

The senior manager for EDI implementation and operation has overall management responsibility for the EDI project. This function is responsible for:

- Obtaining funding required
- Coordinating needed organizational resources
- Serving as liaison to top management
- Acting as EDI advocate

Perhaps the most important function of the Senior EDI team is the role of EDI advocate. EDI requires marketing, both internally and externally. The Senior EDI manager has to be excited about EDI and has to be able to pass that excitement on to others.

EDI Project Manager

The senior EDI manager is supported and assisted by the EDI project manager. The EDI project manager is responsible for the day-to-day operation of the EDI implementation effort. Duties include:

- Developing implementation schedules
- Approving selection of EDI vendors
- Supervising team members

EDI Coordinator

The EDI senior manager and project manager both perform primarily management activities. In support of these management activities, the EDI leadership group needs to have an in-house EDI "expert." This role of EDI in-house expert is performed by the EDI coordinator. As the resident expert, the EDI coordinator needs to be familiar with all aspects of EDI implementation. Specific issues the EDI coordinator should understand include:

- Technical issues such as standards, hardware and software configurations, and third party network options
- Managerial issues such as legal and audit concerns and organizational impact
- Industry issues such as trade group activity and industry guidelines on standards

The EDI coordinator should be actively involved in all EDI decisions. The coordinator should serve in an advisory role in determining the scope and purpose of the EDI implementation project. The coordinator should also have significant input into the EDI implementation plan and schedule, including the priority of transactions and trading partners to be added to the EDI effort.

In many organizations, the EDI coordinator also serves as the standards coordinator. As such, the coordinator attends standards meetings and serves as the organization's spokesperson in the standards development process. The EDI coordinator is also involved, on a day-to-day basis, with the actual implementation of EDI. The coordinator should be involved in the pilot testing of the EDI effort and in making any necessary changes prior to full implementation.

Summary of EDI Leadership Group

As discussed earlier, EDI leadership should come from a business background, rather than an in-depth technical background. Because of the need to coordinate many different functional areas and to sell EDI both internally and externally, most organizations have found that the best EDI managers come from the functional areas rather than the computer or systems areas.

Further EDI leadership must have support of top management. Carol Kromer of *Transport Topics* reports of one EDI attempt that failed because of weak leadership. She reports that:

> "A carrier implemented EDI from the MIS department outward because there was no upper management support. Without that support, there was none from any of the other affected departments. This carrier's program did not go very far and very few customers were added to the system, making it very expensive to develop and maintain. Sales did not know what the EDI capabilities were and did not sell them. Marketing could not answer customers' questions. Accounting did not want to get involved because they did not understand EDI and believed it would only mean more work on their part. This carrier is now a follower instead of a leader when it comes to EDI."[2]

This example demonstrates the importance of having a leadership group with both an understanding of business and strong support from corporate management. Figure 8-2 summarizes the major activities of the EDI leadership group.

OPERATIONS GROUP

In addition to the EDI leadership group, the EDI team must also include a group made up of functional business managers, such as purchasing, accounting, or transportation. These are the users of EDI. Their involvement in the EDI planning process will increase their feeling of "ownership" toward the EDI effort and is likely to decrease resistance to its use. The operations groups comprise functional area managers and functional area coordinators and perform the duties shown in Figure 8-3.

ACTIVITIES OF THE OPERATIONS GROUP

— Identify the EDI applications to functional areas
— Prioritize EDI applications
— Design new functional flows and processes

Figure 8-3   Activities of the operations group.

Functional Area Managers

The role of the functional managers is to identify how EDI can be used within each specific functional area and to act as an advocate of EDI to all others in the functional area. In addition, the functional manager is also responsible for prioritizing alternative EDI options within the specified functional area. The functional area manager is supported by a functional area coordinator.

Functional Area Coordinator

The role of the functional area coordinator is to serve as the functional area expert on the EDI team. Duties include:

• Identifying potential transactions and trading partners
• Determining current information flows with the functional area
• Identifying changes needed to the functional area due to EDI
• Assisting in performing cost/benefits analysis

The EDI operations group represents those people who will actually be using the EDI system. It is in these areas that EDI is going to have the most noticeable, direct, and substantial impact on day-to-day operations, as well as on long-term strategy. For these reasons, it is very critical that the functional representatives play a major role in planning and implementation.

TECHNICAL GROUP

Because the implementation of EDI involves the introduction of new computer technology to an organization, the EDI implementation team should include representatives from the computer and systems areas in the organization. As shown in Figure 8-4, the role of the technical group is to provide advice on the organization's current systems and to assist in the integration of the EDI system into the organization's current system. Three functions are performed by the

```
┌─────────────────────────────────────────────────────┐
│                                                       │
│    ACTIVITIES OF THE TECHNICAL GROUP                  │
│                                                       │
│       — Perform systems tasks                         │
│       — Recommend communications and software options │
│       — Develop/ obtain software                      │
│                                                       │
└─────────────────────────────────────────────────────┘
```

Figure 8-4   Activities of the technical group.

technical group: communications specialist, applications specialist, and technical coordinator.

Communications Specialist

The role of the communications specialist is to be familiar with your organization's current capability for interorganizational communication and to establish EDI communications methods. Issues that are the responsibility of the communications specialist include communications protocols and line speed, network time availability, and network volume capacity.

Applications Specialist

The role of the applications specialist is to be familiar with the various databases currently used in the organization's application programs. It is the responsibility of the applications specialist to program any changes needed to the current databases or software, and to develop or acquire any conversion packages that may be necessary to interface the EDI system to the internal applications systems.

Technical Coordinator

The technical coordinator serves the role of the "systems expert" from both the communications and applications side. Based upon input provided by the communications and applications specialists, the technical coordinator is responsible for selecting specific communications and software options, and for installing the system. The technical coordinator may also provide technical advice to trading partners.

Summary of Technical Group

The technical group represents those who are going to actually get EDI "working." Any changes to MIS systems, any new software, any new hardware are all the responsibilities of the technical group.

LIAISON GROUP

The role of the liaison group is to communicate EDI efforts both within your organization and between your organization and your trading partners. In addition, the liaison group also serves as EDI advocates who help to sell the EDI effort both internally and externally. Figure 8-5 shows the primary duties of the liaison group performed by two functions: salesperson and trading partner coordinator.

EDI Salesperson

The primary function of the EDI salesperson is to increase awareness of and participation in EDI both within and outside the organization. The salesperson, with help from the functional group and the trading partner coordinator, should encourage trading partners to join the EDI effort. This can be done through training seminars, personal visits, or films. For instance, the Aircraft Group of General Electric has prepared a film highlighting the benefits of EDI, which is shown to suppliers to encourage their participation. The film explains how a trading partner can get started in EDI and provides examples of successful use of EDI by GE suppliers. Other EDI users offer similar types of training. In addition to working directly with trading partners, the EDI salesperson should also be involved in EDI trade shows, standards meetings, and conferences. Attendance and participation at such functions is a way in which the EDI salesperson can "announce to the world" that the organization is using EDI and is actively seeking trading partners. Once a trading partner begins to express an interest in doing EDI, then the trading partner becomes the responsibility of the trading partner coordinator.

Trading Partner Coordinator

The trading partner coordinator is responsible for identifying and maintaining EDI trading partners. From information provided by the functional group as well as the EDI salesperson, the trading partner coordinator is responsible for prioritizing potential trading partners and selecting trading partners for the pilot implementation. Normally, the trading partner will then coordinate a trading partner meeting

---

ACTIVITIES OF THE LIAISON GROUP

— Sell EDI internally and externally
— Select trading partners for pilot test
— Maintain trading partner status

Figure 8-5   Activities of the liaison group.

where partner readiness and willingness to participate can be determined. In addition, the trading partner also can, at this point, discuss mutual concerns such as standards to be used, special identification codes that are necessary, communication protocols, and transmission schedules.

The trading partner coordinator is also responsible for identifying any training of trading partners that may be needed and for arranging with the training coordinator to provide such training. The coordinator works closely with a counterpart in the trading partner's organization to schedule transmission testing, to track progress, and to discuss any changes required.

The trading partner coordinator is also responsible for maintaining status information on trading partners. For instance, information on whether a trading partner has been approved, has purchased equipment, has software installed, is in pilot, or has completed the pilot test should be maintained. In addition, the coordinator should also normally track whether the trading partner is using a third party network (and if so, which network), and should also track the standards, including version number, that the trading partner is using. The status of the trading partners should be provided to the functional and leadership groups as well as to the organization's third party network.

Summary of Liaison Group

EDI requires a strong selling effort, both internally and externally. The primary responsibility for this sales job falls to the liaison group.

STAFF SUPPORT GROUP

In addition to the technical and functional groups necessary for a successful implementation of EDI, representatives from staff functions within the organization should also be involved in EDI implementation. Representatives from the auditing and legal staff should be included in the EDI planning process. A contract administrator and a training coordinator should also be included as a part of the EDI team. Their duties are shown in Figure 8-6.

Audit and Legal Reviewers

Because EDI changes paper and data flows, the representatives of the auditing and legal functions of the organization should be included as a part of the EDI team. Although the use of EDI does not decrease an organization's ability to perform an audit on transactions, it does change the method in which the audit is likely to be conducted. The role of the auditing representative is to bring audit concerns to the attention of the EDI team, so that these concerns can be addressed during system design. The same holds true on the legal side.

ACTIVITIES OF THE STAFF SUPPORT GROUP

— Review EDI process for legal and audit sufficiency
— Develop/ obtain training

Figure 8-6   Activities of the staff support group.

The role of the the legal representative on the EDI team is to raise any concerns the legal function may have with the use of electronic documents in lieu of paper documents. Concerns over electronic signatures, data security, and functional control can all be addressed by EDI system design. Having these issues raised during the planning and implementation stages of EDI assures that the new paper and data flows produced by the EDI system are acceptable to the auditing and legal functions.

EDI Contracts Administrator

To assure that all parties understand and agree to their individual responsibilities in an EDI effort, many organizations use EDI contracts. The role of the contracts administrator is to prepare and/or to monitor the various EDI contracts.

EDI contracts can be written between your organization and your trading partners, your third party network, and your software vendor. Although not all companies involved in EDI use contracts with all of the organizations mentioned, a number of organizations strongly support the use of EDI contracts, believing that trading partner contracts provide for a closer and better business relationship. On the other hand, some organizations do not feel that the contracts are necessary, particularly with trading partners with whom they have had a long and cooperative business relationship.

Training Coordinator

One final function that must be performed for your organization to have a success-ful EDI implementation is that of training coordinator. The training coordinator is responsible for determining training needs and arranging for training. Training needs within your organization are likely to range from very detailed technical training on standards to very general overview training on EDI. In addition, the training coordinator may find that a trading partner may need training prior to being brought on-line within your organization. It is the role of the training coordinator to either develop or acquire the necessary training and to schedule the training consistent with the EDI implementation schedule.

Summary of the Staff Support Group

The staff support group is often overlooked in EDI implementation. In fact, in some organizations, attempts are made to deliberately exclude legal and auditing staff in EDI planning. As reported by Tony Seideman of the *Journal of Commerce*, at an "EDI Summit Conference" many speakers emphasized the need to "keep lawyers away from the EDI process." According to those at the conference, agreement can usually be quickly reached between trading partners on new terms and conditions for EDI transactions, as long as lawyers are not involved. One EDI project manager was reported to say, "Our worst troubles have been with our legal organizations or our trading partners' legal organizations getting involved."[3] In many cases it may not be easy to get the legal (or the auditing) staff to understand and to agree to the changes made by EDI, but having their support is important. Involving them in the planning process may initially slow down implementation; however, it should prevent major problems from developing later.

SUMMARY OF STAFFING REQUIREMENTS

The staffing requirements discussed above have been presented as a guide to the type of effort and tasks needed to implement EDI. As noted earlier, multiple roles can be performed by one person. However, it is important that someone is responsible for each of the tasks discussed above, to ensure a successful EDI implementation.

EDI TRAINING

Introduction

As pointed out earlier, the implementation of EDI requires cooperation and work from personnel in a number of functional, staff, and technical areas. It also requires the support of top management. This effort cannot be obtained unless personnel are knowledgeable about EDI.

Yet, numerous studies have shown that although EDI has now become a corporate "buzz word," there is still a significant lack of understanding about what EDI is and how EDI operates. In a study conducted by the Financial Executives Research Foundation of users of either EDI or EFT, the lack of knowledge of EDI was often cited as a reason for delaying implementation.[4] In answer to the question—"Has your company postponed implementation of any functional component of EDI for any of the following reasons?"—training-related factors were identified as "important" by 41 percent of the respondents and as "very important" by 42 percent of the respondents. Training-related factors included lack of knowledge, lack of senior management awareness, and difficulty of educating customers or vendors.

Training and education, therefore, is very important both for gaining acceptance for EDI and for understanding and successfully implementing EDI. This section of the chapter discusses training requirements for different parts of the organization as well as the different groups that make up the EDI team. In addition, sources of EDI training are discussed.

TRAINING REQUIREMENTS

Because EDI affects so many diverse functions within an organization, and because the impact is felt at all managerial levels within the organization, training requirements for EDI are numerous and diverse. The training required by the top management is obviously going to be different from the training required by a functional user of the system. Additionally, even within the EDI implementation team, training requirements will differ. As an example, the training required for the EDI coordinator is going to be much more intensive and detailed than that required by the EDI salesperson.

TRAINING MATRIX

Figure 8-7 shows a training matrix composed of two components: EDI Knowledge Requirements and Organizational Functions.[5] The knowledge requirements identify basic EDI knowledge and skills, and the organizational functions identify the various groups within the organization that require some form of EDI training. Included in the organizational functions are the EDI team groups, along with top management and users. The intent of the matrix is to provide a guideline for EDI training by identifying what knowledge and skills are necessary and which are desired for the various groups involved in an EDI implementation effort. Following is a summary of the information that comprises each of the EDI knowledge requirements.

EDI KNOWLEDGE AND SKILLS

The EDI knowledge and skills concepts are classified into three general categories: EDI Overview, EDI Components, and EDI Implementation Issues. Each category is subdivided into more detailed knowledge areas. Presented below is a discussion of the types of concepts and ideas that should be included in the training for each of the knowledge and skill requirements.

Knowledge and Skills	Organizational Groups						
			EDI Team				
	Top Mgt.	Users	Leadership	Operations	Technical	Liason	Staff
OVERVIEW							
Basic Concepts	R	R	R	R	R	R	R
Strategic Use	R	D	R	D	D	D	D
Examples	R	D	R	R	D	R	D
Costs/Benefits	R	D	R	R	D	R	
STANDARDS							
Role/Function	D	D	R	D	R	D	
Mapping			R	D	R		
Documents	D	R	R	R	R	R	R
SOFTWARE							
Role/Function	D	D	R	D	R		
Options			R		R		
Operations		R	R	R	R	R	
SYSTEM CONFIGURATION							
Options	D		R		R		
Operations		R	R	R	R	R	
Interfacing			R		R		
IMPLEMENTATION ISSUES							
Tasks	R	D	R	R	D	R	
Impact on Process	D	R	R	R	R	R	R
Security Issues	D	R	R	R	R	R	R

R = Required
D = Desirable

(Adapted from "Electronic Data Interchange: Managing Implementation
in a Purchasing Environment. Used with permission.)

Figure 8-7   EDI training matrix.

EDI OVERVIEW KNOWLEDGE REQUIREMENTS

Basic Issues

The EDI overview category includes the knowledge requirements of a basic introduction to EDI, strategic use of EDI, examples of EDI usage, and costs and benefits of EDI. Training on the basic issues of EDI should include an explanation of what EDI is and how it works. Also included should be a discussion of how EDI differs from current technology such as E-Mail and facsimile transmission. The basic components of EDI, including standards, software, hardware configurations, and third party networks, should be introduced and explained. In addition, a brief discussion of implementation issues should be included in the general overview.

Strategic Use

The section on strategic use of EDI should address corporate benefits that can be obtained from the use of EDI. This knowledge requirement addresses issues beyond productivity savings and includes an explanation of the use of EDI to gain competitive advantage due to improved customer service, better and faster information, and the integration of EDI into internal systems.

EDI Examples

Examples of EDI usage should also be a part of the overview training for EDI. Examples provided should include a discussion of organizations in your industry that have successfully used EDI. The examples should address how EDI was implemented, who was involved, costs and benefits that resulted, and any "lessons learned" during the implementation process. Examples outside of your industry can be included to show the wide diversity of organizations using EDI.

Costs and Benefits

The final topic that should be included in the EDI overview is a discussion of costs and benefits of an EDI system. This discussion should be kept at a fairly general level, by presenting the various types of costs that will be incurred during EDI implementation and the identification of expected benefits. Reports from industry action groups that have estimated costs and benefits for specific industry applications should be included in this discussion.

EDI COMPONENTS KNOWLEDGE REQUIREMENTS

This section of the training should address the basic elements or components of EDI necessary for EDI to work. Included in this section should be an introduction to EDI standards, EDI software, and EDI system design.

Standards

One of the major components of EDI is standards, yet this appears to be the most misunderstood of all EDI concepts. Perhaps this is because it is often hard for functional managers to envision "a standard document" which would work effectively in all of the very different purchasing or accounting situations dealt with by an organization. Therefore, training in EDI standards is critical to the successful implementation of EDI. The training should address the issues of the role of standards, the documents that the standards support, and how a paper document is "mapped" to an electronic document.

The discussion of the role of standards should include an explanation of what standards are and how they make EDI possible. The discussion should also include a brief history of the development of standards and a discussion of the various standards developing groups and committees. Also included should be a discussion of what the standards cover in terms of formatting and communications requirements. The purpose of this section is to provide the knowledge that a standard provides a way to put unstructured information into a structured format; however, the purpose is not to explain how that is done.

Another topic that should be included in the standards training is a discussion of which documents are supported by the standards. This should include a presentation of those documents that have approved standards and those documents that are currently under review by the standards committee.

A third knowledge requirement necessary for a full understanding of the standards is that of mapping. The purpose of training in mapping is to provide users with detailed knowledge on how a paper document is mapped or translated into an electronic document. This training should include some practice in working through standards documentation and actually writing a document in EDI standard language.

Software

A second major component of EDI that must be covered in EDI training is that of EDI software. The role of EDI software, the operation of the software, and the criteria for deciding whether to buy commercially available software or to develop the software in-house are all topics that should be included in software training.

One part of the software training should include a general overview of EDI software. Here the use of the software and the translation function it performs should be explained. This should be a nontechnical presentation that can be understood by those without a computer or systems background.

In addition to the general overview on the role of software, additional training on the use and operation of the software should be provided. This would include practice on using the software program to format and to communicate electronic transmissions. Again, this training should be at a nontechnical level.

A third software knowledge requirement needed for successful implementation of EDI is information on various software options. This would include a comparison of the numerous commercially available software packages, as well as a comparison of the costs of buying the software versus building the software in-house. Training for this knowledge requirement should be at a fairly technical level, aimed primarily at systems personnel.

System Design

Training on EDI system design is also important. Understanding of the various options for establishing an EDI link with trading partners is required to understand how EDI operates. This training should include a discussion of the advantages and disadvantages of a PC versus a mainframe design, as well as a discussion of door-to-door versus application-to-application EDI. Discussion of third party networks should also be presented. This discussion should cover the role of the third party and the functions a third party can perform. This discussion should be aimed at a primarily nontechnical audience and be designed to present an overview of third party activities.

IMPLEMENTATION ISSUES
KNOWLEDGE REQUIREMENTS

The final category of knowledge that must be addressed in EDI training is that of implementation. Training in how EDI is to be implemented and its impact on the organization is necessary for a smooth implementation process. Specifically, the implementation training should address implementation tasks, procedural or process changes, and security issues.

Implementation Tasks

Implementation training should begin with a basic overview of the tasks required for implementation of EDI. This should include a timeline for completion of the tasks and a discussion of assignment of the tasks among various EDI implementation team members. This training should obviously be aimed at the EDI implementation team, but is also useful to others who will be affected by EDI.

Impact on Procedures

Implementation training should also include a discussion of changes in procedures and processes that will result from EDI. The use of EDI changes both the traditional paper and data flows within an organization. An understanding of how these flows are to be changed and the organizational impact is critical to the acceptance of the EDI system.

System Security

Further, implementation training should also include a discussion of security issues. Normally, the legal and auditing staffs, as well as functional personnel, are very concerned about how EDI affects the organization's ability to control and track documents and transactions. Training in how EDI provides an audit trail, and on various security measures that can be designed into an EDI system, usually decreases resistance to EDI. As a part of the training, a discussion of how other organizations in your industry have addressed this problem should be included.

SUMMARY OF EDI KNOWLEDGE REQUIREMENTS

While all of the topics presented above should be a part of EDI training, not all topics need to be presented to all personnel. The purpose of the training matrix is not only to suggest topics for EDI training but also to suggest which topics should be presented to which groups.

Obtaining EDI Training

EDI training can be obtained in one of two basic ways: It can be developed in-house or it can be purchased from outside sources.

In-House Development

As a part of your EDI implementation effort, your organization can develop its own EDI training. Information available from a number of outside sources, including third party networks, standards committees, trade shows, and published material, can be used to develop in-house EDI training. The main advantage of in-house training is that the training is tailored to your specific needs. The training can be designed to best fit your implementation schedule and to best fit the specific knowledge requirements of your EDI team, as well as top management and EDI users. A major disadvantage of in-house training is that the trainers are not experts in the area. In addition, in-house training capability is often limited so that EDI training may be competing with other training requirements.

External training in EDI is available from a large number of sources including third party networks, EDI consultants, software vendors, and EDI training organizations. The major advantage of external training is that the training is usually presented by experts in the field. A major disadvantage of such training is that it is sometimes generic in nature and may not address specific needs or problems that may be unique to your organization. However, many EDI educational organizations will customize training sessions to meet your particular needs.

The decision on whether to develop EDI training in-house or to contract out for the training should be based upon an assessment of your specific needs including resources available, time schedule for implementation, and current level of EDI knowledge within your organization. A large percentage of EDI users identify training as the area in which they feel the highest need for outside help. EDI Research conducted a study of Fortune 1000 organization. in which 1094 interviews showed that 39.4 percent of companies using, or planning to use, EDI identified training as the area in which outside help was most needed.[6]

Sources of EDI Information and Training

EDI information and training, for either in-house development or external training, is available from a number of sources. The *1989 EDI Yellow Pages* lists 49 consultants, 26 information sources, and 11 training organizations, all of whom provide training. Further, EDI training and assistance can be obtained from industry action groups, standards committees, EDI trade shows, and professional organizations.

SUMMARY OF TRAINING REQUIREMENTS

Lack of knowledge of EDI has been identified as one of the major barriers to EDI implementation. Yet training is readily available from numerous sources. Whatever your particular training requirements are, they can be met through either in-house or outside training organizations.

9

OVERCOMING EDI BARRIERS

INTRODUCTION

The stage is set for EDI growth. EDI provides benefits; major industries are promoting its use; the components of EDI are readily available. So what is the difficulty in implementing EDI? EDI implementation is difficult because EDI is much more than a technical tool—it is a cultural change.

For most of us, paper is a form of business "security blanket." We like paper. We use it and we keep it. Yet EDI threatens to take away that security blanket. Further, EDI threatens to bring other changes, such as new duties and different procedures, to our jobs as well. These changes all impact people.

In other words, the implementation of EDI will not only have a significant impact on technology and on processes, both within and outside the organization, but it will also impact people and management philosophy. Therefore, for EDI to be successful, its implementation must focus on attitudes and behaviors, not just on implementation steps. And focusing on attitudes means that organizational and personal barriers to EDI must be recognized and overcome if the implementation effort is to be successful. This chapter presents a number of common EDI barriers often raised, and offers suggestions for overcoming those barriers. The following comments reflect barriers and concerns that most organizations that have implemented EDI have faced.

- We've never done it that way before. EDI will change what I do.
- EDI will destroy my relationship with my buyer (seller).
- EDI is someone else's problem—it's not my department.
- EDI is too complex to understand.
- Our trading partners will receive all the benefits from EDI.

- EDI costs too much.
- EDI will give others access to our proprietary data.
- EDI creates all sorts of legal problems.
- EDI eliminates the audit trail.
- EDI communications are not secure.
- EDI takes away my float.
- None of our trading partners are doing EDI.
- EDI standards are always changing—we should wait.

BARRIER:
WE'VE NEVER DONE IT THAT WAY BEFORE!

One of the major barriers to EDI implementation is resistance to change, or corporate inertia. Many organizations are very slow to change due in a large part to employee resistance to new technology, processes, or management. Because the specific impact of change cannot always be predicted, the introduction of change within an organization is often met with strong resistance. "It's the fear of the unknown," according to one manager at Bergen Brunswig, which has caused resistance to EDI.[1]

Resistance to change by functional managers, such as purchasing and accounting, was identified as the major barrier in EDI implementation by early EDI users.[2] These organizations cited strong resistance by managers who saw EDI as a threat to their status, their power base, and possibly to their jobs. For instance, one manager reported that EDI was expected to reduce headcount, yet his salary was tied, in part, to headcount. This manager obviously saw EDI as a threat to his position. Natural resistance to change, coupled with fear of exactly what EDI is and what it is to do, creates a formidable obstacle to EDI. How can this obstacle be overcome?

Solution

Three major steps can be taken to minimize organizational resistance to change: strong top management support, early user involvement, and organization-wide training. Any organizational change is much more likely to be accepted if it has strong and vocal support from top management. High-level support immediately elevates the change into an issue of importance to the whole organization, thus helping to reduce resistance.

In addition to having support from top management, the EDI effort should also have as much support as possible from the functional area managers who are to be most affected by the change. In other words, the potential EDI users should be actively involved in the planning for and implementing of the EDI effort. Involving users in the EDI effort, rather than leaving all of the planning and implementation to the MIS department or to outside consultants, will help the functional managers feel that EDI is "their" project. In this way, the managers are less likely to be against the project and are more likely to become vocal supporters of EDI.

Finally, a strong and early educational program stressing the benefits of EDI and explaining how EDI will be integrated with existing systems will help to reduce the fear of the unknown. By clearly stating the objectives of the EDI program, organizations can minimize the misinformation usually present with any organizational change. This will help to prevent such comments as "EDI is going to put us all out of a job" or "EDI will turn us all into techies."

Resistance to change is present in nearly every organizational change. However, such resistance can be minimized by first recognizing the reasons behind the resistance, and second by working to reduce the "fear of the unknown" through support and education.

BARRIER:
EDI WILL CHANGE WHAT I DO!

The use of EDI clearly impacts roles and functions both within and between organizations. Concerns over exactly how roles and relationships may change often present a barrier to EDI implementation.

A strong concern of functional managers is how EDI will impact their roles within the organization. For instance, one article in a leading magazine for purchasing professionals stated that, "EDI could drastically change the way purchasing professionals (and others) do their jobs."[3] Another purchasing executive stated that, ". . . properly identifying and adjusting to the changing roles of buyers, salesmen, and administrative personnel such as accounts payable people, accounts receivable departments, order entry and order placement functions remain to be resolved—and they are significant issues. . . . The major challenge will be related to people and relationships."[4] Purchasing personnel often raise a concern that EDI will turn buyers into "glorified computer clerks." Salespeople may question whether EDI would eliminate their jobs, since orders will no longer have to be picked up. Functional managers in all areas have worried that EDI will reduce headcount in their departments, which is sometimes used, at least in part, as a basis for salary.

Solution

Although all of these concerns may not necessarily be valid, nor borne out by experience of EDI users, the concerns must be addressed. Because if not resolved, these concerns form a significant barrier to a smooth implementation of EDI. Again, the way of addressing these concerns is through education and top management support.

Use of EDI has been shown to change the roles of functional personnel; however, the changes have been positive. Purchasing personnel have found that EDI "frees them from administrative tasks and provides them with more time for professional buying activities."[5] Likewise, salesmen have found that with EDI, they can spend more time actually selling and less time doing paperwork. Educating personnel on the real impacts of EDI should help to eliminate the concern of functional managers.

However, top management support is also required. EDI does change the role of many functional managers. Top managers need to realize this and be willing to adjust performance measures, if necessary, to reflect an EDI rather than a paper environment. Rewarding productivity gains, in lieu of headcount, could eliminate a concern for loss of salary or position due to EDI.

BARRIER:
EDI WILL DESTROY MY RELATIONSHIP
WITH MY BUYER (SELLER)!

Another significant concern of functional managers is that EDI may adversely change the relationship between trading partners, particularly between buyers and salespeople. EDI is seen by some as representing, "at least to some degree, interventions into on-going exchange relationships."[6] Buyers have expressed a concern that EDI will reduce the number of contacts between buyers and sellers and will thus make the relationship more impersonal. Likewise, salespeople have often expressed a fear that EDI will weaken buyer-seller ties. Again, while these concerns are valid, experience proves that EDI strengthens relationships between trading partners.

Solution

In one study of EDI users, 87 percent of the organizations stated that the use of EDI actually made for a better relationship between trading partners.[7] The primary reasons for the improved relationship were the cooperation and coordination needed to implement EDI, and the increased trust that developed through the sharing of information. Some organizations have actually implemented EDI to improve relationships. One of the main reasons Navistar cites for implementing EDI was to build stronger relationships with trading partners. EDI, then, does change relationships between trading partners. However, the changes tend to reflect a movement away from an adversarial relationship to a more cooperative and stronger relationship. Educating functional managers about experiences of other EDI users should help to overcome this barrier to implementation.

BARRIER:
EDI IS SOMEONE ELSE'S PROBLEM—
IT'S NOT MY DEPARTMENT!

The implementation of EDI faces a major barrier that other organizational changes, such as the introduction of a computer system to the purchasing department, do not face. That barrier is EDI's effect on the basic organizational structure found in most organizations. As shown in Figure 9-1, the use of EDI cuts across traditional departmental boundaries. In other words, to be fully implemented, EDI requires the cooperation of purchasing, accounting, and transportation, marketing, and sales, as well as the support of legal and audit staffs. Further, not only must this cooperation between departments be mirrored in the trading partner's organization, the traditional boundaries between organizations must be eliminated. In other words, a level of trust and support both within and between organizations is required for the realization of all of EDI's potential benefits.

Solution

Obviously, companies that have implemented EDI have not thrown out their organization charts, nor have they removed traditional barriers between functions. However, these organizations have worked to obtain cooperation across functional lines. The use of cross-functional EDI implementation teams, coupled with strong management support, helps to encourage participation and cooperation between departments. Top management encouragement to view trading partners not as adversaries, but as an extension of the company has helped to break down the

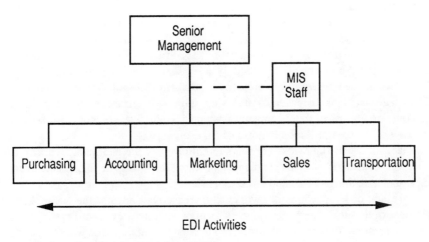

Figure 9-1   Organizational barriers to EDI.

barriers between organizations as well. Further, if a company starts EDI with a level 1 implementation, organizational barriers will not be as great, since usually only one department is affected. After the implementation in that one department has been shown to be a success, other areas are more likely to be less resistant to EDI in their departments.

BARRIER:
EDI IS TOO COMPLEX TO UNDERSTAND!

In many cases, all of the above barriers to EDI can be traced to one fundamental problem: that of lack of knowledge about EDI. Numerous studies have shown that most potential EDI users are ignorant or ill-informed about what EDI is, about the potential benefits of EDI, and also about the potential costs of EDI.

Lack of EDI knowledge is a severe constraint on the growth of EDI. Of over 1200 firms responding to a series of EDI surveys conducted in 1986, only 17 percent of the firms reported that their organizations participated in any industry associations that fostered EDI. Further, the same study also indicated that in 58 percent of the organizations, top management had only limited knowledge of EDI (with only 14 percent reporting considerable knowledge and 28 percent reporting no opinion).[8]

In another study of EDI users, lack of awareness was identified as a major cause of postponing the implementation of EDI in one or more functional areas. The factors of lack of knowledge, lack of senior management awareness, internal training requirements, and difficulty of educating trading partners were identified as an important reason for postponing EDI implementation by 41 percent of the respondents, and were identified as very important by 42 percent of the respondents. The same study also showed that only 30 percent of the firms believed that they had a good working knowledge of ANSI X12 standards, 28 percent of software, and 36 percent of communications facilities for EDI.[9] Further evidence of lack of EDI knowledge is provided by a 1988 study by Ferguson and Hill that indicated that nearly two-thirds of the over 1000 firms responding to a survey on EDI usage stated that they were "not familiar with VAN services supporting EDI"; and only one-fourth of those companies using EDI or actively planning to use EDI were aware of the translation features of EDI software.[10]

This lack of EDI knowledge appears to hold true on the international scene as well. A recent study of British managers indicated that less than 10 percent have a clear understanding of EDI and its benefits.[11]

This lack of knowledge only works to increase resistance to the use of EDI. Because of the lack of understanding, many organizations are overestimating costs and underestimating benefits. Further, not understanding how EDI works tends to increase concerns over the perceived technological complexity of EDI as well as over data security and control issues. As a result, many firms are reluctant to initiate EDI efforts and are waiting to be "forced into" EDI by a trading partner.

Solution

The answer to breaking through this barrier is simply education. While implementing EDI is not a simple task, EDI is not technologically complex. Further, assistance is available from vendors, trade groups, and trading partners. To begin your EDI education or to help your trading partners, consider:

- Attendance at commercially available training courses
- Participation in EDI conferences and trade shows
- Involvement in the standards process
- Meetings with trading partners already using EDI
- Discussion with software and network vendors

BARRIER:
PERCEIVED COSTS AND BENEFITS —

MY TRADING PARTNER WILL RECEIVE ALL THE BENEFITS!

A specific aspect of the general lack of EDI knowledge hindering EDI growth is a lack of awareness of the potential benefits of EDI. The benefits of EDI, from both a productivity perspective and from the perspective of gaining strategic advantage, can be substantial. Yet many organizations are unaware of these potential benefits. One study of functional managers indicated that most managers believed EDI to be only moderately beneficial.[12] This shows a lack of awareness of the significant benefits EDI offers.

Further, in many instances, potential EDI users believe that the benefits of EDI are unevenly split between trading partners, and more significantly, that the majority of benefits accrue to trading partners rather than to their own organizations. In a study in the general merchandising and grocery industries that involved both distributors and manufacturers, nearly "every company . . . indicated that their channel counterparts would benefit more from EDI than they would."[13] This response was received from both the manufacturers and the distributors.

As long as organizations believe that EDI benefits are limited, the growth of EDI is likely to be slow. In addition to the concern over limited benefits, many organizations also have a very strong concern over potential costs of EDI.

EDI COSTS TOO MUCH!

Not only do many organizations believe that EDI benefits will be limited, they also believe that costs will be substantial and will not be offset by benefits. In a number of different surveys, the implementation barrier most often cited is high start-up costs.[14] Further, most organizations citing cost as a significant barrier indicate that hardware costs are the most substantial investment, followed by software development costs.

The belief that hardware costs are a significant barrier to EDI indicates a lack of knowledge of EDI. In most cases organizations already have all of the necessary hardware to perform EDI. In those few cases where an organization has no computer capability, the purchase of a microcomputer and a modem can be made for a few thousand dollars. Although software costs may be substantial if EDI is fully integrated into internal operations, in most applications of EDI, software packages can be purchased and only minimal in-house software development is needed. The implementation of EDI does require a financial investment; however, the actual costs of implementation are often not as great as the perceived cost of implementation.

Solution

A number of methods can be used to overcome incorrect perceptions of EDI costs and benefits. One obvious solution is education. Sharing the costs and benefits experiences of current users can help to alleviate fears of substantial investment with no return. Further, many industry action groups have published "ballpark" estimates of the savings that result from the use of EDI. These figures can be used to show the potential benefits of EDI.

Second, a cost/benefit analysis can be performed. Most organizations have found that they can justify EDI on the basis of direct savings. Third, a pilot test of EDI using a microcomputer stand-alone system linked to a third party network can be initiated. In this way the benefits of EDI will be demonstrated while initial costs of implementation will be low.

Fourth, those wanting to use EDI should suggest patience to those reluctant to use EDI due to costs. EDI costs tend to be highest during early implementation, while benefits are highest much later in the implementation process. Therefore, users should not expect an immediate economic benefit from EDI. Long-term benefits from EDI can be substantial, but they normally follow a time of up-front costs.

Fifth, EDI advocates should avoid justifying EDI strictly on economic terms. While EDI can be justified on a cost-benefit basis, significant nonmonetary benefits in the form of better relationships, improved operations, and strategic advantage are the more important reason for its use.

BARRIER:
EDI WILL GIVE OTHERS ACCESS TO OUR
PROPRIETARY DATA!

In addition to expressing concerns over costs and benefits, functional managers are also hesitant to implement EDI because of a fear of the the loss of data security.

Traditionally, American industry has tended to have a somewhat adversarial relationship between trading partners; as a result most organizations tend to "play their cards close to their vest" when dealing with customers or suppliers. In other words, most companies are usually rather reluctant to share information with those outside of the company. This seems particularly true in such areas as purchasing and accounting, which traditionally have had very tight control over access to information. EDI is often seen as a threat to this tight control of information.

A concern of many managers is that EDI, because it links computers, will allow an outside organization to somehow tap into the company's computer system and to obtain access to confidential or sensitive information. In one study of potential EDI users, the concern most often expressed by purchasing managers was that EDI would provide either suppliers or competitors with electronic access to purchasing files.[15]

Solution

The fear of unlimited access to computer files through EDI is unfounded. However, it is a fear that must be addressed before EDI will be accepted by many functional managers. There are a number of ways the data security issue can be addressed. First, EDI does not provide direct access to internal files. An EDI system can be set up so that no outside computer is ever in contact with the company's computer. By using a third party network as an electronic mailbox, a company can have all messages sent to the mailbox. In addition, the company can arrange to dial-out and to retrieve the messages rather than having the third party network dial-in to the company's computer. In this way, there is no outside access to the company's computer. Further, even if a company does permit dialing-in by the third party network or by trading partners, the use of authorization codes and passwords can limit the activity that can be performed by the outside party. In addition to functional managers' concerns over data security, legal and auditing issues also often arise with the introduction of EDI.

BARRIER:
EDI PRESENTS ALL SORTS OF LEGAL PROBLEMS!

One obstacle to implementing EDI is the concern of the legal staff. As mentioned previously, many EDI users believe that involving the legal staff in the EDI effort guarantees its failure since lawyers often believe that EDI presents insurmountable legal problems. However, it is essential that legal concerns be addressed early in the EDI planning effort. Corporate lawyers have expressed a number of concerns over EDI. The two primary legal issues appear to be a concern over the loss of authorization control and a concern over the legality of electronic documents.

AUTHORIZATION CONTROLS

Most organizations have internal controls established to ensure that only authorized personnel perform certain functions. For instance, in purchasing, a signature is usually required to obligate funds; and often the person who is authorized to sign varies depending upon the dollar value of the purchase order. A concern with EDI is that with an electronic purchase order there appears to be no signature and therefore no control.

Solution

Through the use of authorization codes and passwords, the EDI system can be set up so that only authorized personnel have access to the system. In this way the authority of a person to transmit a specific purchase order can be validated. Just as in the paper world, an EDI system can be designed with built-in checks and balances to ensure that the same person cannot requisition an item, authorize its purchase, document receipt, and authorize payment. Through the use of authorization codes that limit access to the system and through the use of digital or electronic signatures, which positively identify the originating party, the same level of control can be established in the electronic arena.

DOCUMENT LEGALITY

Another concern of lawyers is the legality of electronic documents. Most paper purchase orders contain a section of "boilerplate" or standard terms and conditions. These terms and conditions are usually written on the back of the purchase order and therefore are a part of every order. However, in an electronic purchase order, there is no "boilerplate." What then are the terms and conditions governing the purchase order? Further, there is also a concern over the lack of a "written document" and a "written signature."

Solution

Most EDI users are handling this issue through the use of trading partner contracts. A trading partner contract usually includes the basic terms and conditions that will govern all electronic transmissions. Other users include a reference in the notes data segment to standard terms and conditions. These methods provide a way for including terms and conditions as a part of EDI orders. The American Bar Association is currently investigating whether it should recommend contract and liability issues that should be covered in trading partner contracts.[16] In addition, the Bar Association is studying whether EDI has changed contract formulation enough in terms of signatures and form to warrant a change to the Uniform Commercial Code.

BARRIER:
EDI ELIMINATES THE AUDIT TRAIL!

In addition to concerns from the legal staffs, many companies are also facing resistance to EDI from auditors. The most serious concern of auditors appears to be that electronic transmission of documents eliminates the audit trail. While EDI may change the "look" of the audit trail, EDI does not eliminate the trail. In fact, EDI often provides a better audit trail than does the paper environment.

Solution

In EDI, all transactions are time- and date-stamped automatically. EDI software generally provides for a log of all transactions. These mechanisms allow for an audit trail that is at least as reliable as a paper audit trail, and in many cases much better.

BARRIER:
EDI COMMUNICATIONS ARE NOT SECURE!

In addition, auditors also often express a concern over the integrity of electronic information. In other words, with a paper transmission, it is fairly easy to determine if someone intercepted a transmission and either reviewed or changed the information. However, a concern with electronic transmissions is that a message could be intercepted and the information in the message revealed to an outside party, with neither the sender nor the receiver being aware of the interception. Two methods of data security address this auditing concern: data encryption and data authentication.

Solution

Data encryption ensures the secrecy of electronic transmissions. In data encryption, which ANSI X12 supports, an electronic message is sent in coded form. The sender translates the EDI message into a coded message using a key that is available only to the sender and the receiver. Upon receipt of the coded message, the receiver uses the key to translate the message. In this way, the secrecy of the message is guaranteed.

Data authentication ensures that the message that was sent was actually the same as the message that was received. Here, the emphasis is not on maintaining secrecy of the data, but rather on ensuring that the message was not altered in any way during transmission. Under data authentication, an EDI message is coded using an encryption key. However, both the coded and uncoded messages are transmitted to the trading partner. Upon receipt of the messages, the trading partner uses the encryption key to decode the coded message and compares that to the original uncoded message received. If the two messages match, then the receiver should have confidence that the message was not altered during transmission.

Data encryption and data authentication are methods to ensure the integrity of EDI transmissions. However, their use is not widespread because most of the messages sent via EDI do not require such tight control.

BARRIER:
EDI TAKES AWAY MY FLOAT!

One barrier to EDI implementation often cited as a reason for delaying EDI is that the use of EDI will reduce cash flow. Because EDI reduces the order cycle period, the time during which a buying firm has access to funds is often reduced. This is particularly true if EDI is used for electronic payments as well as for transactions such as purchase orders and invoices. For instance, in the paper environment it is common that payment is due 30 days after the invoice date. However, many companies interpret the payment date to mean the date the payment must be mailed. So, the check is placed in the mail on day 30. Yet, due to mail and processing time, the funds are not actually taken out of the buyer's account for a number of additional days. Moving to electronic transmission and electronic payment removes this float.

Solution

This issue of concern over loss of float can be addressed in two ways, both of which require cooperation and negotiation between the trading partners. First, the trading partners can agree to adjust the payment due date. In other words, the buying company can withhold authorization of the electronic payment until the date on which the paper payment would have been received. Second, new payment terms can be negotiated between the trading partners. For instance, if due to EDI the payment is received 10 days earlier than under a paper system, the seller should be willing to negotiate a reduction in price to reflect the earlier receipt of funds. Organizations currently using EDI are using both methods as an answer to the float question.

BARRIER:
NONE OF OUR TRADING PARTNERS ARE DOING EDI!

EDI is like the telephone in that it requires two parties to work. An organization obviously cannot send an electronic message unless there is someone to receive the message. One barrier many organizations perceive as a hindrance to EDI growth is the lack of trading partners who are interested, willing, and capable of implementing EDI. This can even be a problem in industries with strong EDI efforts underway. For instance, according to the Ford Motor Company, one problem, early on, to its expansion of EDI is the the large number of small, unsophisticated suppliers.[17]

The fact that EDI cannot be implemented unilaterally presents an implementation barrier in another way as well. Many organizations have become aware of EDI and realize that they will eventually have to implement EDI. However, in many cases these organizations are waiting for a request from their trading partners to do so. Meantime, their trading partners have also decided to wait for a request from a trading partner before implementing EDI. In other words, what is often the case is that two trading partners are waiting for each other to make the first move.

Solution

The lack of willing and able trading partners can be overcome in a number of ways. First, one solution is to become aware of those companies who are willing to begin EDI efforts. The *EDI Yellow Pages* lists over 7000 organizations, with names of contact personnel, which are interested in EDI.[18] Your trading partners may already be on that list.

Second, for those trading partners who have not expressed an interest in EDI, training and support may be required. A number of organizations have created training seminars, literature, and videos that are distributed to trading partners. This information is designed to point out the benefits of EDI and to encourage trading partner participation. In addition, a number of organizations are providing trading partners with the necessary hardware and software to perform EDI. For the small initial investment required to establish a microcomputer stand-alone EDI system for trading partners, organizations are finding that they are receiving significant incremental benefits from EDI.

BARRIER:
EDI STANDARDS KEEP CHANGING!

Another barrier that is often a concern to potential EDI users is the lack of *one* common set of EDI standards. Organizations with only a limited knowledge of EDI have often heard of the various types of standards such as TDCC, UCS, VICS, X12, WINS, etc. These organizations often say that they are waiting until there is just one type of standard, because they fear that if they adopt a particular standard now, they may have to change everything at a later date.

Solution

Two responses address this concern. First, the ANSI X12 standard is fast becoming *the* standard for EDI in this country. The various standards committees are working to make sure that the families of standards are compatible, and going with the X12 standard poses little risk. Second, a company that is concerned with evolving and changing standards can shift the risk for such changes to either a third party network or to a software vendor. By purchasing a software package for translation, or by having a third party perform translation services, an organization can minimize the risk and effort involved as the standards change.

SUMMARY

A number of barriers to the use of EDI exist; however, most are actually only perceived barriers. In other words, potential EDI users are often misinformed about EDI. Education and top management encouragement should help to eliminate many of the misconceptions about EDI.

However, a more serious, and harder to overcome, barrier to EDI exists. That barrier is the belief that EDI is a technology that can be added on top of the current organizational structure. For EDI to be fully successful both within and between organizations, traditional boundaries must begin to break down, and organizations must rethink their operations, their processes, and their relationships. This is the real barrier facing EDI.

The next two chapters provide additional implementation guidance. Chapter 10 provides a method for quantifying EDI costs and benefits, which should help to minimize some of the resistance to EDI. Chapter 11 presents two cases outlining the implementation strategies of actual companies. The two cases provide examples of how some EDI barriers were overcome by the companies involved.

10

QUANTIFYING EDI COSTS
AND BENEFITS

INTRODUCTION

Although EDI is often thought of and marketed as a cost-saving technology, nearly every recent survey of EDI users indicates that obtaining cost reductions is *not* the primary reason for implementing EDI. For instance, the 1988 "State of EDI" research study conducted by EDI Research, Inc., showed that improved information management and customer service was cited as the most important benefit of EDI by the largest number of respondents. Cost efficiency was rated second in the study.[1] Another study conducted by INPUT, of MIS managers in Fortune 1000 companies, found that "the reason most commonly cited for implementing EDI is strong demand by customers."[2]

EDI pioneers and advocates also recommend that EDI not be viewed primarily as a cost-reduction exercise. As noted earlier, George Klima formerly of Super Valu Stores has repeatedly stated that any organization which implements EDI just to save money will not realize the full potential of EDI. And Super Valu has documented well over $600,00 in annual savings due to EDI![3]

Among early users of EDI, the recognition that EDI provided significant benefits beyond cost reduction was clearly evident. A study of EDI pioneers in the automotive, grocery, chemical, and other manufacturing industries indicated that only 13 percent of the companies had specifically quantified EDI costs and only 27 percent had specifically quantified EDI benefits, prior to implementing EDI.[4] Typical comments on why a detailed cost/benefit justification had not been performed included:

> "EDI hits at the heart of our business. The benefits are so obvious that cost/benefit documentation is not a worthwhile expenditure of resources."

"Costs are not considered to be significant and benefits are obvious. An intuitive decision was made at the top to pursue EDI."

WHY DOCUMENT COSTS AND BENEFITS

To Help Sell EDI Internally

The focus of many of the early users of EDI was not to reduce costs but to reduce the time involved in the business cycle and to gain other strategic benefits such as improved business relations. While it appears that many of the early pioneers and strong supporters of EDI found that quantifying EDI costs and benefits was not essential, there are a number of reasons why cost/benefit quantification should be performed. First, regardless of how important EDI may be to a firm's survival, most organizations require some type of economic justification. EDI can be economically justified based upon tangible savings. It makes sense therefore to perform the analysis and to use the results in marketing EDI throughout the corporation.

To Help Budget for EDI Activities

Second, even in those firms where no economic justification is necessary (i.e., top management is convinced that EDI is necessary for survival), quantifying costs and benefits is still useful. The cost/benefit analysis will not only indicate the level of resources that must be budgeted for implementation, it will also indicate the financial changes that can be expected as the use of EDI expands within the company.

To Help Set EDI Strategy

A third important reason for doing a cost/benefit analysis is because it can assist in the selection of an EDI implementation strategy. The costs to implement EDI and the resulting benefits vary significantly depending upon the level of EDI system implemented. For instance, costs for a microcomputer stand-alone system are very low (often under $3000), while the costs for a fully integrated, application-to-application EDI system are usually high (well above $100,000). A cost/benefit analysis of the various EDI options, along with a review of resources available, will help to determine the type of EDI system to implement. If resources are likely to be limited in the first year of EDI operation, a company may choose to implement a system with a microcomputer as a front-end to a mainframe. In this arrangement, initial costs would still be low, yet the company has the option of expanding the system to a full mainframe operation in later years.

BEHAVIOR OF EDI COSTS AND BENEFITS

In performing a cost/benefit analysis two important characteristics of EDI must be kept in mind. This is particularly true if EDI is going to be justified on an economic basis. The two points are as follows:

1. Costs come early; savings come later.
2. Costs are easy to determine; benefits are not.

Timing of Costs/Benefits

The implementation of EDI may require considerable up-front resources. This could be true even if a simple microcomputer system is to be used. Training, purchase or development of software, purchase of any needed hardware (such as microcomputers and modem), membership in EDI associations and standards groups will all incur costs before any EDI can actually be done. A large portion of EDI costs tends to be fixed, up-front costs.

On the other hand, benefits tend to be variable as a function of EDI volume. In other words, the benefits will increase as the volume of EDI usage increases. Most EDI implementation efforts begin with the exchange of just a few documents with a limited number of trading partners. Therefore, benefits are going to be the most limited during the time when the costs tend to be the highest. The timing of the realization of costs and benefits is shown in Figure 10-1.

Understanding when EDI costs and benefits occur is important because in the early stages of EDI, it is very likely that EDI will "be losing money." During the time when costs are greater than benefits, the company must remain committed to the EDI effort. It is usually during this time that the strongest internal marketing efforts are required.

Determination of Costs and Benefits

A second important point to consider during a cost/benefit analysis is that it is usually much easier to estimate costs than it is to estimate benefits. Costs tend to be hard figures, which can be directly determined. Costs for EDI training, software, or third party services can be exactly determined because the vendor sends a bill showing the cost. Time and effort from internal staff personnel to perform in-house development or to make modifications to existing programs is also easily tracked.

Benefits, on the other hand, are often "soft." Estimating the amount of inventory that will be saved, the amount of paperwork that will be reduced, and the effect of improved information accuracy is often subjective. Further, the data necessary to fully estimate benefits are often not available or are not necessarily accurate.

This distinction is important because if affects how others view the cost/benefit analysis. In most cases, it is likely that estimated costs will be taken as "gospel,"

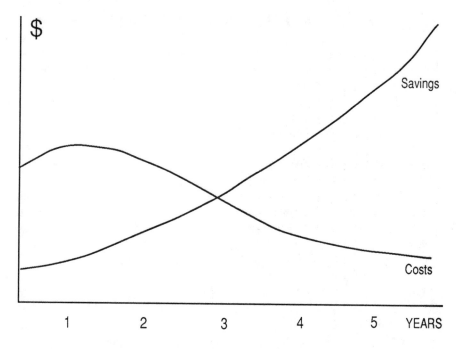

Figure 10-1   EDI costs and benefits over time.

while estimated benefits will be challenged. The EDI team will need to be aware of these differences and be prepared to defend the analysis and to support the estimated benefits.

CATEGORIES OF EDI COSTS

Hardware Costs

EDI hardware costs include the purchase and maintenance of any computer equipment necessary to perform EDI. While most organizations are likely to already have all the necessary equipment, some companies may be faced with the need to purchase either a microcomputer and/or a communications modem. Both of these items can usually be purchased for under $2500.

Software Costs

There are two general categories of software costs: initial software development or purchase and on-going maintenance costs. Two factors determine the level of software costs. The first is the configuration of the EDI system. If a microcomputer system is used, initial software costs for translation software can be as low as $500, while mainframe translation software, whether developed in-house or purchased commercially, will usually cost at least $25,000.

On-going maintenance of software is necessary to ensure that the software can handle updated versions of the standards. Maintenance costs also vary with type of system, with microcomputer costs as low as $200 annually and mainframe annual costs in the $2000 range.

The other factor that will influence software costs is the degree to which EDI is to be implemented into internal applications. If EDI is implemented as a stand-alone function, no additional software, beyond the translation software, is needed. However, if the EDI system is integrated with internal application systems and the internal application systems are bridged, additional software development is necessary. Software development costs for internal applications bridging can easily exceed $100,000.

Communications Costs

Costs will be incurred in the actual transmission of electronic communications between trading partners. In cases where a third party network is used, both one-time and on-going costs will be incurred. Most third party networks charge an initial start-up fee and then also charge a per-message or per-transmission fee. The per-message or per-transmission fee is obviously a variable cost, based upon EDI volume. If a direct link between trading partners is used, the communications costs will vary depending upon whether dedicated communication lines or public communication lines are used.

Training Costs

Nearly every EDI implementation effort is going to require some degree of training for company personnel as well as for trading partner personnel. Training costs include both in-house provided training as well as vendor provided training. The most significant amount of training is usually incurred up-front, with a limited level of on-going training required to keep personnel abreast of changes in standards and technology.

Personnel Costs

The implementation of EDI requires the support of the MIS staff as well as the support and participation of EDI team members. While many companies allocate MIS support to the EDI effort and charge MIS time against the EDI project in computing project costs, most companies do not charge time of other EDI team members (such as functional managers) to the EDI project. However, any new personnel who are hired for the EDI effort are usually charged against the project.

Outside Support Costs

Often companies will obtain the services of an outside consultant to assist in the development of EDI strategy. The cost of hiring a consultant is usually a one-time fixed cost incurred early in the EDI effort.

Membership Costs

Most companies who become active in EDI join and participate in EDI associations. Many of these associations have either a one-time membership fee or annual membership dues. For instance, obtaining a UCS communication identification code from the Uniform Code Council requires a one-time payment ranging from $500 to $10,000 based upon type of organization and annual sales volume. Annual membership dues for ANSI X12 range from $250 to $2500 and annual dues for TDCC range from $500 to $3000, depending again on sales volume or gross revenues. It should be noted, however, that the membership fees and annual dues are voluntary in some cases, and may be waived under certain conditions.

Time Value Costs

One other cost which may be incurred when doing EDI is the loss of float. This is the cost incurred by making earlier payments to suppliers. This variable cost is a function of the percent of payments handled electronically, the amount of cash flow lost, and the organization's cost of money.

Cost Summary of EDI

A cost summary worksheet is shown in Figure 10-2. The worksheet outlines the various costs categories. Exact cost figures will vary from organization to organization depending upon the cost structure of the firm and the specific EDI strategy selected.

CATEGORIES OF EDI BENEFITS

As mentioned earlier, EDI costs are much easier to estimate than are EDI benefits. While some benefits are obvious and measurable, such as a reduction in postal expense, other benefits are much less obvious and much more difficult to compute, such as improved productivity of personnel. Discussed below are a number of types of cost savings that can be realized with the implementation of EDI.

It should be noted that many firms reporting EDI savings do so on the basis of costs saved per document. For instance, RCA has reported that EDI has reduced purchase order costs by over $50 per order; while Douglas Aircraft reports a $5 per

Fixed Costs Generally Not Related to EDI Volume

Cost Category	Initial	Annual
HARDWARE		
Equipment Purchase	_____	
Equipment Mainenance		_____
SOFTWARE		
Development or Purchase		
Translation	_____	
Integration	_____	
Maintenance		
Translation		_____
Integration		_____
PERSONNEL		
MIS Support		
Initial Development	_____	
On going		_____
New Personnel		_____
OUTSIDE SUPPORT	_____	
MEMBERSHIP FEES		
Initial Fees	_____	
Annual Dues		_____

Variable Costs Relating to EDI Volume

Cost Category	Initial	Annual
THIRD PARTY/COMMUNICATIONS		
Initial Fee	_____	
Transmission Charges		_____
TRAINING		
Initial Training	_____	
Upgrading		_____
TIME VALUE COSTS		
Loss of Float		_____

Figure 10-2   Estimating EDI costs.

document reduction.[5] The reported cost savings, however, represents reductions in a number of areas, such as personnel, equipment, mailing, office supplies, etc.; therefore, these are the types of categories discussed below.

Personnel Cost Savings

The implementation of EDI eliminates a number of clerical activities normally performed in a paper-based system. Therefore, the cost of performing these activities can be considered as cost savings under EDI. Activities usually reduced or eliminated by EDI include:

- Rekeying operations of data
- Mail processing costs (stuffing envelopes, addressing)
- Filing costs
- Reconciling various documents
- Follow-up on incorrect, lost, or late documents

The actual savings realized in personnel costs is a function of a number of factors. First, the savings are variable based upon the percentage of EDI volume. The greater the EDI volume, the more savings will be realized. Second, the dollar value of the savings will vary considerably based upon who currently performs the activities listed above. For instance, in some organizations clerical personnel perform follow-up, while in others buyers perform follow-up. A third factor that will influence the actual amount of cost savings experienced is what is done with the "time saved" due to elimination of activities. Some companies have actually been able to cut staff due to EDI. Others have not cut staff, but have been able to assign present staff to additional activities. In these cases savings have been estimated based upon the number of additional personnel who would have been hired, had existing personnel not been reassigned.

Paper Savings

Because EDI replaces paper documents with electronic documents, paper costs are reduced with EDI. These costs include the cost of the paper forms, storage costs, and mailing costs of the paper documents. These costs savings are variable based upon the level of EDI usage.

Inventory Savings

EDI often results in a reduction in inventory levels. Inventory is reduced due to a shorter order cycle time as well as decreased uncertainty in order cycle time. Inventory savings are a function of the number of days of inventory reduced and the cost of carrying the inventory. In addition, a reduction in inventory may also result in a reduction in storage costs.

Time Value Benefits

If EDI is used to receive payments, earlier availability of cash is likely to result. The dollar benefit of earlier payment is a variable based upon the number of payments received earlier. The amount of costs savings is a function of the additional time the money is available and the organization's cost of money.

Information Cost Savings

A number of additional savings are possible from EDI due to the availability of more timely and accurate information. Examples of these savings include:

- Reduction in premium freight charges
- Reduction in out-of-stock situations and lost sales
- Reduction in production line shut-downs

Other Benefits

The benefits discussed above can be quantified by most organizations. EDI provides a number of additional benefits that cannot be easily quantified but are often "factored into" the decision to implement EDI. Improved internal operations, closer relationships with vendors, maintenance of the customer base, and increased sales due to increased productivity of personnel all have a value to the company and should be considered in the EDI decision.

Summary of EDI Benefits

Figure 10-3 provides a summary of the quantifiable benefits resulting from EDI. The summary outlines each type of benefit and offers suggestions for calculating benefits.

PREPARING A COST/BENEFIT ANALYSIS

Figure 10-4 provides a worksheet for combining EDI costs and benefits in order to show the net dollar result of implementing EDI. In computing the total economic impact of EDI, a number of points should be kept in mind.

First, the calculation should be made over a multiple-year period. Costs of EDI tend to be short term, while benefits tend to be long term. Therefore, the analysis should not be done on a one-year basis, but rather for the life of the EDI effort.

Second, the analysis should take into account the rate of growth of the EDI effort. Most of the benefits are variable based upon the level of EDI volume, whereas most of the costs tend to be fixed. The analysis should include an estimate of the volume of transactions that will be converted from paper to electronic each year.

Cost Category	Annual Savings

PERSONNEL SAVING

    Hours or Employees Saved

    X Salary Plus Fringe Benefits   _____

PAPER SAVINGS

    Costs of Paper

    + Storage + Mailing   _____

INVENTORY SAVINGS

    Inventory Reduction

        # Days Reduction X Average Value of

        Inventory X Cost of Capital   _____

    Storage Reduction

        # Days Reduction X Average Value of

        Inventory X Incremental Storage Costs _____

TIME VALUE BENEFITS

    Additional Days of Cash Float

    X Average Daily Cash Float

    X Cost of Capital   _____

OTHER COSTS

    Reduction in Freight   _____

    Reduction in Lost Sales   _____

    Reduction in Production Line Shut Down _____

NOTE: EDI BENEFITS TEND TO BE VARIABLE BASED ON EDI VOLUME. In computing savings, many organizations estimate savings based upon 100 percent conversion from paper to EDI and then adjust the savings to reflect the actual level of EDI volume.

For instance: Assume that at 100 percent EDI personnel savings would be $100,000. In year one, if 5 percent of transactions are to be EDI, the year one personnel savings are $100,000 X .05 or $5,000.

Figure 10-3   Estimating EDI benefits.

Net Resut of EDI Implementation:

Start Up:

    – Total Initial Costs
    + /Initial Savings (usually 0)|
    ―――――――――――――――――

    Start Up Net Loss/Gain

Year One:

    – Total Fixed Annual Costs
    – Total Variable Annual Costs X Conversion Factor
    + |Total Variable Benefits X Conversion Factor
    ―――――――――――――――――

    Year One Net Loss/Gain

Year Two:

    – Total Fixed Annual Costs
    – Total Variable Annual Costs X Conversion Factor
    + |Total Variable Benefits X Conversion Factor
    ―――――――――――――――――

    Year Two Net Loss/Gain

Year Three and Beyond

    (Same as year two , adjusted for conversion factor)

NOTES: FIGURES SHOULD BE COMPUTED ON AN AFTER TAX BASIS AND
              SHOULD BE ADJUSTED TO REFLECT PRESENT VALUE

Figure 10-4   Cost/benefit worksheet.

SUMMARY

While not all companies perform an EDI costs/benefit analysis, such an analysis provides useful information. For most firms, the analysis should provide economic justification for using EDI. This economic justification, coupled with strategic advantages available through EDI, will prove useful in marketing the EDI effort within the organization.

11

IMPLEMENTATION CASE STUDIES

INTRODUCTION

This chapter presents two case studies of the EDI implementation process. The primary objective of the case studies is not to show how different companies are using EDI, but rather to show how different companies have gone through the implementation process. The two cases reflect companies in very different industries and with different implementation strategies. The material in this chapter was abstracted from previously published case studies. The Mervyn's case was prepared by INPUT.[1] The North American Philips Corporation case was prepared by the Council of Logistics Management.[2]

MERVYN'S

Background of Company

Mervyn's, one of the four main subsidiaries of the Dayton Hudson Corporation (DHC), is a popular-priced, value-oriented department store chain that features nationally branded and private label apparel, accessories, and household soft goods. Currently the chain operates over 200 stores in 14 western and southern states. To support these stores, Mervyn's operates four large distribution centers located in California (2), Utah, and Texas. Each of the distribution centers uses state-of-the-art technology and design to support just-in-time delivery of items to individual stores.

Management Philosophy

Mervyn's operates under a strong Mission Statement and set of specific operating principles. According to the Mission Statement, Mervyn's mission is "to achieve superior financial performance by consistently providing the consumer with exceptional value in soft-line general merchandise. Exceptional value is provided by the proper balance of quality, price, fashion, timeliness, and customer service. Superior financial performance is demonstrated by consistent long-range profit growth and a return on investment above the Dayton Hudson standard. We accomplish our mission through the meticulous execution of the Operating Principles."[3]

Mervyn's Mission Statement has a consistent and strong influence on the corporate culture. Each manager is responsible for understanding the Mission Statement and for following its guidelines. The combination of the Mission Statement and the Operating Principles clearly indicate that Mervyn's "focus on profitability and growth is supported by a commitment to using effective systems and a flexible management style as tools to maintain productivity in a rapidly changing environment."[4]

EDI Applications Environment

In support of its objective to use effective systems as a management tool, Mervyn's has computerized a number of diverse internal applications. The majority of Mervyn's application programs are proprietary systems that have been developed in-house. Currently, the programs are run on IBM mainframes under IMS; however, Mervyn's is in the process of switching to a relational database system. Major functional applications that have been computerized by Mervyn's include:

- Merchandise processing
- Stores operating systems, such as point of sale
- Inventory management
- Proprietary credit
- Financial
- Human resources information

MERVYN'S EDI APPLICATIONS

Mervyn's defines EDI as any form of electronic communication between separate entities, whether the parties are external to Mervyn's or not. In other words, electronic communication between the various units of Mervyn's is considered to be EDI, along with electronic communications between Mervyn's and its trading partners and banks.

Externally, Mervyn's electronically communicates order and shipment data with trading partners. In addition, direct transmission of payroll data to banks, charge card authorizations and billings, and credit inquiries are also communicated electronically.

Mervyn's uses both a direct network and third party network for its EDI transmissions. In situations where the communications are essentially one to one, for instance with the largest key trading partners, direct communications through leased lines are used. However, in other cases where Mervyn's is communicating similar information to a large number of trading partners, such as purchase orders to other vendors, Mervyn's uses a third party network mailbox service.

Justification for EDI

Mervyn's adopted EDI because it supports their management philosophy of the effective use of informational tools. EDI was justified primarily based upon "long-range strategic benefits."[5] Even before EDI was widely accepted, Mervyn's MIS department had identified data communications as a technology that was of critical importance to the organization, for both internal operations and for external relationships with trading partners. EDI obviously supported this use of data communications.

Further, Mervyn's also saw EDI as a way of improving internal logistics, which the organization believed was "one of the most important applications a retailer can concentrate on to gain value from its activities."[6] The use of EDI allowed Mervyn's to significantly reduce its inventory level while strengthening ties between Mervyn's and its suppliers.

Implementation Process

Although Mervyn's did not establish a separate and formal EDI team, the EDI effort was assigned project status by the MIS steering committee. The MIS steering committee is composed of the CEO/President, the Chief Accounting Officer, and the Vice President of MIS. The steering committee establishes overall corporate priorities among various functional areas.

The EDI project, as are all IS projects at Mervyn's, was assigned a user Project Control Chairman (PCC). While the MIS department initiated the project, the user PCC is the one responsible for implementation of the effort. By having users responsible for the implementation of EDI, internal resistance was minimized. According to Mervyn's, this "strong partnership approach between user management and MIS provides a constructive environment for applying innovative techniques such as EDI. . . ."[7]

The initial step in Mervyn's EDI implementation process was the development of an overall EDI strategy and the implementation of a pilot test. As part of overall EDI strategy, Mervyn's decided to develop the system completely in-house rather than to purchase software packages. The results of the pilot test "demonstrated the value of EDI as a tool that contributed to Mervyn's overall strategy of relationship building and improving logistics management."[8] Because of the success of the pilot, the EDI effort was expanded to all other applications within the company.

Standards Participation

Mervyn's also became very involved in the standards process during the EDI implementation effort. The importance of industry-wide standards was recognized early, and the MIS department was encouraged to pursue and support the development of industry standards. At the same time, Mervyn's parent company, Dayton Hudson Corporation (DHC) also became interested in EDI and fully encouraged all of its subsidiaries to participate in standards activities. DHC joined the VICS (Voluntary Inter-Industry Communications Standards) committee, while Mervyn's joined ANSI and began work with the X12 committee.

Trading Partner Activity

During EDI implementation efforts, Mervyn's was fairly "aggressive in spurring its trading partners to adopt EDI."[9] Although Mervyn's drive to have trading partner participation in EDI was helped by their "strong culture of relationship building and the large reservoir of understanding and trust that it had built up with suppliers over the years," Mervyn's still encountered some rather strong resistance from its trading partners.[10]

The vendors' greatest concern was over the change in the salesperson's role due to EDI. Vendors appeared to believe that EDI would bypass the salesmen, thus decreasing their control of the account relationship. In addition, salesmen also expressed a concern over the possibility of losing commissions. Mervyn's argued that with EDI support, the salesmen could "provide better service, spend more time addressing customer problems, and have fewer headaches in the process."[11]

To show the importance Mervyn's placed on EDI, several vendor conferences were held to educate trading partners about EDI. The one-day conferences included presentations by top Mervyn's executives who emphasized the importance of EDI in maintaining trading relationships. Other trading partners who were already doing EDI with Mervyn's also made presentations. In addition, Mervyn's makes its technical staff available to trading partners who have specific implementation problems.

Lessons Learned

Based upon their experience in implementing EDI, Mervyn's management has offered a number of suggestions they believe will be helpful to other firms pursuing EDI. First, EDI should be viewed as "a linchpin to make other things happen."[12]

Specifically, EDI can be used as the impetus for just-in-time or quick response systems. Therefore, EDI should not be justified on the basis of direct savings or simply as a substitute for a paper-based system. Second, EDI will not succeed without strong top management support on both sides. It is important to get active participation by the top management of your trading partner if EDI is to succeed.

Third, after top management support, education is the next most important factor in implementing EDI. This includes both in-house education as well as trading partner education. Fourth, "EDI is a matter of details."[13] Everyone, from the top down, must focus on the detail. While vision and commitment are important, they are not enough if the details are ignored. And finally, as in any project, the key to its success is careful planning.

NORTH AMERICAN PHILIPS CORPORATION INTRODUCING EDI IN A MULTIDIVISIONAL ORGANIZATION

Background of the Company

North American Philips Corporation (NAPC) ranks among the top 100 industrial firms in the country. With efforts concentrated in the areas of consumer products, lighting products, electrical and electronic components, and professional equipment, NAPC had sales of over $5 billion in 1987. Some of NAPC's more widely known products include Magnavox, Philco, and Sylvania home entertainment products; Norelco electric razors and coffee makers; Philips lamps, medical systems and electronic instruments; and Genie garage door openers.

Development of EDI Efforts

NAPC began its EDI efforts in 1984 and has been active ever since. The NAPC EDI effort has three major components. The first major component is a proprietary EDI system used for communication within the Philips organization on a worldwide basis. The second major component of NAPC's EDI effort is to work closely with both domestic and international standards committees. The objective of this activity is to ensure that NAPC's interests are represented in the standards development process. The seriousness of NAPC's commitment to this effort is evidenced by the fact that Dennis McGinnis of NAPC was the U.S. representative to international standards setting committees for a number of years. The third major component of NAPC's EDI effort is to work with divisions who want to implement EDI efforts with customers and outside vendors.[14]

EDI Staffing

When NAPC began its EDI efforts, it considered four options in managing the implementation process. The first option was to delegate all EDI development to the divisions. In other words, each division that wanted an EDI effort would be responsible for its own development and implementation effort. Second, NAPC also could have hired a third party vendor to develop and manage the EDI effort. A number of such vendors were available and offered a solution to the EDI implementation problem. Third, NAPC could have assigned all EDI activity to a staff-level MIS function. Finally, a fourth option, and the one selected by NAPC, was to use a combination of the above implementation approaches.

Implementation Responsibility

At NAPC all EDI development is a staff responsibility within the MIS group.[15] However, in EDI efforts involving specific divisions, the implementation is "co-managed" by MIS staff and division personnel. The staff personnel include an MIS-Electronic Business Communications manager and a full-time assistant, who are supported by six corporate MIS programmers. Division personnel are managers from the functional areas implementing EDI. A listing of staff MIS EDI services is shown in Figure 11-1.

Responsibilities of the EDI Staff

The EDI staff group is responsible for providing "timely and accurate response to EDI inquiries."[16] The staff group receives EDI inquiries from a number of sources including external customers, senior level functional management, and corporate top management. The staff group is responsible for prioritizing the various EDI requests and also must remain current with "changes in hardware, software, new third party products, and shifting internal and external needs."[17] Further, the group often acts as a marketer of the EDI process to those both within and outside of NAPC. To support the various EDI requests, the EDI staff has developed a basic six-step implementation process which is used when working with either a request from a division or a request from the corporate functional area.[18]

NAPC EDI Implementation Process

Step 1—Situational Analysis   The first step is for the EDI staff group to analyze the background of the request. This involves determining the source of the request and the scope, as well as estimating the level of resources required to implement the requested effort. Specific questions addressed by the EDI staff group at this point include:

MIS-Electronic Business Communication Services Available

DEPARTMENTAL FUNCTIONS

Planning and project co-management
Research and communications of EDI developments
EDI policy administration
Education
Billing
Problem management

CORPORATE OFFERINGS

Central communications facilities
Purchase/develop EDI products
Maintain currency of EDI standards in all products
Support all products in a global environment
Implementation assistance

CONTRACT PROGRAMMING

Contracted directly with NAPC or an outside software company

DAY-TO-DAY OPERATIONS

Information center for EDI
Oversee NAPC Support of communications facility and hotline
 services to EDI user community
Interface with communications vendors
Oversee support of EDI community

Source: *Customer Service: A Management Perspective*
         Reprinted with permission

Figure 11-1   NAPC's EDI staffing.

- What is driving the EDI request?
- Is it in response to a customer's demand?
- How broadbased is the requested EDI effort?
- What resources will be needed to support the effort?
- When does the EDI project initiator need a response from the staff group?

Step 2—Problem Approach   The second step in the EDI process is to develop a basic EDI strategy for the EDI project. The strategy includes issues of system configuration, scope of the project, and level of education required. The strategy for implementing EDI varies depending upon the nature of the EDI project. For instance, if the EDI request is in response to a customer's demand and therefore a quick implementation is required, the strategy often includes the use of outside support, such as third party networks or software vendors. However, if the request does not require a very rapid response, more in-house development is likely. Specific questions addressed by the EDI staff group at this point include:

- How much time is required for customer education?
- What type of education is needed?
- Are resources available in-house, in the time required?
- Should third party support or products be used?
- What is a realistic timetable for project execution?
- Can the EDI effort be expanded to include other divisions or other end users?
- Who should be the major divisional players involved in the implementation effort?

Step 3—Initial Meeting with the Division   After doing some of the initial background investigation and planning, the EDI staff conducts a meeting of all the parties affected by the EDI effort. Normally the meeting includes representatives from the MIS staff, customer service, finance, and staff system support, as well as the EDI staff group. In addition, divisional personnel representing the initiator of the EDI request are also in attendance. Specific questions addressed by this group include:

- What is the specific implementation approach that will be used?
- What is the specific schedule of implementation?

Step 4—Problem/Solution Clarification   Often the EDI staff group finds that the development of the EDI strategy and implementation plan requires additional input beyond that received with the initial request and the information obtained during the divisional meeting. Obtaining any additional information or support needed is the responsibility of the EDI staff group. Obtaining the additional support often requires the following activities:

- Additional discussions with divisions on overall strategy
- Visits to the division's customers who would be using the EDI system
- Meetings with the third party networks used by the division's customers
- Discussions with outside software and hardware vendors

Step 5—Divisional Implementation   While the EDI staff group, working with divisional representatives, is primarily responsible for the planning of the EDI strategy and implementation, the division is actually responsible for the EDI implementation effort. Once all of the planning has been completed and agreement on strategy has been achieved between the staff group and the division, responsibility for the EDI effort is passed from the staff to the division. The majority of the EDI efforts implemented by NAPC divisions required a three- to six-month implementation process and included an extensive pilot test.

Step 6—Progress Monitoring   Although the responsibility for the EDI effort passes to the division once the actual implementation effort begins, the EDI staff group remains involved in the effort. The Staff MIS-Electronic Business Communications Group meets with divisional representatives in charge of the EDI effort on a monthly basis during the implementation process to determine if the effort is progressing as planned. Specific items discussed at the monthly meetings include:

- Scheduling problems
- Resource problems
- Customer problems
- Special implementation problems

Additional EDI Staff Activities

NAPC's EDI staff is currently considering a number of additional activities to support the implementation of EDI efforts. The changes being made are designed to "make the support function more efficient by broadening the base of [EDI] 'experts' and providing a better level of communications within the organization."[19] Three additional types of support are being considered. The first is a standardized EDI educational package. This package would be a "starter kit" for EDI users and would include a video on EDI applications, hard copy implementation information, and a list of other corporate users. The second item being developed is an internal EDI newsletter. The newsletter will be distributed to all functions and divisions that are either using EDI or are interested in using EDI. The newsletter would discuss new EDI products and new EDI applications within NAPC. The third support item being developed is the scheduling of periodic user meetings within NAPC. The meetings would bring together all EDI users within the company to facilitate networking and the exchange of lessons learned in the EDI implementation process.

EDI Lessons Learned at NAPC

Based upon the situations encountered in implementing EDI at NAPC, the company offers a number of suggestions for others involved in EDI efforts. First, EDI represents the type of change where the technology is changing rapidly and where there is constant pressure for activity from both internal and external sources. In these types of situations a "programmed approach to managing change" is necessary.[20] For EDI, this means that the company should have a basic implementation process developed that is followed for all EDI efforts and projects.

Second, the management of EDI and the related changes EDI causes, frequently require marketing skills. Therefore, if the change is to be managed by staff personnel, emphasis must be placed on involving users in the planning and implementation process and on aggressive internal marketing efforts.

Third, in implementing EDI or any other effort where there is rapid change in technology, educating all of the parties involved, both internally and externally, is necessary before the effort can be successfully implemented.

Fourth, when EDI change is customer-driven, a "crisis aura" may result.[21] In other words, when a customer demands that EDI be implemented, the organization is often faced with the necessity of implementing EDI on a much faster timetable than would normally be desired. If possible, customer requests for EDI should be anticipated and planned for as a part of the overall EDI strategy and implementation process.

Fifth, justifying the EDI effort on a costs/benefits basis is sometimes difficult because "most of the costs were at the front end and the benefits were at the back. Further, the costs were short-run costs and the benefits were long-run benefits."[22] This often makes it difficult to sell EDI efforts to top management and to functional executives.

Sixth, because EDI requires support from a number of areas, such as MIS and the functional areas, networking across functional boundaries is important to EDI implementation. And seventh, the services of third party EDI vendors should be considered in any EDI effort. These vendors cannot only reduce the start-up time required to implement EDI, they can also help to improve the interface between an organization and its trading partners.

Summary

Although these cases represent different industries and different types of organizations, there are a number of similarities between the implementation approaches. The cases illustrate a number of important points about EDI implementation:

1. Some form of EDI project team is needed. The team can be a part of an existing committee or it can be organized as a separate function. However, the team should have a cross-functional membership and should have distinct organizational visibility.
2. User involvement is critical to the success of EDI. Users must be actively involved in planning as well as in the actual implementation process.
3. Top management support is critical. In both cases, strong top management support was evident. The support from top management must be more than just approval—it must be active participation.
4. EDI should not be justified on only a costs/benefits basis. First, this may be difficult to do since costs are up-front while benefits are realized later. Second, the real benefits of EDI are more strategic in focus.

5.   Implementation of EDI requires a close relationship with trading partners. Organizations must be willing to help train and to support trading partners.

SUMMARY OF EDI IMPLEMENTATION

This section has presented guidelines and recommendations for developing an EDI implementation strategy. The implementation guidelines and case examples are presented as a starting point for you to adapt to your particular circumstances.

The following section presents two specific applications of EDI: EDI for electronic payment and EDI in international trade. In addition, where EDI is going in the future is discussed.

IV

THE FUTURE OF EDI

12

EDI AND ELECTRONIC FUNDS TRANSFER

INTRODUCTION

Electronic data interchange is currently being used in many organizations for the transmission of all documents involved in the business cycle. EDI is used for everything from the transmission of a request for quotation by the buyer to the transmission of the invoice by the seller. However, some companies would like to see electronic transmission expanded even further. In the words of one banking official, "If every other aspect of the communications between companies is electronic—invoices, orders, and so on—a corporation won't want its payment information to be paper based."[1]

Due at least in part to EDI, interest in electronic payment systems, often referred to as electronic funds transfer, has been growing. Electronic funds transfer (EFT) is the electronic transfer of value between a company and its bank, or between two banks. While EDI and EFT are not the same, they are very closely related. They both require similar types of technology, as well as similar implementation strategies. They both require a high degree of trust and cooperation between trading partners. And they both offer the potential for significant savings and improved performance. Further, EDI has, in many cases, become the driving force behind EFT. According to James P. Witkins, Senior Vice President of Manufacturers Hanover Trust, EDI "is truly significant in terms of the effect it will have on payment systems evolution. EFT is becoming inseparable from EDI."[2]

This chapter presents an overview of EFT and its relationship to EDI. Payment methods are introduced and the various formats that can be used for EFT are discussed. EFT usage, benefits, barriers, and participants are also outlined. While EFT can be used for a variety of payments, the focus of this chapter is on corporate trade payments.

PAYMENT METHODS

This country's payment system transfers over one trillion dollars each day.[3] The three basic methods of payment transfer include coin and currency, paper-based methods such as checks and check-like instruments, and electronic transfer. While electronic transfer currently accounts for nearly 90 percent of all of the dollar value being transferred, electronic transfer accounts for less than 2 percent of all transactions. Corporate trade payments are one type of payments that account for a large portion of the paper-based transactions.

PAPER-BASED SYSTEMS

Paper-based payments include checks, drafts, and credit card drafts. Checks are the traditional methods for corporate trade payments. Approximately 40 billion checks are written each year, and of those nearly one-fourth are corporate trade payments.[4]

Advantages of Checks

The use of checks for corporate trade payments has a number of advantages. First, checks are a relatively low-cost way to transmit value, in terms of both processing and transmission costs. Bank charges for processing of corporate checks is low; and transmission of checks is done by the postal service at a nominal cost. Second, with the requirement for a signature on the check, and the capability of including multiple signatures, checks provide for authorization security.

Third, the check itself provides room for all needed information, and the check can easily be attached to a remittance advice if additional information must be provided. Fourth, the use of checks offers one additional benefit, which most companies consider to be significant—check float. As shown in Figure 12- 1, three types of float exist in payment by check.[5] The first type is mail float: the time it takes to get from the payer to the payee. The second type is processing float: the time it takes for the payee to process and deposit the check. The third type is clearing float: the time it takes for the bank to clear the check and for the funds to become good. Because a mailed check may take up to five days of mailing time and another one to eight days of processing time and clearing time, the payer retains the use of funds for a longer period of time (assuming that the payee accepts the mailed date as the payment date).

ELECTRONIC PAYMENT METHODS

For an electronic payment system to become a practical alternative to checks, the system must offer at least the same level of benefits as do checks. In other words,

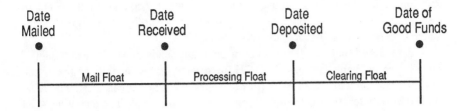

Figure 12-1   Check float.

the system must provide a low-cost, secure transfer method that provides for the transfer of both payment and additional information.

There are currently two major systems for making electronic payments: wire transfers and the automated clearing house. The automated clearing house (ACH) system was designed as an alternative to checks; the wire transfer system was designed primarily for moving large dollars in single payments.

Wire Transfers

Wire transfer systems were developed to allow for instantaneous transfers of a limited number of large dollar volume actions. Organizations traditionally use wire transfers when both speed and security are needed, for instance for cash concentration transfers. Wire transfers are made through two-way communication networks that permit confirmation of receipt and sender notification.[6]

Two major wire transfer systems used by U.S. banks are the Fedwire and SWIFT. Fedwire uses the Federal Reserve's communication system and reserve accounts held by all banks to allow for domestic corporate transfers. The Society for Worldwide Interbank Telecommunications (SWIFT) performs a similar function internationally.[7] Because the wire transfer systems were developed primarily to handle single-transaction, large dollar value transfers requiring same day handling, the wire transfer system is not a practical alternative to checks; and is not often used for repetitive corporate trade payments. The ACH, on the other hand, is designed to handle large-volume repetitive corporate trade payments.

Automated Clearing House

The automated clearing house was developed as a computer-based alternative to the paper-based check-clearing process. Under paper-based systems, checks are sorted by financial institution, and bundles of paper checks are exchanged among the various banks. Under ACH, electronic images of the checks are sorted and then the electronic records are exchanged.

The ACH replaces checks with a series of electronic images or impulses transmitted either over data links or by magnetic tapes or floppy disks. In general, participants in a clearing house use a common format for converting the check to electronic images and follow operating guidelines set up by the National Automated Clearing House Association (NACHA).

Under the ACH network the originating company sends an ACH file to its bank.[8] The originating bank can send the ACH file directly to the receiving bank or can combine the file with other ACH files and forward it to a local ACH. The local ACH then transfers the file to an ACH near the receiving bank. The receiving ACH sends the file to the receiving bank, which credits the receiver's account and sends the advice to the receiver.[8]

ACH Development

The ACH system was developed in the late 1960s due to a concern that the traditional check-clearing facilities would not be able to handle the increasing volume of checks in the future.[9] Realizing that some alternative method of check clearing was necessary, the San Francisco and Los Angeles Clearing House Associations created a joint committee to investigate paperless exchange. In 1970,

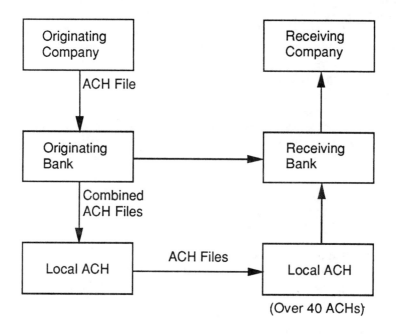

Figure 12-2   The ACH process.

ten California banks formed a committee on paperless exchange and developed software for the ACH to use for interbank paperless entry exchange. In 1972, the Federal Reserve Bank of San Francisco and the Los Angeles Branch began to offer the first automated, electronic, clearing house services.

During this time, efforts were underway in other parts of the country as well. The Federal Reserve Board also became involved. The Fed believed that it should take an active role in the clearing house process to ensure the "safety and soundness of the payments mechanism."[10] The Fed agreed to provide space, equipment, and management for the various ACHs because it believed that "electronic systems at the local level would create 'nodes' that the Federal Reserve could then link together through its communications network into a national electronic payments system."[11]

As the development of electronic exchange systems by local and regional ACHs grew, it became obvious that strong national coordination was necessary. In 1974 the National Automated Clearing House Association (NACHA) was formed to develop national standards and policy for electronic payment exchange, to conduct educational programs, and to provide technical assistance to local and regional ACHs.

The growth of ACHs progressed significantly in the mid-1970s. In 1975, 13 ACHs began operations. Also in 1975 the federal government began to use ACHs for direct deposit of Social Security payments. In September 1978 the Federal Reserve established electronic exchange between regions, thus establishing a nationwide automated clearing house system. Management of the ACH network is divided between NACHA and the Federal Reserve. NACHA, a confederation of the regional clearing house associations, performs marketing, policy making, and lobbying activities. Actual operating responsibility for the ACH network rests with the Federal Reserve.

ACH Requirements

Since the ACH system was designed primarily to replace a check-based system, ACH processing must provide all of the attributes of a check-based system if it is to be widely used. One of these attributes, which is particularly important in processing corporate trade payments, is its ability to transfer additional information (the payment advice if payer and the remittance advice if payee) along with the actual payment.

The remittance advice identifies the invoice or invoices being paid by the check and may reflect additional information such as discounts taken, freight adjustments, and other such information. When only one invoice is being paid, and the advice is short, the advice is usually connected to the check. When the payee receives the check, the advice is retained and the check is sent on to the payee's bank. However, in complex transactions where one check is being used to pay a number of different invoices, a computer printout of some kind is usually used as the payment advice. The check is attached to the printout and both are sent to the payee; or alternatively, a computer tape containing the advice records is forwarded to the payee.

The ability of the payment system to handle advice information and payments for multiple invoices is particularly important for corporate trade payments. In a recent survey of members of the National Corporate Cash Management Association, 75 percent of the respondents reported that they regularly pay more than one invoice with a single check; and 65 percent stated that they received checks for more than one invoice.[12]

A number of payment formats can be used through the ACH network. Some of the formats address the requirements necessary for corporate trade payments, and others do not.

ACH Formats

Cash Concentration or Disbursement (CCD)   From its initiation in 1974 until 1983, the ACH system provided for only one payment format, referred to as Cash Concentration or Disbursement (CCD). The CCD format permitted single payment transactions only, with a limited trailing record. The format for the electronic translation of the check consisted of only 94 total characters of information, with a maximum of 34 for advice information. Further, no standards existed for the formatting of the message within the 34 spaces allowed; thus, the advice information could not be processed automatically upon receipt.[13] With these limitations, it was obvious that the ACH system would not be extensively used for corporate trade payments because of the system's inability to handle advice information and the fact that it was limited to a single payment.

Cash Concentration or Disbursement plus Addendum (CCD+)   To accommodate more advice information, the CCD format was modified. One 80-character addendum was added to the CCD format. The new format was referred to as the Cash Concentration or Disbursement plus Addendum (CCD+) format.[12]

This format is currently used by the federal government for payment to vendors. However, although the CCD+ format does allow for additional information, it is still limited to a single payment. In 1984 a new ACH format was developed to significantly expand the information that could be transmitted with the payment.

Corporate Trade Payment (CTP)   The Corporate Trade Payment format allows a payer to include up to 4999 additional message records of 94 characters each for each payment. In this format, the payer "packs" the advice information into the additional records. The additional records, along with the payment transaction, are then sent through the ACH system. The receiving ACH passes along both the payment transaction and the additional records to the payee's bank. In this way, the payee could receive electronically the same information normally included in a paper-based payment advice.[15] It was expected that the introduction of the CTP format would significantly increase the use of ACHs for corporate trade payments, but this did not occur.

Two major factors contribute to the lack of interest in the CTP format. The first is the lack of a standard format for the message information. Just as the original ACH format contained no standard for the short advice message that was allowed, neither does the CTP format. In other words, the method of "packing" the advice information into the additional records varies from company to company. This means that the advice information cannot be automatically processed upon receipt.

The second major factor limiting the use of CTP is that few banks handle the CTP format. There is no established procedure for the banks to follow in passing the advice message onto payees. As a result, banks tend to be generally inconsistent in both willingness and ability to pass the information along. In other words, although there is room for advice information with the CTP format, there is a chance that the payee may not readily receive the information and if the information is received, it cannot be automatically processed. In 1987 a new ACH format was introduced that provides a standard format for advice messages.

Corporate Trade Exchange (CTX)   The Corporate Trade Exchange (CTX) format is a variable length format that supports the ANSI X12 standard for remittance advice. In essence, the CTX format provides an electronic envelope for the ANSI X12 820 Payment Order/Remittance Advice. This means that companies receiving electronic payments in CTX formats through ACHs can automatically process the advice information through their EDI systems.[16]

The development of the CTX format means that the ACH is now an appropriate alternative to checks for corporate trade payments. With the CTX format, EFT advice information can now be transmitted through EDI.

EXAMPLES OF EFT

Given the different ACH formats that are available, there are a number of ways EDI/EFT can be done. The examples following show the various ways ACH formats can be used in conjunction with X12 formats to transfer payment and advice information.

U.S. Treasury

In 1987 the U.S. Treasury launched an effort to convert from paper checks to electronic payments for federal government vendor payments. As of late 1988 the agency was electronically processing over 1.5 million vendor payments annually. The agency hopes to increase EFT to include all of the 77 million payments made to vendors annually. The agency estimates that with full implementation of EFT, over $20 million will be saved annually.[17]

The program, referred to as Vendors Express, uses the CCD+ format with the addendum information structured, in part, in the X12 820 format. The combined format is used to pay single invoices.

According to Charles Schwan of the Financial Management Service of the Treasury Department, "the addenda record is set up to be a very simple process. The record code and the addendum code are standard codes. They just tell the financial institution that there is information here that has to be passed on, has to be read. The second identifier . . . is from X12.4 [remittance]. We use the same separator and common data elements."[18]

Although the program currently uses only the CCD+ format, it is expected that other formats will also be used. According to Schwan, "Our goal is to convert the government's vendor payments to electronics, and we believe that it can be done by using all of those formats [CTX, CTP, CCD], not using just one."[19]

Department of Defense (DOD)

Each year the DOD makes approximately 26.3 million payments to over 300,000 vendors. These payments are made directly from DOD rather than through the Treasury Department. In order to "streamline its disbursement operations, enhance productivity, and to improve relations with its vendors," the DOD is exploring the use of EFT.[20] Another reason why DOD is investigating EFT is that many vendors have asked to be paid electronically. Consistent with the experiences of industry, one of the primary concerns the DOD has in implementing EFT is "the handling of the nonfinancial data," according to one DOD official.[21] Because of this, the agency is favoring the use of the CTX standard. This standard is preferred because many of the agency's payments require advice information applicable to multiple invoices.

Further, the selection of the CTX format also supports the DOD's EDI efforts. According to Ronald Adolphi, "The DOD Comptroller will not pursue EFT in isolation of the various EDI applications being studied by other DOD elements."[22] Criteria used in the selection of the EFT format included that it is supported by NACHA and the Federal Reserve Board, that it will handle multiple invoices, that it allows for encryption of data, and that it has EDI linkages.

Industry Use of EFT

In addition to the EFT initiatives established by the government, industry has also embraced EFT. Substantial EFT efforts are underway in entire industries, as well as by individual corporations.

Oil Industry   The American Petroleum Institute, an industry action group for the oil industry, has outlined what it is calling Preferred Payment Procedures, which are recommended for anyone in the industry implementing EDI. The procedures have been established to meet the criteria that (1) a single payment may cover multiple invoices, (2) the remittance advice must accompany the payment, and (3) the process will be float neutral. These procedures recommend that the ANSI X12 standards and the ACH CTX format be used for all payments. Under the procedures, the vendor will send an ANSI X12 810 invoice to the buyer's mailbox at the third party network. The buyer will send an ANSI X12 820 payment order/remittance advice to its originating bank, which in turn will either send the 820 through the ACH using the CTX format, or will send the 820 directly to another participating bank. The receiving bank will either get an 820 or a CTX transaction, and will then translate that into the format requested by the seller.[23]

General Motors   General Motors is currently one of the strongest corporate users of EFT. GM has an arrangement with six core banks through which it initiates electronic payments to its suppliers. Approximately 1600 suppliers are currently receiving nearly 5000 payments monthly, representing $425 million, from 13 GM divisions. The goal of the company is to be completely electronic on the payment side by 1990.[24]

As shown in Figure 12-3, GM has arranged with six core banks to handle its payments to suppliers.[25] Each participating bank handles designated GM divisions who forward payment information to their assigned banks in X12 820 format. If the payee uses the same bank as the division forwarding the payment, the supplier's account is credited and the bank delivers a payment advice in X12, paper, or other format. If the payee uses one of the other six banks, the payment information is directly transferred between the two banks and the advice is delivered in any of the methods mentioned above. If the payee uses a nonparticipating bank, the GM bank transmits the payment via the ACH in CCD format, or via CTX or CTP format to the payee's bank.[26]

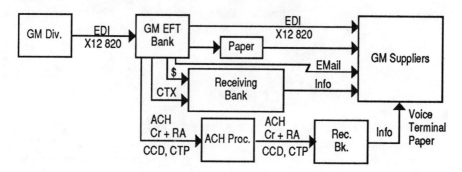

Figure 12-3   GM's payment system.

General Electric   General Electric is another company active in the electronic payments arena, on both the receiving and the disbursement side. GE is actively pursuing EFT as an extension of its EDI activities. According to a GE executive, "GE made a corporate commitment to EDI for all standard business transactions, including electronic payments."[27]

On the disbursement side, GE uses the ANSI X12 820 along with a cash concentration or disbursement (CCD) as the format for transmissions to vendors. One of the major reasons for the selection of the 820 format was its compatibility with other EDI transactions. Under the system, the 820 will be used as the payment advice, with the CCD being used as the payment transaction. GE will send the payments through a third party network, GE Information Services, which will convert the 820s into the vendor's accounts receivable format.

On the receiving side, GE receives the largest percentage of its payments through pre-authorized direct debit, with over 8000 commercial customers and 34,000 consumers paying through an ACH debit system. For its remaining customers, GE has established a system designed to accept electronic remittance advices. The advices are used to create the ACH CCD debit that transfers money from the customer's account to GE's account on the agreed to settlement date.[28]

R. J. Reynolds   R. J. Reynolds (RJR) is also extensively using EFT. Its EFT program was introduced in 1986 and uses the CCD format, which was the only one widely available at that time.

Currently over 650 accounts representing more than 40 percent of sales are being collected through EFT. Under the program, a trading partner signs a contract giving RJR the authority to initiate debit or credit transactions against the partner's account. Under the system, RJR debits the customer's account for the payment amount on the date of delivery of the product to the customer's warehouse. The early payment is offset by a half-point discount provided by RJR. The system is flexible enough to allow customers to decide, order by order, if the EFT transaction will occur on the date of delivery. At the time of order placement, the customer has the option of choosing to accept the discount and authorizing early payment or not. According to one report, "EFT has reduced the company's [RJR] accounts receivable balance at least 25 percent, while generating an additional corresponding cash flow increase."[29]

EFT PLAYERS

The examples above show the various types of EFT payment systems. The examples indicate that, at this point, no one ACH format is dominant. However a recent survey by Phoenix-Hecht on corporate EFT preferences indicated that 21 percent of those questioned preferred the CTX/X12 format, with 6 percent preferring CCD, and 2 percent preferring CTP. (The largest percentage of respondents was unfamiliar with any of the formats.)[31]

The examples also show that EFT can be done in a number of different ways, using a number of different players. As the use of EDI grows, there will be a need for someone to take on the responsibility of translating information between the various formats. This task is similar to the functions currently performed by third party networks in translating information back and forth between EDI format and company-specific format. Two likely candidates for playing this role are the banks themselves and EDI third party networks.

Banks in EFT

While most banks are waiting to enter the EFT/EDI arena, a number of banks have been very aggressive in offering EDI-related services to customers. One such bank is the National Bank of Detroit (NBD). NBD has put together a system that allows customers to initiate and/or receive electronic payments and the remittance advice information in any format desired by the customer. The system is designed to support all ACH formats, ANSI X12 formats, and others such as the Bank Administration Institute (BAI) format (used primarily in lockbox operations). For instance, under this system a customer receiving ANSI X12 payments from General Motors, CTP payments from Sears, and CCD+ payments from the federal government would receive electronic transmissions detailing all of the payments and advices in ANSI format, in BAI format, or in a customized format.[31]

Banks are beginning to realize that there is a need to offer EDI services. In the words of Sabra McConnell, Vice President and Product Line Manager for EFT at Mellon Bank, "... companies understand that EDI can reduce their operating costs, and have asked their customers and suppliers to develop EDI applications. If we [banks] don't, they will take their business to a bank which will."[32]

Value Added Networks in EFT

Value added networks are also stepping up to perform EFT functions. With the development of the X12 compatible CTX format, EDI third party networks are finding that they can play a significant role in EFT. In other words, the VAN can act as a clearing house for both EDI and EFT messages, thus making it potentially possible for VAN customers to communicate directly only with a VAN, rather than also communicating with a bank.

BENEFITS OF EFT

Cost Savings

Electronic payment offers a number of significant benefits. One substantial benefit of EFT is cost reduction. On the receiving side, electronic payments can save between 75 cents and $5 per item, compared to a check system. Also, EDI/EFT can save an additional $1 to $2.50 per item in internal applications such as matching receivables against outstanding invoices.[33] On the disbursement side, savings usually aren't as large but can still be significant. Estimates of per item savings on the disbursement side usually range between 60 and 80 cents.[34]

Improved Cash Management

In addition to reducing costs, EFT also improves cash management. Electronic payments remove payment timing uncertainty and ensure funds availability. With EFT both parties know the exact date on which funds will transfer from one account to the other. This information can improve cash management practices for the payer and the payee.

Reduction in Problems

The use of EFT offers additional benefits as well. Lost or stolen checks are eliminated with EFT. Questions on the settlement date when a prompt payment discount is taken are also eliminated.

While EFT offers significant benefits, its use is still limited. There are a number of obstacles to electronic payments which will need to be overcome if EFT usage is to grow significantly.

BARRIERS TO EFT

Incompatibility with EDI

In a recent study conducted for the Financial Executives Research Foundation, corporate financial managers were asked what factors would make them reluctant to either disburse or receive through the ACH system.[35] The most important reason for not using the ACH network for disbursements was the inability to transmit data in ANSI format. This was also expressed as a concern on the receiving side of EFT.

Data Security

The lack of data encryption and authentication capability was also considered to be a significant barrier for both disbursement and receipt of EFT. In addition, the inability of the ACH system to automatically integrate payment data with accounts receivable systems was considered a problem with the ACH network.

EDI applications, along with the use of the CTX format through the ACH network, are eliminating a number of these barriers. With EDI, data encryption and authentication are possible. Further, a functional acknowledgment confirming receipt of payment is provided. The ACH CTX format allows for the remittance information to be communicated in standard format, thus providing for a link to other applications, such as accounts receivables. The growing use of EDI, along with the CTX format, is helping to break down these EFT barriers; however, others still exist.

Legality of EFT Payments

One concern of many financial managers is that electronic payments are not currently covered by either the Uniform Commercial Code or by a body of case law. Applicable sections of the UCC are currently under review with revisions expected within 12 months. In the meantime, the NACHA has developed guidelines for contract language that can be used between trading partners using the ACH network. The guidelines cover the rights, responsibilities, and liabilities of parties involved in ACH payments.[36]

Loss of Float Due to EFT

Many cash managers have expressed a fear that the use of EFT will result in a loss of cash float. As discussed in the earlier chapter on overcoming EDI barriers, this concern can be handled through an adjustment in timing or through negotiation of payment terms.

Capability of Banks to Perform EFT

Another barrier that will take time to overcome is the limited number of banks currently set up to handle EDI/EFT transactions. Banks participating in the ACH network are only required to handle the CCD format. While a number of banks have been aggressive in this area, others are taking more of a "wait and see" attitude. To encourage bank participation in electronic payments for corporate trade, the NACHA has developed a program under which banks will be tested for their ability to receive and process CTX payments. A list of CTX-capable banks will be maintained and published by NACHA.[37]

THE FUTURE OF EDI/EFT

Although a number of barriers to EFT exist, the future for EFT looks promising. Based upon a 1988 survey of over 200 financial managers in over 24 major U.S. industries, EDI Research, Inc., has concluded that EDI/EFT is here to stay.[38] The study showed that 19 percent of firms with sales between $100 million and $500 million annually (middle market firms), and 34 percent of firms with sales greater than $500 million annually (large firms) are already using EDI. In addition, nearly

42 percent of the middle market companies are currently using the ACH network, while 55 percent of the larger market companies are using the ACH.

Another survey conducted by *American Banker* found similar results.[39] According to telephone surveys conducted with 413 corporate treasurers of companies with at least $10 million in annual sales, electronic cash management services, including EDI, are becoming more important to corporate finance officers. One-third of the treasurers named electronic services as the most important financial service for the coming years, with a large number specifically referring to EDI capability. A separate study of nearly 500 treasurers showed that 44 percent expressed some interest in receiving electronic payments and nearly one-third were interested in sending electronic payments.[40]

RELATIONSHIP OF EDI AND EFT

Obviously, electronic funds transfer can be done without EDI. The wire transfer system and all payments made through the ACH system, regardless of format used, are electronic payments. However, many of the significant benefits of electronic payments are not realized unless EFT is combined with EDI.

According to James Witkins of Manufacturers Hanover Trust, "in some cases EFT is pushing EDI, but in most cases EDI is driving EFT."[41] This belief is shared by Philip C. Ahwesh, Assistant Vice President and Senior Automated Clearing House Manager of Mellon Bank. Ahwesh states that, "EDI/EFT generally serves as a complement to an overall EDI strategy and not as a stand-alone or lead service."[42] Not only do EDI and EFT work together to provide significant benefits, they must be used together if U.S. industry is to remain competitive in the global marketplace. According to Robert H. Harvey, GM's Director of Worldwide Banking and U.S. Cash Management, General Motors believes that, "the application of EFT and EDI in the corporate trade cycle must be an integral part of American business, if it is to survive."[43]

SUMMARY

Electronic Funds Transfer is a logical extension for those companies involved in EDI. The investment in technology, the learning obtained, and the implementation procedures from the EDI effort will all transfer over to EFT applications. So any company already doing EDI has a headstart on EFT.

EDI/EFT will complete the "paperless" process. It is the final step in improving and managing the entire business transaction cycle.

13

INTERNATIONAL EDI

INTRODUCTION

Activity in electronic data interchange is not limited to just the United States. EDI efforts are underway in nearly all industrial sectors of the world. According to Jack Shaw of EDI Strategies, Inc., "The British like to note that, on a per-capita basis, they have more companies using EDI than the United States. Canada, western Europe, Japan, and the Pacific rim nations are only a year or two behind."[1] In addition, EDI efforts are also underway in the Soviet Union and eastern Europe.

This chapter presents an overview of international EDI activities beginning with a discussion of the importance of international EDI. The standards used for international communications are also discussed. Finally, some general and some specific applications of EDI on an international basis are presented.

IMPORTANCE OF INTERNATIONAL EDI

As companies worldwide continue to compete on a global basis, the importance of EDI in international trade will increase. According to John Naisbitt, author of *Megatrends*, "The global information economy of the future will rest on a global network and EDI will be behind this."[2]

Documentation Costs

EDI will become a significant factor in international trade for a number of reasons. First, the sheer volume and cost of processing international paperwork will cause companies in all countries to move toward EDI. International paperwork costs have been estimated to be as high as $140 billion out of $2 trillion in international trade. These costs alone "will lead to a single worldwide network" in five years, according to Shaw, who predicts that the network will "consist of at least 25 different national and international EDI network service providers exchanging data on a worldwide basis."[3]

Trade Barriers

Second, EDI is seen as a way of overcoming traditional barriers to international trade. According to Hak Jung Lee, senior manager for the VAN Development Group of the Data Communications Corporation of Korea, "as long as good business communications channels can be maintained, EDI will facilitate the flow of goods back and forth [between international countries]."[4] He further suggests that "EDI trading partners will be able to cut through cultural, language, and bureaucratic barriers that can (and do) inhibit the distribution of products and services."[5]

Global Competition

Global competition is another factor leading to increased importance of EDI. In recent years companies in numerous countries have begun to feel the impact of "foreign competition." This increased competitiveness has led to a search for ways to improve productivity, and in many cases that has led to EDI. For instance, according to Etienne Dreyfous, chair of the United Nations' Group of Experts, "EDI is seen in Europe not just as a convenient way of replacing paper . . . it is seen as a new form of management."[6] And in the Far East, "competition among Hong Kong, Singapore, and other Pacific rim countries has created peer pressure to get involved in EDI," says another international EDI representative.[7]

International EDI is growing in importance and also growing in use. According to a 1988 INPUT report, "U.S. involvement in international EDI is expected to grow from $2.5 million in 1988 to $220 million in 1992, representing an annual growth rate of 147 percent."[8] Further, of the 400,000 companies expected to be using EDI by 1995, 35 percent will be European and 15 percent will be Pacific rim companies, with the remaining being U.S. companies.[9]

INTERNATIONAL STANDARDS

The format standard used in international EDI is EDIFACT, EDI for Administration, Commerce, and Transport. In essence, EDIFACT is a combination of the ANSI X12 standards and the Trade Data Interchange standards developed in Great Britain and used throughout Europe. As shown in Figure 13-1, EDIFACT standards development is the responsibility of two groups. The syntax and the data dictionary are the responsibility of the International Standards Organization. The development of standards and the message registration is the responsibility of the United

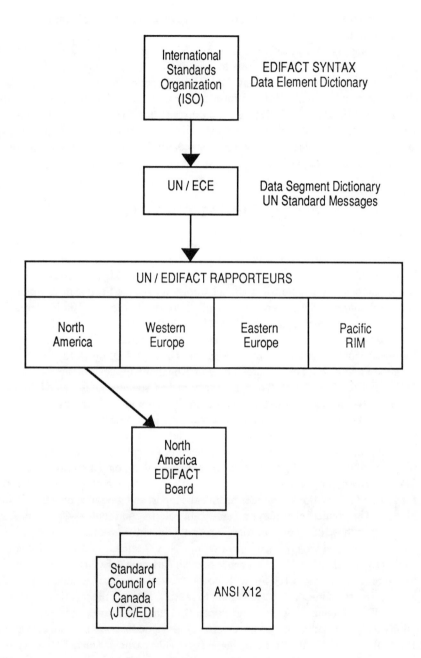

Figure 13-1   International standards development.

Nations Economic Commission for Europe. Western Europe, Eastern Europe, North America, and the Pacific rim currently have representatives in the standards-setting bodies.

According to Dennis McGinnis, a former North American representative, "It is important for North American users to keep abreast of international standards."[10] In this country EDI standards have shifted from company- or industry-specific formats to more general, common formats; the same is happening on the international scene. In other words, X12 is becoming, in effect, a subset of the EDIFACT standard, with EDIFACT providing all of the X12 data requirements.[11] According to McGinnis, a movement from the X12 standard to the EDIFACT standard by a user will "require some effort" but should not be extremely traumatic.[12]

INTERNATIONAL EDI ACTIVITY

As mentioned earlier, EDI activity is expanding in all corners of the globe. In Europe, EDI is seen as a way of enhancing the movement toward a Unified European Community by 1992. According to a statement by Karl-Heinz Narjes, commissioner responsible for high technology within the European community, "new technological developments are leading to cross-border information services, such as EDI, which play an increasingly important role in our economic competitiveness."[13] Estimates by a British research firm indicate that 80 percent of European retailers will be conducting business through EDI by 1992.[14]

In the Pacific rim, both Hong Kong and Singapore are developing nationwide EDI networks. The Hong Kong government has stated that its TRADELINK project will "link up the country's entire trading community."[15] In Japan, over 200 private telecommunications and EDI service companies have entered the market to meet the rising demand for intercompany electronic communications.[16]

In Canada, membership in the EDI Council of Canada has soared over the last two years. "Currently it [the council] is almost growing out of control" reported Marshall Spence, president of the council.[17] The council, which acts as a "funnel" for 18 trade associations, provides technical support and guidance on EDI-related matters. The council also plays a significant role in coordinating Canadian EDI efforts with those of other countries, especially the United States.

A national EDI group is being formed in New Zealand, and an EDI council similar to Canada's has recently been formed in Australia.[18] Even the Soviet Union has embraced EDI. Over 100 Soviet Bloc transportation executives attended a 1988 shipping meeting in London. According to INPUT, "Before the meeting was over, the EDIFLOT concept was being worked on, and executives representing the ministries of air, land, rail, and ocean travel all signed a communiqué endorsing UN/EDIFACT."[19] INPUT predicts that Eastern Bloc participation in EDI will grow rapidly once central planners give the go-ahead.

These brief examples show the widespread use of EDI internationally. Discussed below are three detailed examples of how EDI is currently being used on an international basis. The examples were selected to show the diversity of current international EDI efforts.

SPECIFIC EXAMPLES OF INTERNATIONAL EDI

U.S. Customs

In February of 1988 the U.S. Customs Service announced that it endorsed the use of EDIFACT for international EDI. Currently, Customs is piloting EDI tests with three U.S.-based multinational firms. Texas Instruments, Inc., ICI Americas, Inc., and North American Philips Corporation are all testing the use of the EDIFACT standard.[20]

The initial phase of the pilot involves the transmission of messages only (no cargo) to the Customs Service for a period of 90 days. In the pilot test, the three companies are using EDIFACT for only a limited number of items, coming in through a limited number of ports. Texas Instruments, for instance, is testing EDIFACT with the port of Houston on shipments of foreign-made semiconductors. North American Philips is testing EDIFACT on shipments of compact disks arriving in New York, while ICI is doing the test for chemicals arriving in Charleston, SC.

Under the test, the three companies will "electronically transmit to the Customs Service all of the paperwork and accompanying invoices needed for importing goods. This information will be sent in a format called a Customs Declaration Message, which is defined by EDIFACT."[21]

It is hoped that the use of EDIFACT will eliminate the costly delays caused by the large volume of paperwork required on imported items. Typically, an importer sends a Customs Declaration Message to the port three or four days prior to expected arrival of the shipment. When the goods actually arrive, the customs inspector prints out a listing showing the contents of the shipments and the corresponding tariffs. Without EDI, importers usually have to manually fill out many long documents specifying the cargo and provide inspectors with copies of all of the invoices. Often this required special delivery of documents by couriers. Having the information delivered electronically should eliminate time, work, and errors.

According to Karen Hiatt, director of the commercial services division of the Customs Service, the Customs Service believes that "EDIFACT will greatly ease the enormous barriers to trade found in customs paperwork and thus help lubricate the world economy."[22]

Because the test is using the international standard, it is expected to gain worldwide attention. Other EDI users throughout the world are likely to view this as the first real test of EDIFACT.

Canadian-Korean Pilot

Currently, international EDI is being conducted between buyers in Canada and sellers in South Korea. In a pilot test, Sears Canada is sending electronic purchase orders to South Korean suppliers, who are responding with acknowledgments and advance shipping notices. Upon receipt of the goods, Sears will acknowledge electronically and will also send electronic invoices. The second stage of the pilot will include the use of EDI to clear goods through both Korean and Canadian customs. Currently, all transactions will be conducted using the ANSI X12 standards.[23]

The international EDI effort was initiated by the Data Communications Corporation of Korea (DACOM) which is partially owned by the Korean Government.[24] According to Hak Jung Lee, a senior EDI manager for DACOM, the company first became aware of EDI in 1985, and since that time has been actively pursuing EDI efforts. The company has been aggressive in introducing "full scale, intercorporate networks to Korean and international clients."[25] According to Lee, by 1986 DACOM recognized EDI as a way to "solve the data communications needs in Korea" and as a "vital element for the enhancement of [Korean] industry's competitiveness."[26]

Having decided that EDI offered significant potential, DACOM began to investigate ways to begin an international EDI effort. The company sent representatives to both European and North American EDI meetings and gatherings. After reviewing activities both in Europe and in North America, DACOM decided to approach North American companies about establishing an EDI relationship using the ANSI standards.

DACOM chose to begin EDI on an international basis, rather than domestically, for two major reasons. First the Koreans believed that they could take advantage of the learning of the North American trading partner. Second, DACOM realized that there would need to be "substantial adjustment to existing standards to accommodate Korean applications."[27] The company also decided that performing a pilot test with a Canadian firm would allow DACOM to "learn how Canada learned from the United States." DACOM decided to go with the ANSI standards rather than EDIFACT because ANSI "currently exists and is operational."[28]

Lee believes that it is essential that Korea become involved in EDI efforts. He feels that the country will lose its competitiveness if it doesn't embrace EDI. "I have been telling Korean industry that although our economy has been performing well in the international arena, within five years if we do not develop EDI relationships with our international partners, it could begin to cost us. U.S. companies could impose a surcharge for transacting business on a paper-based system, which would destroy our competitive edge."[29]

This truly international EDI effort should have a number of important impacts on the countries involved, as well as all others involved in international EDI. An international EDI network should allow U.S. trading partners to differentiate products and services on the international market, just as is now done in the domestic market. For Korea the advantage of the EDI system is increased competitiveness. According to Lee, Korea feels that if they "implement EDI faster than Japan does, we can have a competitive edge over Japan."[30]

The Canadian-Korean EDI effort also represents a number of important firsts in the EDI world. According to Ralph Notto, President of EDI, Inc., as quoted in an exclusive interview with *EDI News*:[31]

"It is the first time standards will be used in Korea."

"This will be the first international EDI relationship of its kind."

"It is the first time that X12 standards will be used outside of North America."

"It is the first time that EDI is used in a bilingual and cross-cultural environment."

European Transportation EDI

In the fall of 1988 shipowners, shippers, freight forwarders, and exporters from all areas of western Europe began a pilot test of EDI transmission of transportation data across international borders. The EDI project, referred to as COST-306, is "aimed at achieving standardization at the West European level that eventually will form the basis for a worldwide electronic transmission system."[32] Major backers of the project include Europe's two biggest ports, the European Railway Federation, the European Customs Union, forwarding associations in France and West Germany, and Scandinavian companies. According to Henk C. van Maaren, project manager, it is "the first serious attempt to transcend industry barriers."[33]

The COST-306 project is based upon the EDIFACT syntax, using the U.N./Economic Commission of Europe and the U.N./Trade Data Elements Directory. The project will use electronic transmissions of "ordering of transport, invoicing, and reporting."[34]

The above examples indicate that international EDI is being performed and is doing well. However, a number of barriers are often encountered in international EDI.

BARRIERS TO INTERNATIONAL EDI

In addition to the barriers faced in implementing any EDI effort, international EDI faces additional hurdles. First, not all international trade agencies are believers in

EDI or in EDIFACT. For instance, according to *EDI News*, "the Commerce Department's Census Bureau data collection process is not compatible with the customs agencies' systems, nor is it consistent with any of the ANSI X12 or EDIFACT standards."[35]

Second, overseas telephone and mail agencies have often placed restrictions on EDI networks. Because these agencies have a vested interest in promoting the use of public rather than private networks, they are often reluctant to allow private networks.

Third, many countries have laws that may restrict EDI operations. For instance, the Canadian-Korean effort could not have been started prior to April of 1987. Before that time companies in Korea could only do intracompany EDI; intercompany EDI was prohibited.[36]

Fourth, in addition to the problem of numerous different standards on the international side (just as there are a number of different families of standards domestically), there is also the problem of different cultures, languages, and business practices.

SUMMARY

International EDI efforts have been initiated in a number of different areas and for a number of different applications. Over the long term the international market is going to demand one international EDI standard—and it appears that the standard will be EDIFACT. Even if your company is not directly involved in international activity it is wise to be aware of what is happening with international EDI. In the words of Dennis McGinnis, "Everyone is impacted by international trade in some way . . . [so] we all have to remain knowledgeable of the international requirements relevant to our business."[37]

14

THE FUTURE OF EDI

INTRODUCTION

Where is Electronic Data Interchange headed? Up and out and in! EDI is headed "up" in terms of volume of usage. It is headed "out" in terms of applications of usage. It is headed "in" in terms of integration with other management concepts and technologies. This chapter provides specific examples of each of these areas of growth. Also discussed in this chapter is how management can continue to gain a competitive advantage from EDI even when it reaches the point where "everybody is doing it."

GROWTH IN VOLUME

Exponential growth is expected in EDI usage in the next few years. It is predicted that by 1993 over 70 percent of U.S. firms will be making *significant* use of EDI.[1] By 1995, over 400,000 companies worldwide will be communicating electronically.[2] The growth is expected to come from a number of directions.

Additional Trading Partners

First, current EDI users will be adding more trading partners. According to studies by EDI Research, Inc., current EDI users plan to at least double their number of trading partners, each year over the next three years.[3] Further, many large U.S. corporations are still in the pilot stage of implementation, testing EDI transactions with a limited number of selected suppliers or customers. Once these companies are satisfied with pilot results, they are likely to begin fast, widespread expansion.

Additional Industries

A second source of growth will come from the entry of new industries into the EDI arena. While a number of industries have been involved in EDI for a long while, some are just beginning to take strong action toward EDI. For instance, the petroleum industry established an EDI action group, for the first time, in mid-1988. Endorsement and encouragement of an industry action group has been shown in the past to be a significant stimulus to EDI activity by individual companies within the industry.

Additional Countries

A third source of growth in EDI volume will come from the international arena. The United States is currently ahead of all other countries in terms of level of EDI use. However, other areas of the world are beginning to catch up. Major EDI efforts are underway in Canada, western Europe, the Pacific rim, and the Soviet Bloc, as well as in other parts of the world.

Summary of Growth in Volume

All of these factors are contributing to the growth of EDI. Taken together these factors suggest that EDI volume will expand significantly for a sustained period. One estimate places the annual growth rate of EDI worldwide at about 88 percent a year over the next three years.[4]

GROWTH IN APPLICATIONS

EDI is also going to expand "out." In other words, new and different applications of EDI will be used. Currently, EDI is used for the communication of standard business documentation in a structured format. The communication is done using EDI standards and EDI networks. However, much of what is communicated in business does not fit that category.

Electronic mail, voice imaging, and videotext are all methods currently being used to some degree for business communications. It is expected that EDI technology will eventually expand to allow for the incorporation of such communications methods.

While EDI has not reached the point of incorporating all such techniques, some activity is already underway that expands the use of EDI beyond standard, structured communications. For instance, current work is being done to integrate the electronic mail standard X.400 into EDI networks. And other activity is underway to expand EDI usage to include free form information. Two specific applications in this area demonstrate EDI's potential.

CAD/CAM

Computer Aided Design/Computer Aided Manufacturing (CAD/CAM) is becoming a critical component of many manufacturing activities. Obviously the ability to send engineering drawings, specifications, and graphics between trading partners is essential to CAD/CAM.

As currently structured, EDI does not provide for the communication of drawings or graphics, since these do not fit a standard structured format. However, the expansion of EDI to incorporate such items appears to be underway.

At least one software supplier has announced that its EDI software can be used for the transmission of engineering drawings and graphics in CAD/CAM format. Supply Tech's microcomputer software STX12™ has the capability of transmitting CAD/CAM files between EDI trading partners.[5] A special data segment is included in the EDI transmission. The data segment identifies how many bytes of non-EDI information follow. Trading partners agree in advance on the format of the non-EDI data. When the computer reaches the special segment, it "sends the specified number of bytes transparently and then resumes normal EDI transmissions."[6]

Other activity is also underway in the CAD/CAM–EDI area. The X12 Product Data Project Team is currently working on developing a specific transaction set for the transmission of graphics data. According to Mike Gerus, chairman of the project team, "We're trying to make a transaction set that lets you move all the information you need to make a quote or build a database for design engineers." According to Gerus, the transaction set will "fit into the X12 environment, but not necessarily in the X12 format."[7]

This example shows how EDI is being expanded to new applications. Graphics are not what EDI was designed for. However, EDI users and groups have realized that expansion beyond the original foundation is necessary. Expansion to cover graphics applications is particularly important because it offers a significant potential for increased EDI use. First, it should help increase the use of EDI in industries that are heavily dependent upon the use of graphics and CAD/CAM, such as the aerospace and electronics industries and the federal government. Second, the transmission of graphics through EDI could possibly provide a way for documents to have a "real" signature. This will particularly help the spread of EDI in international trade, since in many cases a document must have a signature in order to be valid.

Product Catalogs

Another example of the expansion of EDI technology beyond its original intent is in the retail industry. Product catalogs are an essential part of purchasing in the retail industry and communicating the catalog item descriptions has always been a problem in the industry.

The average retailer normally selects items from over 450,000 possible options, taking into account different vendors, different styles, colors, sizes, etc.[8] To better manage these items, the retail industry has begun to use the Universal Product Code (UPC). The UPC is a unique identifier for each item. Although the use of the UPC helps to better manage items, the retail industry still needed some way for a retailer to have convenient access to all of the 450,000 likely UPCs.

According to James L. Lovejoy, Director of Quick Response for IBM, the retail industry had considered a number of options for providing UPC information to retailers. Paper catalogs, bar codes on shipping advices, magnetic tape, and direct exchange between the vendor and the retailer were considered. However, while "every one of these solutions is viable at low volume . . . high volumes pose the challenge."[9]

The retail industry found the answer to its challenge in EDI. The retail industry is planning to use the EDI network, specifically value added networks, as a central database for product information. Under this system the vendor would transmit UPC catalog information to the VAN. As needed, a retailer can "choose one or many vendors' catalogs to work with via a series of interactive screens."[10] When the retailer has made a selection of catalog information, the information can be downloaded from the VAN to the retailer's computer for use in the retailer's application systems and for transmittal via EDI.

This example shows how EDI applications have been expanded to include new types of information. Although the catalog information is not being transmitted via EDI, the technology of EDI allows the UPC electronic catalog system to be used. EDI usage will not only grow as new applications of the technology are found, it will also grow due to the integration of EDI technology with other forms of systems.

GROWTH THROUGH INTEGRATION

The use of EDI is also going to grow inward. As companies become familiar with EDI and become comfortable with its use, they are finding innovative ways to integrate EDI with their existing systems and with other technologies. Numerous examples can be found where companies, and entire industries, have integrated EDI to the point where it is much more than just a way of exchanging documentation between trading partners. Two industries that have been particularly aggressive in integrating EDI into internal operations are the automotive industry and the retailing industry.

JIT through EDI in the Automotive Industry

One of the major reasons behind implementing EDI in the automotive industry was to improve the operations of just-in-time (JIT) systems. Because JIT calls for frequent and rapid delivery of items, a method of rapid and accurate communication was also needed. EDI provided this communications ability. Numerous JIT users, in the auto industry as well as in other industries, have stated that JIT is very difficult to do without EDI. Now that EDI has become an accepted and fairly standard method of communication within the auto industry, more efforts are being undertaken to closely integrate EDI within internal systems, including JIT scheduling and information systems. One example of how EDI is being effectively integrated with internal operations to make JIT work is Chrysler's "fast-batch" operation.[11]

Chrysler's Fast-Batch

Chrysler has so closely integrated its EDI system with its JIT system that it has modified the EDI system to be more responsive to the JIT schedule. The modification has made the EDI system closely resemble an interactive system, rather than the batch system that it is.

Because the JIT operation involves shipping parts to the production line only as they are needed, rapid processing of a vendor's shipping notice becomes critical to the success of JIT. Further, accuracy in the ship notice is also important.

According to one EDI source, "If a shipping notice contains an incorrect part number, and the mistake isn't corrected promptly, the wrong parts could arrive at a plant, causing production difficulties. Or the right parts might arrive, but because they carried a shipping notice with a wrong number, no one would know."[12]

Under the original EDI arrangement between Chrysler and its suppliers, suppliers would dial-in to Chrysler's mailbox and deposit a ship notice. Chrysler would retrieve the ship notice, and if there was an error, would send a return message back to the supplier's electronic mailbox. However, since in most cases mailboxes were checked only once a day, the supplier did not realize that there was a problem until the next day.

With fast-batch, the supplier's computer forwards a ship notice to Chrysler and then remains on-line for up to three minutes while the ship notice is reviewed for accuracy. If there is an error, Chrysler's computer immediately notifies the supplier's computer. According to James R. Oravec, an AIAG director, the system sets into motion a series of events that ensure proper product identification by the time the shipment has arrived. Chrysler has found that most of the errors have been incorrect information on the ship notice rather than incorrect shipments.[13]

While this is not a completely interactive system, it does show how EDI can be modified and be integrated into existing systems to provided additional benefits. Another automotive company that has integrated EDI into other internal systems is Ford.

Ford's CMMS

Ford Motor Company has initiated a new program designed to improve operational efficiency. The program, which is called Common Manufacturing Management

Systems (CMMS) integrates a number of information collection and management technologies, including EDI.[14] The program consists of eight core modules, including a master file and bill of materials, manufacturing planning, shop floor scheduling, supplier releasing, receiving, inventory control, shipping, and nonproduction materials.

Plans call to have a direct link between the CMMS program and four separate EDI transaction sets. In other words, as an EDI transaction set is received, the CMMS modules will be automatically updated. Ford says that the "new CMMS initiative is the most complex material management systems effort ever undertaken by a company in the automotive industry."[15]

Ford's integration of EDI into this complex and innovative system shows how EDI's use can be expanded through integration with other systems. Another industry that has extensively linked EDI with other systems is the retailing industry.

Quick Response in Retailing   The retailing industry has done such a good job in integrating EDI with other technologies that its use has been given a new name. Quick Response in the retailing industry is the combination of the use of Universal Product Coding (UPC) and EDI.

By using UPC and EDI in combination retailers and their manufacturers have been able to gain substantial benefits. The UPC is used to mark all items sold at the retail level. The code is scanned at the point of sale. In most cases, the retailer's inventory records are automatically updated based upon the sale. Further, orders are automatically generated based upon the inventory records.

Then EDI comes into play. Once orders are generated, they are sent electronically through EDI to the manufacturers. The fast transmission of orders provides a way for retailers to quickly replenish stocks as items sell.

Acceptance of Quick Response has been widespread in the retailing industry. In most retailing applications of UPC, EDI will also be found. This example shows how EDI can be integrated with other techniques to provide benefits that are greater than if either technique was used alone.

Summary of Integration of EDI

Because of EDI's ability to be easily and profitably integrated with other management techniques and systems, the use of EDI should grow. EDI is not a stand-alone, unifunctional technology. Its adaptability and its widespread applicability across industries and functions will contribute to its fast and explosive growth.

EDI FOR COMPETITIVE ADVANTAGE

It has been said repeatedly, here and by others, that EDI is a source of "competitive advantage." All companies are encouraged to implement EDI in order to gain a strategic advantage over competitors. Yet it would seem that if everyone has EDI, no one has a competitive advantage. How then, can your company continue to achieve long-range, strategic advantages through EDI? To obtain long-term advantages of EDI, EDI must be thought of and used as an evolutionary process.

EDI as a "Means," not an "End"

Strategic advantage comes not from having EDI or from implementing EDI but from the changes that EDI precipitates. EDI is not an end in itself. It is a means by which organizational structure, process, and policies can change.

Seeing EDI as the software, as the networks, as the standards, as the electronic transmission of documents is viewing EDI as a form of technology rather than as a process. EDI should be viewed as a process by which strategic partnerships and linkages are formed and through which the efficiency of the entire logistics chain is improved. The process of EDI allows a company to achieve long-term strategic benefits because those improved relationships and logistical efficiencies continue beyond the transmission of electronic messages.

EDI is Evolutionary

According to Jane Hagen of Temple, Barker, and Sloan, EDI is a "continuous evolutionary [process] with its own life cycle."[16] In other words, there is no standing still with EDI. There have already been numerous examples of companies that have gained additional benefits from EDI by using EDI in new and unique ways. Continual innovation is just as important in the management of information and relationships as it is in the management of manufacturing operations. EDI should be viewed as a continually changing process that provides management with opportunities to forge strategic alliances and to develop innovative management techniques.

SUMMARY

Electronic Data Interchange is here to stay. Explosive growth of EDI is on the near-term horizon. At least in this country, EDI is fast reaching the point where it will become a requirement to do business. Significant benefits, in the form of reduced costs, improved productivity, and better information, result from EDI. While all of these points are important and should be considered in your decision to implement EDI the real message of EDI is this:

> EDI is changing, for the better, how America, as well as the rest of the world, is doing business. The change is irrevocable. Your company needs to be a part of that change.

GLOSSARY

ACH Automated Clearing House. An organization that acts as a storage and transfer facility for electronic payments.

AIAG Automotive Industry Action Group. Trade association in the automotive industry that investigates ways U.S. manufacturers can remain competitive with foreign manufacturers. Currently has project groups dealing with EDI, JIT, Bar Coding, and Quality Circles.

ANSI American National Standards Institute. Coordinator and clearing house for information on national standards. Serves as the U.S. representative for the International Standards Organization. Chartered a committee (X12) to develop EDI standards. Has final approval over X12 EDI standards.

application-to-application EDI An EDI system which links application programs between trading partners (i.e., buyer's purchasing system with seller's order entry system). Eliminates rekeying of data between parties.

applications programs Programs used within a company to perform various functions. For instance: purchasing, accounts payable, accounts receivable.

ASC Accredited Standards Committee. A group that has been chartered by ANSI to develop standards. ASC X12 is the group with responsibility for EDI standards.

asynchronous transmission A communication protocol for sending messages. Each message begins with a start bit and ends with a stop bit.

authentication Process to ensure that the exact message that was sent was received. The sender uses an encryption key to code a message. Both the original

authentication   Process to ensure that the exact message that was sent was received. The sender uses an encryption key to code a message. Both the original and the coded message are sent to the receiver. The receiver uses the same key to decode the message. The decoded message is compared to the uncoded message. If the two match, no change in the data has occurred during transmission.

bar code   A form of identification where a series of lines are printed on an item. Various formats are available—a common format is the Universal Product Code.

baud rate   The speed of transmission of data between computers measured in bits per second. Common rates are 300, 1200, 2400, 4800, 9600.

bisynchronous transmission   A communications protocol that moves information in blocks of characters. Provides for error checking.

bridging software   Software used to connect internal application programs. Normally must be custom-designed to each company.

CAD/CAM   Computer Aided Design/Computer Aided Manufacturing.

CCD   Cash Concentration or Disbursement. An ACH format for electronic payments that provides for a limited trailing record.

CCD+   Cash Concentration or Disbursement plus Addendum. An ACH format for electronic payments. Expansion of CCD. Allows additional remittance information. Addendum can be done in X12 format.

CIDX   Chemical Industry Data Exchange. EDI in the chemical industry.

communications protocol   Establishes the parameters of communications between two computers. Includes baud rate, type of transmission, parity setting, etc.

communications software   Software that manages communications between two computers.

conversion software   Software used to take data out of a company's internal database and reformat the data into a fixed-field format file that can then be translated.

CTP   Corporate Trade Payment. An ACH format for electronic payments. Allows for considerable remittance information, but information is not in standard format.

CTX   Corporate Trade Exchange. An ACH format that allows for the transmission of payment information and remittance information. Supports the ANSI X12 remittance advice. Remittance data are in a standard format.

data dictionary   A document that defines the precise content of each data element.

data element   The smallest unit of information in a transaction set, such as quantity or ZIP code. Data elements are combined to make data segments.

data element separator (delimeter)   A character used to indicate that a new element of data has started. The most common separator is the *.

data segment   A line of information in an EDI message. Comparable to the address line, for instance, in a paper document.

data segment diagram   A schematic that shows the sequencing and the contents of the data elements in each data segment.

data segment directory   A document that provides the definitions and formats of the data segments used to create a transaction set.

direct link   Communications between two trading partners where the message is transmitted, usually through a modem, directly from one computer to the other computer.

direct store delivery   In the grocery industry, delivery of items directly from the manufacturer to the retail level (as opposed to going through a distributor or broker). An area of expansion of EDI.

DISA   Data Interchange Standards Association. The secretariat for the ANSI ASC X12 committee.

door-to-door EDI   EDI not integrated into internal application programs. Data are manually entered into a PC for the generation of an EDI message. Upon receipt of an EDI message, the message is printed out and then manually entered into an application program.

download   Transfer information from a mainframe computer to a microcomputer.

EDI   Electronic Data Interchange. The computer-to-computer exchange of standard business documentation in machine processable form.

EDICC   EDI Council of Canada. Canadian trade association for the development of EDI.

EDIFACT   EDI for Administration, Commerce, and Transport. The international standard for EDI. Developed based upon ANSI X12 and the Trade Data Interchange standards used in Europe.

EFT   Electronic Funds Transfer. The company-to-company or company- to-bank electronic exchange of value.

electronic envelope   A pair of data segments that designate a transaction set, a functional group, or an interchange.

electronic mail   The transfer of messages over computer networks. Messages are usually in free format.

electronic mailbox   A designated holding location for electronic messages. The mailbox can either be on the user's computer or, as is more common, on a third party network computer.

electronic payments   Any method of making payments electronically. Includes wire transfers and ACH payments.

encryption   A method of ensuring data secrecy. The message to be sent is coded using a key available only to the sender and the receiver. The coded message is sent to the receiver and then decoded upon receipt.

flat file   A data file in prescribed fixed-field format. Is necessary if data entry to translation software is from a data file rather than from manual input.

float   Access to funds by a payer after a check has been written due to mailing and processing time.

formatting software   Software that translates data from a company specific format to a standard format. Can normally accept input from either a data file or from manual entry.

front-end processor   The use of a microcomputer as a way to communicate with a mainframe computer. In EDI a front-end processor would normally perform translation and communications functions.

functional acknowledgment   An electronic message that confirms receipt of an earlier message. Indicates that a functional group was received and either accepted or rejected.

functional group   A group of like transaction sets. Represents the transmission of a group of similar documents such as purchase orders.

gateway   A connection between two third party networks that allows messages from one to be communicated to the other.

industry convention   A modification to a standard to reflect special needs of a specific industry. VICS is an industry convention of the X12 standards.

interchange   An electronic exchange between two companies. The interchange is indicated by an interchange control header and an interchange control trailer. Comparable to an outer envelope in paper transmissions.

ISO   International Standards Organization. Responsible for the development of international standards including EDIFACT.

just-in-time   A manufacturing and inventory philosophy in which inventory is scheduled for delivery only as needed on the production line.

lockbox   A postal box to which customers send payments. The payments are collected and processed by a financial institution.

machine processable format   Data in designated fields so that that data can be automatically processed by a computer without interpretation or rekeying.

mailbox   A location for holding electronic messages. (See electronic mailbox.)

mapping   Taking data from company-specific format and fitting it to standard format.

microcomputer   A personal computer.

MODEM   Modulator-demodulator. A device that converts information from a computer into an audio tone that can be passed over telephone wires.

NACHA   National Automated Clearing House Association. Confederation of regional clearing house associations, responsible for marketing, policy making, and lobbying activities.

ODETTE   Organization for Data Exchange by Teletransmission in Europe. An EDI trade group in the automotive industry. Similar to AIAG in the U.S.

pilot   A test of the EDI system where both paper and electronic documents are transmitted. Usually done with a limited number of trading partners to test the EDI system.

proprietary EDI   EDI using company-specific format. Normally done between a major player in an industry and its trading partners. Many companies and industries that had strong proprietary EDI networks have now converted to standard EDI.

quick response   A program in the retailing industry that combines the use of the Universal Product Code and EDI. UPC is used to track items as they are sold, and EDI is used to transmit orders.

stand-alone EDI   Using a microcomputer-based EDI system where there is no linkage to company internal systems. A good way to test EDI or to start an EDI effort quickly. Low cost but also low benefits.

TDCC   Transportation Data Coordinating Committee. Industry trade group, which originally led the development of standards and EDI in the transportation industry.

Also a type of standard used primarily in the transportation industry.

Now known as TDCC/EDIA (Electronic Data Interchange Association) and primarily involved in EDI training and marketing.

TDI   Trade Data Interchange. EDI standards developed in Great Britain and currently used throughout Europe. Has been used in the development of EDIFACT.

third party network   A service provider that serves as a clearing house for EDI messages. Will normally provide both mailbox and value added services such as translation of data from one format to another.

trading partner   Any company with whom another company is doing business. EDI links trading partners electronically.

transaction set   An EDI document. A group of data segments that form one complete document such as a purchase order or an invoice. Identified by a transaction set header segment and a transaction set trailer segment.

translation software   Software used to take data from a flat file and put it into EDI format. Can be easily purchased.

UCC   Uniform Code Council. Association which performs the administrative functions for UCS, WINS, and VICS. Also provides UCS identification codes and UPCs.

UCS   Uniform Communications Standards. The EDI format used in the grocery industry. Also used as a reference for EDI in the grocery industry.

UPC   Universal Product Code. A bar code that identifies manufacturer, item, style, color, etc.

upload   Transfer data from a microcomputer to a mainframe.

user group   A group of users of a particular software vendor or third party network. Can also refer to a trade group.

VAN   Value Added Network. A third party network performing services beyond transmission of data—for instance, translation, training, encryption, etc.

VICS   Voluntary Interindustry Communication Standards. The EDI standards for the retailing industry. Based on ANSI format and administered by the UCC.

WINS   Warehouse Information Network Standards. The EDI standards for the warehouse industry. Administered by UCC.

X12   Short for ANSI X12. Standard for EDI. Also refers to the committee that develops the standards.

X400   An international standard for electronic messages in free format.

ENDNOTES

CHAPTER 1

1. "Respondent Report The State Of U.S. EDI: 1988," EDI Research, Inc., 1988, p. 8.
2. Brown, Warren and Brown, Anna Lee. "Electronic Pulses Replacing Paper in Workforce," *Washington Post*, September 2, 1988.
3. "EDI Stats," *INPUT EDI Reporter*, November, 1988, p. 5.
4. Milbrandt, Ben. *Making Business More Efficient*, Willowbrook, Il, 1987, p. 6.
5. Hough, David. Manager, Implementation Programs, McDonnell Douglas, personal interview.
6. History developed based primarily upon material from Davis, Henry A. *Electronic Data Interchange and Corporate Trade Payments*, Financial Executives Research Foundation, 1988 and from EDI Group, Ltd.

CHAPTER 2

1. Hillkirk, John. "Electronic Exchanges Trimming Costs," *USA Today*, August 26, 1988.
2. "EDI Is Coming At You," *Information Week*, October 5, 1987, p. 23.
3. Emmelhainz, Margaret A. *The Impact of Electronic Data Interchange on the Purchasing Process*, Ohio State University, 1986, p.130.
4. Seideman, Tony. "Study Predicts Big Boom for EDI," *The Journal of Commerce*, September 12, 1988.
5. "Ford Motor Co. To Impose EDI On All Its Suppliers," *Computing Canada*, September 9, 1988, pp. 37–38.
6. "Toys-R-Us: Its Recent Turnaround Wasn't Child's Play," *Information Week*, December 14, 1987, pp. 24–26.

7. LaLonde, Bernard J., Martha C. Cooper, and Thomas G. Noordewier. *Customer Service: A Management Perspective*, Council of Logistics Management, 1988, p. 30.

8. *Computer World*, August 29, 1988, p. 98.

9. "Electronic Data Interchange," *Shipping Digest*, August 22, 1988, pp. 54–57.

10. "Most Users Still Testing Technology But Interest High In Getting Involved," *The Journal of Commerce*, September 12, 1988.

11. "Respondent Report For The State Of U.S. EDI: 1988," EDI Research, Inc., p. 9.

12. Byles, Torrey. "DuPont Finds EDI Links Offer The Right Chemistry," *The Journal of Commerce*, August 10, 1988.

13. "EDI: The Cost Saving Way for OEMs To Talk To Suppliers," *Electronic Business*, July 15, 1988, p. 14.

14. Same as endnote 1.

15. Brown, Warren. "Electronic Pulses Replacing Paper in Workplace," *Washington Post*, September 2, 1988, p. F-1.

16. Same as endnote 13.

17. Same as endnote 1.

18. Same as endnote 13.

19. Davis, Henry A. *Electronic Data Interchange And Corporate Trade Payments*, Financial Executives Research Foundation, 1988, p. 43.

20. Same as endnote 19 at p. 51.

21. Brown, Warren. "Paper Pushed Aside By Pulses," *The Washington Post*, September 5, 1988.

22. Craig, Anthony. Remarks at the American Electronics Association Productivity Colloquium, April 19, 1988.

23. "DEC, IBM Praise EDI To The Sky," *Computer World*, August 9, 1988.

24. Same as endnote 21.

25. "Electronic Data Interchange For The Grocery Industry Feasibility Report," Arthur D. Little, Inc., 1980, p.10.

26. "EDI: Data on the Fast Track," *Distribution*, June 1987, pp. 38–41.

27. Same as endnote 3 at p. 158.

28. Klima, George. Former Director of Accounting Systems, Super Valu Stores, presentation, October 1988.

29. Same as endnote 4.

30. Same as endnote 23.

31. "The Electronic Connection," *Traffic Management*, September 1986, pp. 58–65.

32. Same as endnote 15 at p. F-2.

33. Carroll, Paul B. "Computers Bring Changes To Basic Business Documents," *The Wall Street Journal*, March 6, 1987, p. 33.

34. Same as endnote 28.

35. Wallace, Bob. "EDI User Faces Wary Suppliers," *Network World*, August 19, 1988.
36. Milbrandt, Ben. *Making Business More Efficient*, Willowbrook, Il, 1987, p. 2.
37. "FAHS Leads Way for Industry Wide Electronic Data Interchange System," *Federation of American Health Systems Review*, May/June 1988, pp. 56–58.
38. Same as endnote 1.
39. Same as endnote 11 at p. 13.
40. Craig, Anthony. "EDI Increases Productivity and Competitiveness," *The EDI*Update*, June 1988, p. 1.
41. Ball, Michael. "EDI Takes Root," *Computerworld*, September 7, 1988, p. 26.
42. Same as endnote 41.
43. Emmelhainz, Margaret A. *The Impact Of Electronic Data Interchange On The Purchasing Process*, Ohio State University, 1986 (interview with chemical executive).
44. Svinicki, John. "Integrating EDI Into the Second Supplier Tier," *Systems/3X World*, September 1988, pp. 70–76.
45. "How Ford Buys Electronics," *Electronics Purchasing*, August 1988, pp. 46–53.
46. Same as endnote 44.
47. Same as endnote 13.
48. "Maintenance and Purchasing Can and Do Work Together," *Maintenance Technology*, September 1988, p. 40.
49. Same as endnote 1.
50. Same as endnote 28.
51. "The New Sales Function," *Electrical Distributor*, August 1988, p. 38.
52. Hencir, Sheila. "3M Says More, More, More," *Computer User*, July 1988.
53. Same as endnote 7 at p. 6.
54. Same as endnote 7 at p. 6.
55. Reda, Susan. "Decoding UPC and EDI," *Apparel Merchandising*, August 1988, pp. 51-53.
56. Chanko, Ken. "Don't Wait for QR to Come to You, Go Out and Get It," *Discount Store News*, August 22, 1988.
57. Lesch, Susan. "Electronic Data Interchange: What's In It For You," *Discount Store News*, September 12, 1988, p. 39.
58. Emmelhainz, Margaret A. *The Impact Of Electronic Data Interchange On The Purchasing Process*, Ohio State University, 1986, p. 125.
59. Same as endnote 41.
60. "... Speakers At X12 Forum Emphasize Business Opportunities Of EDI," *EDI News*, April 27, 1988, p. 3.

61. "Xerox Stresses Business Benefits Of EDI," *EDI News*, April 27, 1988, p. 3.
62. Same as endnote 40.
63. Same as endnote 22.
64. Same as endnote 22.
65. Canna, Elizabeth. "Union Carbide Goes Paperless In Four Stages," *American Shipper*, August 1988, p. 34.

CHAPTER 3

1. "EDI Stats," *INPUT EDI Reporter*, Volume 3, No. 11, November 1988, p. 5.
2. Same as endnote 1 at p. 7.
3. Harrington, Lisa H. "EDI: Up And Running At Last," *Traffic Management*, August 1988, p. 65.
4. Same as endnote 3.
5. Same as endnote 3.
6. "The Electronic Connection," *Traffic Management*, September 1986, pp. 58–65.
7. "EDI Puts Buyers In Control," *Purchasing World*, March 1987, pp. 46–48.
8. "EDI: Data On The Fast Track," *Distribution*, June 1987, pp. 38–41.
9. Same as endnote 6.
10. Same as endnote 6.
11. Same as endnote 8.
12. Same as endnote 6.
13. Same as endnote 6 at p. 65.
14. Medford, Cassimer J. "EDI Keeps On Trucking," *Information Week*, September 26, 1988, p. 24.
15. Same as endnote 14.
16. "Union Carbide Goes Paperless In Four Stages," *American Shipper*, August 1988.
17. Graves, Newton in Ben Milbrandt, *Making Business More Efficient*, 1987, pp. 61–65.
18. Same as endnote 17 at p. 61.
19. Weart, Walter. "Procter and Gamble's War On Paper," *Distribution*, May 1988, pp. 88–89.
20. Same as endnote 19.
21. Canna, Elizabeth. "Union Carbide goes Paperless In Four Stages," *American Shipper*, August 1988.
22. Dunlap, Craig. "Brokers Backing Test Of Processing Proposal," *The Journal of Commerce*, October 11, 1988.
23. "ACES Debuts At The B-State Port," *VIA Port of NY-NJ*, August 1988.

24. Same as endnote 23.
25. "Seaway Investigates EDI Benefits," *Seaway Review*, Summer 1988, p. 31.
26. Same as endnote 25.
27. Same as endnote 21.
28. "Electronic Data Interchange For The Grocery Industry Feasibility Report," Arthur D. Little, Inc., 1980.
29. Same as endnote 28 at p. S-1.
30. Same as endnote 28.
31. Davis, Henry A. *Electronic Data Interchange And Corporate Trade Payments*, Financial Executives Research Foundation, 1988, p. 50.
32. Klima, George. Former Director of Accounting Systems, Super Valu Stores, Inc., presentation, October 1988.
33. Same as endnote 32.
34. "Direct Store Delivery Store-Level Study," Arthur D. Little, Inc., 1987, p. ix.
35. Same as endnote 34.
36. Same as endnote 31 at p. 52.
37. Wallace, Bob. "EDI User Faces Wary Suppliers," *Network World*, August 19, 1988.
38. Same as endnote 37.
39. Same as endnote 37.
40. Same as endnote 37.
41. "Eli Lilly Launches New EDI Program," *Wholesale Drugs*, September 1988.
42. "Hospital Suppliers Work Together Toward Electronic Standard," *Modern Healthcare*, August 1988.
43. Thill, Mark D. "EDI Dogfight Bringing Industry Closer To Dream," *Hospital Purchasing News*, September 1988, p. 37.
44. "Eye on EDI: Multi-Hospital Buyers Endorse EDI." *Federation of American Health System Review*, September/October 1988, pp. 46–47.
45. Same as endnote 44.
46. Same as endnote 44.
47. Same as endnote 44.
48. "EDI Coming Of Age In Automotive Industry With AIAG's Fine-Tuning," *EDI News*, June 2, 1988, p. 7.
49. Hillkirk, John. "Electronic Exchanges Trimming Costs," *USA Today*, August 26, 1988.
50. Brown, Warren. "Paper Pushed Aside by Pulses," *Washington Post*, September 5, 1988.
51. "Ford Aims To Further Streamline Business Operations Via CMMS," *EDI News*, May 18, 1988, pp. 1–2.
52. Haber, Holly. "Retailers Sold On Standards For EDI," *Daily News Record*, September 20, 1988.

53. Same as endnote 52.

54. Culicchio, Georgia. "The Quiet Giant Dillards Innovation," *Retail Information Systems News*, October 1988, p. 21.

55. Same as endnote 54.

56. "Mervyn's Moves With EDI," *Retail Information Systems News*, October 1988.

57. "EDI and Retail: A Long History," *Retail Information Systems News*, September/October 1988.

58. Same as endnote 57.

59. Same as endnote 57.

60. Same as endnote 57.

61. Baker, David F. "Keynote Address," at Electronic Data Interchange: Bringing It Together In Government, Gaithersburg, MD, May 26, 1988.

62. Betts, Mitch. "EDI Shreds Federal Paperwork," *ComputerWorld*, September 5, 1988, p. 51.

63. Same as endnote 61.

64. Same as endnote 61.

65. "Number 2 Man In DOD Directs All Components To Make Maximum Use Of EDI," *EDI News*, June 15, 1988, p. 1.

66. Hostetter, Ralph. "EDI For Purchasing," at Electronic Data Interchange: Bringing It Together In Government, Gaithersburg, MD, May 26, 1988.

67. Foote, Lee. "EDI At Dupont," at Electronic Data Interchange: Bringing It Together In Government, Gaithersburg, MD, May 26, 1988.

68. Same as endnote 67.

69. "Military Stores Advance On EDI," *EDI Executive*, October/November 1987, p. 5.

70. Long, John E. "We Enjoyed Our Best Year," *Military Market*, July 1988, p. 32.

71. "Marine Stores Now Centralized," *Military Market*, July 1988, p. 33.

72. Wallace, William. Systems Analyst, Army and Air Force Exchange System, Dallas, TX, telephone interview, April 1988.

73. Strombaugh, Ken. "OSD Transportation Policy," at Electronic Data Interchange: Bringing It Together In Government, Gaithersburg, MD, May 26, 1988.

74. Same as endnote 73.

75. Same as endnote 74.

76. Bartley, Jack. "EDI In The Department Of Defense," at Electronic Data Interchange: Bringing It Together In Government, Gaithersburg, MD, May 26, 1988.

CHAPTER 4

1. "An Introduction To Electronic Data Interchange," ANSI ASC- X12, July 1987, p. 2.

CHAPTER 5

No endnotes

CHAPTER 6

1. Hough, David. Manager, Implementation Programs, McDonnell Douglas, personal interview.
2. Same as endnote 1.
3. Same as endnote 1.
4. Emmelhainz, Margaret A. *The Impact of Electronic Data Interchange On The Purchasing Process*, Ohio State University, 1986.

CHAPTER 7

1. Norris, Richard. "An Electronic Pipeline That's Changing The Way America Does Business," *Business Week*, August 3, 1987, p. 82.
2. Emmelhainz, Margaret A. *The Impact of Electronic Data Interchange On The Purchasing Process*, Ohio State University, 1986 (personal interview with grocery executive).
3. Seideman, Tony. "Production, Marketing Crucial To EDI Systems," *The Journal of Commerce*, October 19, 1988.
4. Hough, David. Manager, Implementation Programs, McDonnell Douglas, personal interview.
5. Emmelhainz, Margaret A. *The Impact Of Electronic Data Interchange On The Purchasing Process*, Ohio State University, 1986, p. 141.
6. Same as endnote 3.

CHAPTER 8

1. EDI roles based upon functions included in EDI*Net Implementation Guide, McDonnell Douglas, used with permission of David Hough.
2. Kromer, Carol. "Management Must Back EDI Effort," *Transport Topics*, September 28, 1988, p. 20.

3. Seideman, Tony. "EDI Exchange," *The Journal of Commerce*, August 2, 1988.
4. Davis, Henry A. *Electronic Data Interchange And Corporate Trade Payments*, Financial Executives Research Foundation, 1988, p. 83.
5. Adapted with permission from Monczka, Robert M. and Joseph R. Carter. *Electronic Data Interchange: Managing Implementation In A Purchasing Environment*, National Association of Purchasing Management, 1987, p. 28.
6. "Respondent Report For The State Of U.S. EDI: 1988," EDI Research, Inc., 1988, p. 21.

CHAPTER 9

1. Wallace, Bob. "EDI User Faces Wary Suppliers," *Network World*, August 19, 1988.
2. Emmelhainz, Margaret A. *The Impact Of Electronic Data Interchange On The Purchasing Process*, Ohio State University, 1986, p. 141.
3. Reich, Caroline. "How To Get Started In EDI," *Purchasing World*, June 1985, p. 72.
4. Wright, Michael, "DSD/USC: A Marriage Made In Heaven," *Direct Store Delivery*, September 1985, p. 14.
5. Same as endnote 2 at p. 117.
6. Stern, Louis W. and Patrick J. Kaufmann. "Electronic Data Interchange in Selected Consumer Goods Industries: An Interorganizational Perspective," in *Marketing In An Electronic Age*, Cambridge, MA, Harvard University Press, 1985, p. 15.
7. Same as endnote 5 at p. 160.
8. Hill, Ned C. and Daniel M. Ferguson. "Survey Evidence Suggests Barriers To EDI Usage," *International Trade and Transport*, January 1988, pp. 15–20.
9. Davis, Henry A. Electronic Data Interchange And Corporate Trade Payments, Financial Executives Research Foundation, 1988, p. 79.
10. "Respondent Report For The State Of U.S. EDI: 1988," EDI Research, Inc., 1988, pp. 17, 19.
11. *Electronic Data Interchange: A Management Overview,* Digital Equipment Company Limited, Berkshire, England, 1989, p. 31.
12. Same as endnote 11 at p. 18.
13. Same as endnote 6 at p. 24.
14. See endnotes 5, 8, 10, and 11.
15. LaLonde, Bernard J. and Margaret A. Emmelhainz. "Electronic Purchase Order Interchange," *Journal of Purchasing and Materials Management*, Volume 21, Number 3, Fall 1985, pp. 2–9.

16. "Lawyers Study EDI Agreements," *EDI Executive*, April 1988, p. 6.
17. "EDI: Data On The Fast Track," *Distribution*, June 1987, pp. 38–41.
18. *EDI Yellow Pages*. EDI, Spread The Word, Dallas, TX, 1989.

CHAPTER 10

1. "Respondent Report For The State Of U.S. EDI: 1988," EDI Research, Inc., 1988, p. 13.
2. Seideman, Tony. "EDI Exchange," *The Journal of Commerce*, October 11, 1988.
3. Klima, George. Former Director of Accounting Systems, Super Valu Stores, presentation, October 1988.
4. Emmelhainz, Margaret A. *The Impact Of Electronic Data Interchange On The Purchasing Process*, Ohio State University, 1986, p. 137.
5. Brown, Warren. "Paper Pushed Aside By Pulses," *The Washington Post*, September 5, 1988.

CHAPTER 11

1. "EDI Implementation Case Studies," INPUT, Mountain View, CA, 1988.
2. LaLonde, Bernard J., Martha C. Cooper, and Thomas G. Noordewier. *Customer Service: A Management Perspective*: Council of Logistics Management, Oak Brook, IL, 1988.
3. Same as endnote 1 at p. 59.
4. Same as endnote 1 at p. 59.
5. Same as endnote 1 at p. 65.
6. Same as endnote 1 at p. 67.
7. Same as endnote 1 at p. 66.
8. Same as endnote 1 at p. 65.
9. Same as endnote 1 at p. 63.
10. Same as endnote 1 at p. 63.
11. Same as endnote 1 at p. 64.
12. Same as endnote 1 at p. 68.
13. Same as endnote 1 at p. 68.
14. Same as endnote 2 at p. 122.
15. Same as endnote 2 at p. 122.
16. Same as endnote 2 at p. 124.
17. Same as endnote 2 at p. 124.
18. Same as endnote 2 at p. 125.
19. Same as endnote 2 at p. 126.
20. Same as endnote 2 at p. 126.

21. Same as endnote 2 at p. 127.
22. Same as endnote 2 at p. 124.

CHAPTER 12

1. Cage, Theodore Justin. "Increased ACH Use Presents Challenge Few Banks Can Meet," *Cash Flow*, August 1988.
2. "EDI To Have Major Effect On EFT, Manny Hanny Official Predicts," *EDI News*, May 4, 1988, p. 5.
3. Davis, Henry A. *Electronic Data Interchange And Corporate Trade Payments*, Financial Executives Research Foundation, 1988. p. 18.
4. Same as endndote 3 at p. 19.
5. Figure provided by Daniel M. Ferguson, President, EDI Group, Ltd.
6. Stone, Bernell K. "Electronic Payment Basics," *Economic Review*, Federal Reserve Bank of Atlanta, March 1986, pp. 9–18.
7. Same as endnote 6.
8. Information and figure provided by Daniel M. Ferguson, President, EDI Group, Ltd.
9. Frisbee, Pamela S. "The ACH: An Elusive Dream," *Economic Review*, Federal Reserve Bank of Atlanta, March 1986.
10. Same as endnote 9 at p. 5.
11. Same as endnote 9 at p. 6.
12. Same as endnote 3 at p. 22.
13. Stone, Bernell K. "Corporate Trade Payments: Hard Lessons In Product Design," *Economic Review*, Federal Reserve Bank of Atlanta, April 1986, pp. 9–21.
14. Same as endnote 3 at p. 21.
15. Same as endnote 13 at p. 11.
16. Stone, Bernell K. *One To Get Ready: How To Prepare Your Company For EDI*, Core States Financial Corporation, 1988, p. 21.
17. "Vendor Express Charges Full Steam Ahead," *Corporate EFT Report*, October 12, 1988, p. 1.
18. Schwan, Charles. "EDI In The Treasury Department," Electronic Data Interchange: Bringing It Together In Government, Gaithersburg, MD, May 26, 1988.
19. Same as endnote 18.
20. "DOD Announces Several EDI/EFT Pilots for Vendor Payments," *EDI News*, May 4, 1988, pp. 4–5.
21. Same as endnote 20.
22. Same as endnote 20.
23. "EDI And The Oil Industry," *Corporate EFT Report,* November 9, 1988, pp. 2-3.

24. ". . . Meanwhile, GM Boasts Growth In Electronic Trade Payments," *EDI News*, January 1988, pp. 9–10.
25. Same as endnote 5.
26. Same as endnote 24.
27. "GE Designs New Systems To Increase Electronic Payments And Collections," *Corporate EFT Report*, October 12, 1988, p. 6.
28. Same as endnote 27.
29. "EFT Helps RJR Stay Ahead Of Competition," *Corporate EFT Report*, November 23, 1988, p. 1.
30. "Corporate EFT Preferences Emerge," *Corporate Cashflow*, July 1988.
31. "National Bank Of Detroit Commits To EDI Payments With Wide Range Of Format Offerings," *EDI News*, January 1988, p. 7.
32. Korzeniowski, Paul. "Banks Invest In EDI," *Communications Week*, August 8, 1988.
33. "How To Analyze EFT Costs, Benefits," *EDI Executive*, July 1988, p. 5.
34. Same as endnote 33.
35. Davis, Henry A. *Electronic Data Interchange And Corporate Trade Payments*, Financial Executives Research Foundation, 1988, pp. 83–84.
36. Same as endnote 35 at p. 27.
37. Same as endnote 36.
38. Ferguson, Daniel M. News Release, EDI Research, Inc., October 24, 1988.
39. Kantrow, Yvette D. "Electronic Cash Management Is High On Corporate Wish List," *American Banker*, September 1988.
40. Same as endnote 39.
41. Same as endnote 2.
42. Siedeman, Tony. "Fund Transfer, EDI Marriage Promises Bliss," *The Journal of Commerce*, October 24, 1988.
43. Same as endnote 24.

CHAPTER 13

1. Shaw, Jack. "EDI's Future: The Torch Is In Your Hands," *Executive Briefing*, p. 2.
2. Naisbitt, John. Quoted in *INPUT EDI Reporter*, November 1988, p. 3.
3. Same as endnote 1.
4. "The Pacific Rim Pilot: The Korean Perspective," *EDI News*, May 18, 1988, p. 8.
5. Same as endnote 4.
6. Lamb, John. "IBM Eyes EDI In Europe," *Datamation*, July 1, 1988, pp. 48–12.
7. Gaynor, Mark. "EDI Poised To Take Off Internationally," *EDI Executive*, July 1988, p. 4.

8. "EDI To Experience Dramatic Growth In International And Domestic Marketplaces," *EDI News*, May 18, 1988, p. 4.
9. "EDI" *Seaway Review*, Summer 1988, p. 34.
10. "McGinnis Expresses Optimism On The Progress Of International EDI Efforts," *EDI News*, March 1988, p.1.
11. Same as endnote 10.
12. Same as endnote 10.
13. Lamb, John. "IBM Eyes EDI In Europe," *Datamation*, July 1, 1988, pp. 48–52.
14. Same as endnote 13.
15. Porter, Janet. "Asia Catching Up With US, Europe In EDI Technology," *The Journal of Commerce*, September 16, 1988.
16. Dysart, Joe. "EDI Takes Hold In Europe, Pacific Rim," *The Journal of Commerce*, August 29, 1988.
17. Same as endnote 7.
18. Same as endnote 7 at p. 4.
19. "Soviet EDI Takes Off—'EDIFLOT' Launched," *INPUT EDI Reporter*, November 1988, p. 4.
20. Crockett, Barton. "US Customs In Joint Pilot Test For EDI Standard," *Network World*, August 8, 1988, pp. 1–3.
21. Same as endnote 20 at p. 3.
22. Same as endnote 21.
23. Same as endnote 7 at p. 3.
24. Same as endnote 4 at p. 6.
25. Same as endnote 24.
26. Same as endnote 4 at p. 7.
27. Same as endnote 26.
28. Same as endnote 26.
29. Same as endnote 26.
30. Same as endnote 4 at p. 8.
31. "Intercontinental EDI Pilot Program Between Korea and North America On Horizon," *EDI News*, April 19, 1988, p. 2.
32. Barnard, Bruce. "European Companies Launch Trans-Border EDI Program," *The Journal of Commerce*, September 8, 1988.
33. Same as endnote 32.
34. Same as endnote 32.
35. Same as endnote 8 at p. 5.
36. Same as endnote 7 at p. 4.
37. Same as endnote 10.

CHAPTER 14

1. Shaw, Jack. "EDI's Future: The Torch Is In Your Hands," *Executive Briefing*.
2. "EDI," *Seaway Review*, Summer 1988, p. 34.
3. "Respondent Report For The State of U.S. EDI: 1988," EDI Research, Inc., 1988, p. 9.
4. Seideman, Tony. "EDI Exchange," *The Journal of Commerce*, October 11, 1988.
5. "Supply Tech's ED/Graphics Approach—AT&T Too?" *INPUT EDI Reporter*, November 1988, pp. 4–5.
6. Same as endnote 5 at p. 5.
7. "EDI Evolves Toward Design Data," *EDI Executive*, April 1988, p. 2.
8. Lovejoy, James L. "EDI And UPC—Partners," *RIS News*, July/August 1988, p. 31.
9. Same as endnote 8.
10. Same as endnote 8.
11. "Chrysler Takes On-Line Approach To EDI," *EDI Executive*, April 1988, p. 4.
12. Same as endnote 11.
13. Same as endnote 11.
14. "Ford Aims To Further Streamline Business Operations Via CMMS," *EDI News*, May 18, 1988, pp. 1–2.
15. Same as endnote 14 at p. 1.
16. "Successful Companies Will Take Advantage Of Changing Business Environments," *EDI News*, April 6, 1988, p. 5.

INDEX

Abbott Laboratories, 51
Accredited Standards Committee (ASC) X12, 22, 64, 76, 77, 79-80
  standard development process, 76-79
Air industry, standards, 85-86
American Bankers Association, 21
American National Standards Institute, 64
Analytical Systems Automated Purchasing, 51
ANSI X12, 16, 23, 54, 57 60
  See also Accredited Standards Committee.
  Applications specialist, role of, 142
Army and Air Force Exchange Service, 59
Asynchronous transmission, 100
Audit
  audit reviewers, role of, 144
  EDI, 130
  software feature, 94
Audit trail
  concern about 165
  mailbox services, 111
Authentication, value added network (VAN), 113

Automated clearing house, 197-201
  development of, 198-199
    Cash Concentration or Disbursement (CCD), 200
    Cash Concentration or Disbursement plus Addendum (CCD+), 200
    Corporate Trade Exchange (CTX), 201
    Corporate Trade Payment, 200-201
    preferred formats 204
    requirement of 199-200
Automotive industry, 22 52-54
  Common Manufacturing Management Systems, 221-222
  Ford Motor Company, 54
  General Motors, 53-54
  just-in-time systems, 220-221
Automotive Industry Action Group, 22, 29, 53

Banks, electronic funds transfer, 205
Bar coding, 37 56 200 222
Barriers to EDI use
  audit trail concerns, 165
  cost misconceptions, 161-162, 166

difficulty of EDI, 160-161
legal concerns, 163-164
organizational resistance, 156-157
organizational structure concerns, 159-160
relationship concerns, 158, 166-167
role concerns, 157-158
security concerns, 162-163, 165-166
standard-related concerns, 167-168
Baxter Healthcare, 22, 51
Bergen Brunswig, 31, 50-51
Bisynchronous transmission, 100
Bridging software, 92-93
Burlington Northern, 43
Business survival, EDI, 25-28

Canadian-Korean pilot test, EDI, use of, 214-215
Cash Concentration or Disbursement plus Addendum (CCD+), ACH format, 200
Cash Concentration or Disbursement (CCD), ACH format, 200
Channel relationships, 37-38
improvements, 38
vendor base, reducing, 38
Checks, a payment, 196
Chrysler, fast-batch, 221
Coact Plus, 51
COBOL, 91Common Manufacturing Management System, 54
and EDI, 221-222
Communication, software function, 91
Communications Committee, 76
Communications specialist, role of, 142
Communication standards, 15-16

Communication Transport Protocols, 75
Components knowledge requirements, scope of, 150-151
Computer Aided Design/Computer Aided Manufacturing (CAD/CAM), and EDI, 219
Conrail, 43
Contracts, establishing, 134
Contracts administrator, role of, 145
Conversion, software function, 91
Coordinator, role of, 139
Corporate divisions, for EDI, 132
Corporate Trade Exchange (CTX), ACH format, 201
Corporate Trade Payment (CTP), ACH format, 200-201
COST-306 project, 215
Cost/benefit analysis
determination of benefits, 171-172
EDI, 131, 149
necessity of, 170
preparation of, 177
timing of costs/benefits, 171
Costs
communications costs, 173
cost misconceptions 16-162 166
EDI, 21
hardware costs, 172
membership costs, 174
outside support costs, 174
personnel costs, 173
savings, 28-33
document processing costs, 29-30
error costs, 32
importance of, 33
information costs, 177
inventory costs, 31, 176
paper savings, 176
personnel costs, 30-31, 176
time value savings, 177

software, 96-97 172
third party networks, 117-118
time value costs, 174
training costs, 173
Cross industry standards, standards, 87
Customer service, 36-37
Customizing ease, software feature, 94

Data Communications Corporation of Korea, 214
Data element, definition, 66
Data element directory, 72
Data Interchange for Shipping (DISH), 81
Data Interchange Standards Association, 23, 76
Data segment directory, 6-72
Defense General Supply Center, 58
Department of Defense, 58, 59
    electronic funds transfer, 202
Dial-out services, value added network (VAN), 113
Digital Equipment Corporation, 29, 30, 31, 35
Dillards Department Stores, EDI use, 55
Direct exchanges, 107-108
Document processing costs, savings and EDI, 29-30
Douglas Aircraft Company, 29
dpANS, 77
Dummy transactions, pilot test, 135
Du Pont, 58

EDIFACT, 210, 212, 213, 215
EDI for Administration, Commerce, and Transport (EDIFACT), 81
Editing capability, software feature, 93-94
EDX, 36
Electronic Data Interchange

application-to-application ED1, 4-5
barriers to/solutions, 156-158
benefits, 20
    channel relationships, 37-38
    customer service, 36-37
    international competition, 38-40
    operational improvements, 33-36
    sales increases, 37
business survival, 25-28
costs, 21
development of, 21-23
documents for transmissions, 18
door-to-door EDI, 5-6
efficiency in use, 10-13
enveloping, 74
versus fax and E-Mail, 13-14
functional acknowledgment, 13
future use, 27-28
growth of, 217-223
international EDI, 209-216
networks, 17-18
software, 16-17, 89-97
versus traditional document flow, 6-10
Electronic Data Interchange Association, 80
Electronic Data Interchange standards
    ANSI ASC X12 standards, 82-83
    communication standards, 15-16, 74-76
    development of, 63-64
    development process
        changes to standards, 79
        committees, 76
        new standards, 77-79
    formatting standards, 15, 64-65
    industry-specific standards, 16
    industry standards, 79-80
    international standards, 80-81
    proprietary standards, 16, 80

TDCC standards
   air industry, 85
   business applications, 87
   cross industry standards, 87
   freight claims transaction
      sets, 87
   motor industry, 85-86
   ocean industry, 86
   rail industry, 86
terminology of, 65-67
transaction set standards, 67-73
   data element directory, 72
   data segment directory, 67-
      72
Uniform Communications Standard, 83-84
Voluntary Interindustry Communications Standards, 85
Warehouse Information Network
   Standards, 84-85
X.400 standard, 81-82
Electronic Data Interchange users
   automotive industry, 52-54
   government usage, 57-60
   grocery industry, 47-49
   health care industry, 49-52
   level of 19-20
   numbe of 3-4
   retail industry, 54-57
   transportation industry, 42-47
   type of 19
Electronic funds transfer, 196-208
   automated clearing house, 197-
      201
   banks, 205
   barriers to, 206-207
   benefits of, 205-206
   EDI/EFT examples
      Department of Defense, 202
      General Electric, 203
   General Motors, 203
      oil industry, 203
      R.J. Reynolds, 204

   U.S. Treasury, 201-202
   EDI/EFT relationship, 208
   future view, 207-208
   value added networks, (VAN),
      205
   wire transfer systems, 197
   See also Automated clearing
      house.
Electronic Partnership Program, 50
Electronic test, pilot test, 135
E-mail, 14
Encryption services, value added net-
   work (VAN), 113
Enveloping, levels of, 74
Error costs, savings and EDI, 32
European Customs Union, 215
European Railway Federation, 215
European transportation EDI, use of
   215

Fast-batch, and EDI, 221
Fax, 13-14
Federal Supply Service, 58
Fedwire, 197
Ford Motor Company
   Common Manufacturing Man-
      agement Systems, 221-222
   EDI use, 26 34 54
Formatting, software function, 90-91
Formatting standards, 15, 64-65
Fortune 1000 firms, 28
Freight claims transaction sets, stan-
   dards, 87
Functional area coordinator, role of,
   141
Functional area managers, role of,
   141

Gateways, 114
General Electric, 22
   electronic funds transfer, 203
General Motors, 28
   EDI use, 53-54

electronic funds transfer, 203
General Services Administration, 58
GE segment, 74
Government usage, 57-60
  procurement uses, 58-59
  resale activities, 59
  standards, support of, 57-58
  transportation, 59-60
Great Lakes maritime industry, 46
Grocery industry, 22, 28, 47-49
  development of EDI, 47-48
  future view, 49
  use of EDI, 48-49
Growth of EDI
  applications
    CAD/CAM, 219
    product catalogs, 219-200
  integration
    Common Manufacturing
      Management Systems,
      221-222
    fast-batch, 221
    just-in-time systems, 220-
      221
    Quick Response, 222
  volume
    international EDI, 218
    new industries, 218
    trading partners, increases
      in, 217
GS segment, 74
GTE Valenite Corporation, 35

Hardware
  costs, 172
  mainframe, 97
  microcomputer, 97-100
    as front-end processor, 99-
      100
    stand-alone system, 98-99
  modems, 100
Hasbro, Inc., 30
Health care industry, 49-52

hospital suppliers EDI, 51-52
  wholesale drug EDI, 50-51
Hewlett-Packard, 29
Hills Discount Chain, EDI use, 55-56
Hospital suppliers EDI, 51-52

ICI Americas, Inc., 213
IEA segment, 74
Implementation issues knowledge requirements, scope of, 151-152
Implementation of EDI
  audit, 130
  case examples
    Mervyn's Department
      Stores, 181-185
    North American Philips Cor-
      poration, 185-191
  contracts, establishing, 134
  cost/benefit analysis, 131
  deciding EDI strategy, 126, 128
  education about EDI, 129-130
  expansion of usage, 135-136
  interdepartmental coordination,
    128
  management support, 128
  operational decisions, 131-133
  payback period, 128
  pilot tests, 134-135
  projection team, 129
    area representatives, 129
    team leader, 129
  publicizing efforts, 136
  trading partners, mapping with,
    133
Industry-specific standards, 16
Information costs, savings, 177
Installation services, value added network (VAN), 113
Interamerican Transport Systems,
  Inc., 43
Interconnectibility, and third party
  networks, 114-115
International EDI

barriers to, 215-216
competitive aspects, 38-40 210
cost documentation and, 209-210
current activity, 212-215
   Canadian-Korean pilot test, 214-215
   European transportation EDI, 215
   U.S. Customs Service, 213-214
   design/production speed 39
documentation improvements 39-40
standards, 210-212
trade barriers and, 210
International Standards Organization, 81 210
Inventory costs, savings and EDI, 31, 176
ISA segment, 74

Johnson and Johnson, 51
Just-In-Time, 34
   and EDI, 220-221

K mart, 55
Korea, Canadian-Korean pilot test, 214-215

Leadership group, members roles of, 138-140
Legal concerns, 163-164
Legal reviewers, role of, 144
Levi Straus & Co., 37
Liability, and third party networks, 117
Liaison group, members roles of, 143-144
LTV Steel Company, 30, 31

McDonnell Douglas, 58
Mailbox services, 108-111
   advantages of, 110-111

audit trail, 111
communications compatibility, 110-111
one call needed, 111
security buffer, 111
process in, 108-110
Mainframes, PC as front-end processor, 99-100
"Management of Federal Information Resources," 57
Management support, for EDI, 128
Materials Requirements Planning, 34
Membership, costs, 174
Mervyn's Department Stores
   EDI use, 55
   implementation of EDI, 181-185
Message Transfer Agent, 81
Message Transfer System, 81
Microcomputer, 97-100
   as front-end processor, 99-100
   stand-alone system, 98-99
Modems
   asynchronous transmission, 100
   baud rate, 100
   bisynchronous transmission, 100
Montgomery Ward, 54
Motor carrier EDI, 44-45
   examples of use, 44-45
   standards, 85-86

National Automated Cicaring House Association, 21, 22, 199
National Bank of Detroit, 205
National Customs Brokers and Forwarders Association of America, 45
National Data Corporation, 22
Navistar International Corporation, 31
Networks, value added network (VAN), 17-18
1989 EDI Yellow Pages, 153
North American EDIFACT Board, 76

North American Philips Corporation, 213
  implementation of EDI, 185-191

Ocean shipping EDI, 45-46
  ocean forwarders, 45
  ocean ports, 46
  standards 86
Oil industry, electronic funds transfer, 203
Operational decisions, 131-133
  corporate divisions, 132
  trading partners, selection of, 132-133
  transaction sets, 132
Operational improvements, 33-36
  access to accurate information, 36
  integration with other systems, 34-35
  internal reassessment, 33-34
  productivity, 35-36
Operations group, members roles of, 140-141
Organizational resistance, 156-157
Organizational structure concerns, 159-160
Organization for Data Exchange and Teletransmission in Europe (OD-ETTE), 81
Originator/Recipient Name, 81
Overview knowledge requirements, scope of, 149

P1 Message Transfer Protocol, 81
Paper conversion services, value added network (VAN), 112-113
Paperless Ordering Purchasing System, 58
Paper savings, 176
Parallel test, pilot test, 135
Payback period, EDI, 128
Payment methods

checks, 196
electronic funds transfer, 196-208
Personnel
  costs, 173
  savings and EDI, 30-31, 176
Pilot test, 134-135
  dummy transactions, 135
  electronic test, 135
  parallel test, 135
  review of, 135
Port Authority of New York and New Jersey, 46
Procedures Review Board, 76, 77
Procter & Gamble, 45
Procurement uses, government, 58-59
Product catalogs, and EDI, 219-220
Project manager, role of, 139
Project team, implementation of EDI, 129
Proprietary standards, 16
Publicizing efforts, EDI, 136

Quick Response, 56, 220
  and EDI, 222
Quik Link, 51

RAILINC, 22, 42
Rail industry EDI, 42-44
  growth of, 43-44
  intermodal EDI, 43
  rail transactions, 43
  standards, 86
RCA, 29
Relationship concerns, 158, 166-167
Resale activities, goverment, 59
Retail industry, 54-57
  Dillards Department Stores, 55
  Hills Discount Chain, 55-56
  Mervyn's Department Stores, 55
  proprietary EDI, 54-55
  Quick Response, 56 222
  R.J. Reynolds, electronic funds transfer, 204

Role concerns, 157-158

Sales increases, 37
Salesperson, role of, 143
Sears, 54
Security
    concern about, 162-163, 165-166
    mailbox services, a security
        buffer 111
    and third party networks, 115-
        116
    training aspects, 152
Segment diagram, components of, 69-
    72
Senden, 54
Senior manager, role of, 139
SE segment, 74
Society for Worldwide Interbank
    Telecommunications (SWIFT), 197
Software
    bridging software, 92-93
    comparisons of available pack-
        ages, 101-105
    costs, 96-97, 172-173
    definition of, 89
    features
        audit options, 94
        customizing ease, 94
        editing capability, 93-94
        table-drive structure 93
    functions of, 89-93
        communication, 91
        conversion, 91
        formatting, 90-91
    in-house developed versus pur-
        chased, 94-95
    training aspects, 150-151
    vendor selection, criteria for, 95-
        96
Staffing, 137-146
    leadership group, 138-140
    liaison group, 143-144
    operations group, 140-141

role designations, 137-138
staff support group, 144-146
technical group, 141-142
Staff support group, members' roles
    of, 144- 146
Stand-alone system, microcomputer,
    98-99
Standard-related concerns, 167-168
Standards
    international EDI, 210-222
    training aspects, 150
    Seals Electronic Data Inter-
        change standards.
Standards Maintenance Group, 83
Steering Committee, 76ST segment,
    74
Super Valu Stores, 29, 30, 31, 33, 35,
    48-49 169
System design, training aspects, 151

Table-driven structure, software fea-
    ture, 93
Technical Assessment Committee, 76
Technical Assessment review, 77
Technical coordinator, role of, 142
Technical group, members roles of,
    141-142
Texas Instruments, Inc., 34 213
Third party networks
    costs, 117-118
    direct exchanges 10-108
    issues/concerns
        interconnectibility, 114-115
        liability, 117
        security, 115-116
    mailbox services, 108-111
    role of, 108
    selection of, 118
    uses of, 119
    value added network (VAN),
        111-113
3M company, 36
Time value

costs, 174
  savings, 177
Touche Ross & Co., 37
Toys-R-Us, 26
Trade Data Interchange (TDI), 81
TRADELINK project, 212
Trading partners
  coordinator, role of, 143
  mapping with, 133
  selection of, 132-113
Training, 146-153
  components knowledge require-
    ments, 150-151
  costs, 173
  external training, 153
  implementation issues knowl-
    edge requirements, 151-152
  in-house training, 152
  overview knowledge require-
    ments, 149
  requirements, 147
  sources of information on, 153
  training coordinator, role of 145
  training matrix, 147-148
  value added network (VAN), 113
Transaction set
  choosing, 132
  definition, 65
Transaction set standards, 67-73
  data element directory, 72
  data segment directory, 67-72
Translation
  services, value added network
    (VAN), 112
  software, 92
Transportation, goverment, 59-60
Transportation Data Coordinating
  Committee 16 21-23, 63, 79
    standards
      air industry, 85
      business applications, 87
      cross industry standards, 87

freight claims transaction
  sets, 87
motor industry, 85-86
ocean industry, 86
rail industry, 86
Transportation industry, 42-47
  motor carrier EDI, 44-45
  ocean shipping EDI, 45-46
  rail industry EDI, 42-44

Uniform Code Council, 64, 83, 84
Uniform Communications Standards
  Committee, 22, 48
Uniform Communication Standards,
  16 64
    Advisor Council 83
    Union Carbide, 39-40, 44
Union Pacific, 43
Universal Product Code, 37, 56, 220
  222
Updates, standards, 79
U.S. Customs Service, EDI, use of,
  213-214
User Agent (UA), 81
U.S. Treasury, electronic funds trans-
  fer, 201-202

Value added network (VAN), 111-
  113
    authentication services, 113
    dial-out services, 113
    electronic funds transfer, 205
    encryption services, 113
    installation services, 113
    paper conversion services, 112-
      113
    role of, 111
    training services, 113
    translation services, 112
Vendor selection, software, criteria
  for, 95-96
Wal-Mart, 54

Warehouse Information Network
   Standard, 64
Wholesale drug EDI, 50-51
Wire transfer systems, 197
Woodbridge Group, 34

X12 committee; See Accredited Stan-
   dard Committee
X12 Product Data Project Team, 219
X12 standard, 212
Xerox Corporation, 38

Yellow Freight Systems, 44